Hannah Senesh, Israel's national heroine and subject of a major motion picture, is remembered as a poet and a martyr. Safe in Palestine during World War II, she volunteered for a mission to help rescue Jews in her native Hungary. She was captured by the Nazis, stood up to imprisonment and torture, and was executed at the age of twenty-three.

"An authentic story of rare heroism and self-sacrifice, one whose poignancy and meaning will affect many readers." —*Publishers Weekly*

"The comparisons . . . not only to Joan of Arc but to Anne Frank are justified [by] the universality of the legend she achieved." —*The Kirkus Reviews*

"This is an exalting volume, a record of a noble life. . . . It stirs the heart, lifts the soul and makes fascinating, exciting reading." —*Judaism*

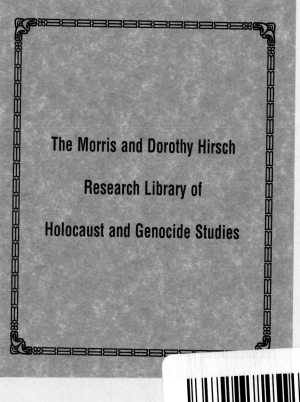

The Morris and Dorothy Hirsch

Research Library of

Holocaust and Genocide Studies

D0112177

Hannah Senesh
Her Life & Diary

Introduction by Abba Eban

THE MORRIS AND DOROTHY HIRSCH
RESEARCH LIBRARY OF
HOLOCAUST AND GENOCIDE STUDIES

SCHOCKEN BOOKS · NEW YORK

English translation copyright © 1971 by Nigel Marsh
Introduction copyright © 1972 by Schocken Books Inc.

All rights reserved under International and Pan-American Copyright
Conventions. Published in the United States by Schocken Books Inc., New York.
Distributed by Pantheon Books, a division of Random House, Inc., New York.
Originally published in Israel by Hakibbutz Hameuchad Publishing House Ltd.,
Ramat Gan, in 1966. Copyright © 1966 by Hakibbutz Hameuchad
Publishing House Ltd. English translation originally published in Great Britain
by Vallentine Mitchell and Co., Ltd., London, in 1971. This edition originally
published in the United States by Schocken Books Inc. in 1973.

Library of Congress Catalog Card Number: 77-179076
ISBN 0-8052-0410-5

Manufactured in the United States of America

First Schocken Paperback edition published in 1973
9 8

CONTENTS

Introduction   vii

Translator's Preface   1

Memories of Hannah's Childhood   5
   Catherine Senesh

THE DIARY   13

THE LETTERS   135

The Last Border   170
   Reuven Dafne

How She Fell   180
   Yoel Palgi

Meeting in Budapest   202
   Catherine Senesh

SELECTED POEMS   243

Introduction

Wait on the Lord: be of good courage,
and He shall strengthen thine heart.
Psalms 27:14

Courage is the scorner of
things which inspire fear.

—Seneca

"I don't know whether I've already mentioned that I've become a Zionist." Hannah Senesh was seventeen years old when she confided this calm news to her diary. She went on: "One needs to feel that one's life has meaning, that one is needed in this world."

The note of dedication is spoken in simple prose. Indeed, from the first shy awareness of her identity right up to the tragic end, she never spoke a single pompous or grandiloquent phrase. Nothing, therefore, can be less apt than the trite comparison with Joan of Arc. It is true that after her execution in Budapest at the age of twenty-three, Hannah became a consecrated image in her people's memory. A whole generation came to see her as the symbol of a vast martyrdom. The personal symbol was necessary precisely because the Jewish bereavement is quite incomprehensible when its dimensions are measured in six million. It comes far more within the scope of perception when it is distilled in recognizable terms into a single life and death.

There is a terrible pathos in any torture or death, but the effect is somehow sharpened when the victim has the innocence of youth and the fragile grace of femininity. So it is not hard to understand how the individual Hannah came to epitomize the total disaster. Yet she sought no particular role. Unlike the Maid of Orleans, she claimed no privilege of divine revelation. She was not even attracted by heroism.

To die . . . so young to die . . . no, no, not I.
I love the warm sunny skies,
Lights, songs, shining eyes.
I want no war, no battle cry—
No, no . . . Not I.

The verses were written in Nahalal in 1941. In the Valley
of Jezreel the summer is languid and gentle, and the wind
seldom gives movement to the cypress trees which make a
circle around the newly planted fields. The presentiment of
death sounds strange amid such peace. Hannah Senesh had
reached Nahalal from Hungary two years before. Nobody
could have foreseen the full horror of the oncoming Jewish
disaster, and Hannah's migration to Palestine a few weeks
after the outbreak of war was more in the nature of an
escape from the European danger than of an advance toward
greater risks. Jewish Palestine in the early 1940's was a scene
of relative comfort and security, and its sense of ease was
enlarged by a creative vitality that never came to rest even
in years of war. But from the first day of her arrival, Hannah
ceased to be a girl enjoying the "love of warm sunny skies."
She was caught up in the predicament of Jewish survival
and identity, as were so many of her generation who would,
by their own temperament, have preferred a private destiny.

A book about Hannah Senesh is essentially a commentary
on the holocaust. Two and a half decades after Hitler's down-
fall, the terrible mystery is still unexplained. All the human-
istic philosophies tell us that man is pulled both upward and
downward by elements in his own nature. The Hebrew
legend proclaims that man is "like unto the stars of heaven
or the dust of earth." The movement of men between
nobility and degradation takes up a great part of literature,
art, and, especially, drama. But no generalization is sufficient
to explain why the Jewish people is such a constant target
of the barbaric assaults: nor how so savage a fury could have
sprung from the German heart and been sustained by mil-
lions of individual cruelties including the flinging of babies
into furnaces. Nothing in human history is even remotely
similar to the ghastly violence committed by the Nazis against

the Jews. The legacy of the holocaust is still acutely relevant
to an understanding of Israel's consciousness today. It explains the obsessive concern with physical security; the
innate suspicion of Gentile intentions; the firm conviction
that Israel's small sovereignty is a minimal justice in comparison to the vast inheritance of Arab freedom in eighteen
states; the strong accent on historic recollection and on
anniversary occasions; and the fear lest the sharpest and
deepest of all injuries be forgotten not only by the outside
world, but by the Jews themselves. Israel and Diaspora
Jewry, despite all outward signs of vitality and exuberance,
are gripped by an overriding melancholy that passes over
them like an intermittent but never-ending cloud. Above
all, if six million people are killed only because they are
Jews, then being Jewish must obviously be something very
important indeed. For its own health and sanity, mankind
must come to terms with the Jewish condition.

These are some of the cosmic issues which erupt out of
the story of Hannah Senesh's life and death. But the poignancy of the story comes from the normal, human, modest
stature of its unwitting heroine. When all is said and done,
she is a girl like countless others—restless, volatile, and of
inconquerable charm. And, like countless others, her nobility is evoked by circumstance and ratified by sacrifice. She
bequeathes to her survivors, especially the youth among them,
the lesson of inescapable responsibility. In Cicero's words,
"No man can be brave who considers pain the greatest evil
of life; or temperate who regards pleasure as the highest
good."

All the definitions of giant courage come together in
Hannah's life. But the main impression is of a small and
lonely figure. It was thus that a comrade-in-arms described
her: "I watched her march confidently towards her unknown
fate, and at the bend in the road she turned and waved
farewell. I didn't know I would never see her again."

ABBA EBAN

December 1971

Translator's Preface

In the national military cemetery, situated on top of the highest of the Judean Hills overlooking Jerusalem, there is a small circle set apart; within it are seven graves in the shape of a V, the outline of a parachute carved on each headstone. Buried in that circle are seven of the thirty-two Palestinian-Jewish parachutists, members of the British Armed Forces, who were dropped into Nazi-occupied Balkan countries during World War II in an effort to save their people from the Nazi holocaust. Of the thirty-two sent, seven fell. One of the seven was Hannah Senesh, aged twenty-three and the only one of the seven about whom there is clear, definite testimony regarding her fate from the time of her capture until her execution.

Hannah Senesh has been called the Joan of Arc of Israel; she is a national heroine who has inspired books and plays. There are few in Israel who have not read her diary and poems, which have been translated into many languages. A ship, a forest and two farming settlements have been named after her; thirty-two streets in Israel bear her name. The leading members of the government of Israel saluted her memory when she was buried with highest military honours among thousands of Israeli soldiers—her body having been brought from the 'Martyrs' Section' of Budapest's Jewish Cemetery where she was buried by unknown hands after her execution in 1944.

Hannah Senesh was born on July 17, 1921, and began her diary when she was thirteen. It opens the door to a surprising Jewish world that continued to exist, relatively normally, while the rest of Europe's Jewry was being decimated. At the same time it explains why the talented daughter of a distinguished, assimilated Hungarian family chose to leave home, friends and country to become a pioneering farm worker in Palestine.

When Hungary joined the Axis, Hannah, long since in Palestine, noted in her diary, 'Sometimes I feel like one who has been sent . . . to perform a mission. What this mission is, is not clear to me. . . .'

Although by then Palestinian Jews were fighting together with the Free French, the British, Tito's partisans, and operating in the vast European underground, it was not until August 16, 1942, when a group of Polish women arrived in Palestine and brought positive and shattering reports of the systematic decimation of European Jewry, that a decision was made by the Palestinians to attempt to rescue their brethren.

In January 1943 Hannah wrote in her diary, 'I have had the sudden idea of going to Hungary. . . . Regardless of how clearly I see the absurdity of this idea, it still seems possible and necessary to me.' And at that very moment a group in Palestine was making plans to reach the remaining Jews in the Balkans and in Hungary—by parachute—in order to help them flee for their lives. Hannah Senesh immediately volunteered for this mission.

It was a military operation without precedent, a crusade in which each member was a novice, and his own commanding officer. None had been drafted—all had begged and demanded to be chosen. They had been selected with infinite care. Each had outstanding physical and mental attributes, each required special linguistic qualifications. They had to be parachutists, secret agents and saboteurs. And they had to have that special brand of courage possessed only by those who are willing to die for a cause.

Their first objective, and the sole condition upon which the British military granted approval and cooperation, was the liberation of Allied pilots shot down behind Nazi lines and the organization of resistance in all occupied countries. Only after this mission was completed were they free to attempt rescuing, via the underground in partisan territory, the million and a quarter Jews still believed to be alive in Rumania, Hungary and Czechoslovakia.

The parachutists, among them Hannah, took off on their mission from Brindisi, Italy, on March 13, 1944, and were dropped into Yugoslavia. Reuven Dafne, a fellow-parachutist whose account appears in this volume, said during a conversation: 'We parachutists were not supermen—nor superwomen. Supermen exist only on television. We were small, frail, inexperienced romantic people with all the shortcomings of the average person. None of us was unique—excepting perhaps Hannah. She was different . . . a spiritual girl guided almost by mysticism. Perhaps one can say she had *charisma* . . . She was fearless, dauntless, stubborn. Despite her extraordinary intelligence and prescience, she was a kind of tomboy—a poet-tomboy—which sounds rather odd, I know. A girl who dreamed of being a heroine—and who was a heroine.'

Dafne parted from Hannah on June 9, 1944, at a village near the Hungarian border, just before she crossed into Nazi-occupied territory. 'When we said goodbye she pressed a piece of paper into my hand saying, "If I don't return, give this to our people." I was amazed by her attitude. It was so unlike her. I looked at the piece of paper and was even more surprised. At a time like that she had written a poem. I had had no idea she even wrote poetry. I almost threw it away. It was *Blessed is the Match,* the poem every Israeli, young or old, can now recite from memory.'

MARTA COHN

Memories of Hannah's Childhood

Catherine Senesh

The idea of chronicling my memories concerning Hannah—not
for the sake of public acclaim, but merely to have a permanent
record—has been haunting me for years, sometimes vaguely,
sometimes acutely. Whether what she did was the consequence of
circumstances, early environment, or a specific feeling of mission,
she herself answers in her diary and other writings. There were,
however, certain events in her richly endowed and tragically cur-
tailed life to which I was the most intimate witness, and thus it is
probably right that I should record them.

From earliest childhood Hannah's environment was warm and
cheerful. With her brother, George, a year her senior, the question
of a playmate was completely solved, and the gay, cheerful nursery,
filled with joyous laughter, was not only their domain, but a
wellspring of happiness for my husband and myself, and for 'Fini
Mama'—my mother—who lived with us. Hannah's father was an
author and playwright. He used to work mainly in the evening and
often late into the night, and because of this, as well as because
of a serious heart condition caused by an illness suffered in early
youth, he would stay in bed most of the morning. Thus, unless
rehearsals or the heat of work drove him to bed at dawn, the
children were part of his morning routine. They would sit on his
bed while he bantered with them and told them a wealth of stories
created solely for their pleasure.

Foreseeing that his sick heart would take him from us at an
early age, my husband knowingly attempted to provide the children
with as many rich and happy memories as possible. There were
all sorts of excursions, visits to the amusement park and the
delightful Budapest Zoo, and innumerable 'story-telling' after-

noons arranged in our home for the entertainment of the children and their friends. But all this ended cruelly and suddenly in May of 1927, when a heart attack, suffered in his sleep, snatched their father from them. He was thirty-three.

A few days earlier my husband had risen very early, anxious to get to work on a half-finished play which was giving him trouble. I watched him in the mirror opposite my bed as he knotted his tie, so completely immersed in thought that he did not, consciously, see himself. I happily observed how well he looked, tanned from a recent holiday at Lake Balaton. Suddenly he said, 'You know, I was just thinking—I could end my life now. I've attained everything a Jewish writer possibly can in Hungary. I'm a respected columnist on the foremost newspaper,* my plays are performed at the Comedy with casts of my own choosing . . . the ink barely has time to dry before my work is in print. What more can there be? The gates of the National Theatre will never be open to a Jewish writer; but even if I had a choice, I think my plays are really far better suited to the Comedy Theatre. So what more can happen? Success abroad? Films? Money? I've had it all. Really, I could calmly go now.'

This was not the first time he had talked of death, and there are many posthumous poems that bear witness to a mood of resignation which—who knows how often?—engulfed him. But outwardly he seemed unchanged, his writing invariably filled with unstinted wit and humour.

Forcing back tears I asked, 'And don't you even think of us? Of what would become of us without you?'

'Naturally, that's the painful part,' he answered. 'But I entrust the children to you with complete confidence. I know they'll be in the best of hands.' (Had he but guessed!) He ended the grimly serious conversation with a humorous remark, and went to his study. A few days later the tragedy occurred. George was seven, Hannah barely six.

While their father was alive the children didn't see any of his plays. After all, they were written for adults. But after his death I took them to see those still running, to revivals, and to per-

---

* Bela Senesh wrote a popular humorous column in the Sunday magazine section of *Pesti Hirlap*, a paper with a circulation of 100,000.

formances of posthumous comedies, so they could retain some memory of their father's theatrical success. However, this actually proved to be unnecessary, since they heard about the plays—still very much alive in people's memories—wherever they went. Thus they not only guarded his memory with profound love, but were also enormously proud of him.

In early childhood George and Hannah heard little about religion and Jewishness. Although we considered ourselves good, steadfast Jews, we did not feel it important to observe the outer formalities of religion. My husband's creed, his guiding principle, was humanism, and he worshipped at its altar by deed, the written word, and in speech. Thus, it was at school that the children were versed in the foundations of religion and religious life. From the very beginning Hannah participated in all Jewish movements, but then she was in the vanguard of all school activities. Despite the great loss of an outstanding father—which undoubtedly affected her profoundly—Hannah's childhood was varied and happy. She completed the four elementary grades of school without the slightest effort, as she later completed the higher ones, and her teacher wrote a warm, friendly recommending letter attesting to her qualities and abilities, stressing her excellence in composition and poetry, which (they said) reminded one of her father's talents.

At that particular time the new quarters of an important Protestant girls' school was being completed in the immediate vicinity of our house, which, after a great many years of strict segregation, opened its doors to Catholic and Jewish pupils. There was, however, the stipulation that in this denominational school those of Christian faiths other than Protestant had to pay double the normal tuition fees, the Jewish students treble. Nonetheless, I decided to enrol Hannah.

At the end of the first year, when she brought home her usual outstanding report, richly annotated with the praise of her teachers, I felt the moral issue of discrimination—quite apart from the financial burden—to be intolerable. I called on the principal and said that whereas in any other school Hannah would have been awarded a scholarship, in this one I was paying a three-fold tuition fee. Because of this, regardless of how much I valued the high standards of the school, I said I felt compelled to enrol elsewhere—whereupon the teacher Hannah loved more than any other of her 'favourite' teachers said, 'No, no, we won't allow her to leave. She is our finest student and sets an example to the entire school. There has never been a precedent, but please submit a written request stating your point of view, and we'll bring it up at our next meeting.'

Considering that, according to the rules formulated by the school's founders, only Protestant girls were permitted to pay the minimum fee, it was some satisfaction—though not very much—that thereafter Hannah's tuition fees were to be the same as those of the Catholic girls. But whenever the teachers were not restricted by constraining rules they demonstrated their recognition of her abilities by awarding her prizes for the various scholastic competitions.

At home she was completely involved, and obviously happy, interested in everything that concerned the family. She was considerate, gentle, conscientious, responsible. She managed her time amazingly well, making use of every moment. When she came home from school she spent the half-hour before lunch at her desk finishing the day's homework, and apart from that I rarely saw her study. Instead, she coached others. From the age of eleven on she always had pupils.

Was Hannah pretty? At first glance, no. But if one scrutinized her and knew her well, one discovered a winning appeal, and sensed great attraction. Her face was dominated by large, expressive eyes, which mirrored her intelligence; at times they were green, at times blue-green. Her wide forehead was framed by soft, wavy hair; her face was attractively oval, her smile charming, her figure excellent, her manner, behaviour, personality and character in general, appealing. When she spoke she was listened to attentively.

Until the age of seventeen Hannah enjoyed fully the delights, pleasures and amusements of youth, and then her diary speaks most eloquently of the radical change of direction in her life. She acquainted me only gradually, over a period of months, with her thoughts, and finally with her plans for future emigration to Palestine. At first I was strongly opposed to her decision, but her many intelligent and convincing arguments weakened my objections. Once she said that even if she had not happened to be born a Jew she would still be on the side of the Jews because one must help, by all possible means, a people who were

being treated so unjustly now, and who had been abused so
miserably throughout history. On another occasion, when I
asked what had become of her ambition to be a professional
writer (considering one had but one mother tongue) she
answered, 'That question is dwarfed by present burning
problems.' Finally she tackled me with this statement, 'Mother,
if you don't agree to my going, of course I won't go. But I want
you to know I feel miserable in this environment, and don't wish
to live in it.'

She became totally immersed in Zionism and the problem of
emigration to Palestine. She wrote repeatedly to the Agricultural
School at Nahalal in Palestine concerning admission, went often
to the Maccabee Society, diligently studied Hebrew, and read a
tremendous number of books—almost all concerning Zionist and
Jewish matters. Though she was physically still with me, she
was actually already living in another world. Outwardly she
appeared controlled, as always, but anyone close to her could
sense the excitement and stirrings within her. Among her circle
of friends many were influenced by her and also joined the
Zionist Movement.

Here I must mention a school incident that occurred in 1937
when she was in the 7th Form, and which undoubtedly pre-
cipitated matters. According to tradition, one of the offices in
the school's Literary Society was generally held by a 7th-Form
pupil. As expected, the 7th Form elected Hannah to the post.
The 8th Form, however, under the influence of the existing
political climate, considered only one factor of any real importance: a Jewish student could not hold office. Thus, at the
very first meeting she attended, Hannah was greeted by the
surprising fact that a new election was scheduled for the office
to which she had been duly elected. Apparently calm and controlled, she sat through the meeting, and when one of her classmates was elected, and tearfully approached Hannah declaring
she would not accept the appointment because she knew she
was not deserving of it, Hannah said, 'Accept it calmly, and don't
think for an instant that I begrudge it to you. Not at all. If you
don't accept it, someone else will. After all, it has nothing to do
with whether Hannah Senesh or Maria X is more capable of
fulfilling the assignment, but whether the person is a Jew or a
Gentile.'

Her form mistress vehemently condemned the behaviour of
the 8th Form. But obviously she could do nothing about the
decision of the self-governing student body. 'I hope, Hannah,
you'll continue to participate in the activities of the Literary
Society, despite what has happened,' she said. 'How can you
imagine such a thing,' Hannah responded. 'Naturally I can't
possibly work with the members of the 8th Form.'

When she told me of the incident I realized how deeply hurt
she had been by the whole affair, though she never spoke of it
again.

During the Easter holiday of 1939 we went to visit George,
who was studying in France. Hannah was delighted to learn
that he had also become a dedicated Zionist. I watched them
indulgently as they discussed and planned the future with profound, youthful zeal, eyes sparkling. They decided Hannah
would emigrate within a few months, and that George would
follow when his studies were completed. Their great concern
was for me to join them. Would we ever again sit together like
this, I wondered, the three of us? Where . . . when . . .?

After graduating *summa cum laude*, Hannah said goodbye to
the school, and to all her teachers. By then her plans were
general knowledge, but the teachers were reluctant to accept her
decision to emigrate. Each in turn tried to prevail upon me to
prevent her from taking this step, emphasizing that they would
positively guarantee her acceptance by the university. (During
those years the *numerus clausus*, which restricted the number of
Jewish students permitted to enter university, was observed with
increasing strictness.) When I later related all this to Hannah
she said, 'Perhaps I ought to be impressed that in view of
graduating *summa cum laude*, and with a plethora of recom-
mendations from teachers and friends, I can get into the university, while a Gentile who just barely squeezed through the exams
can sail in! Besides, are they really incapable of understanding
that I don't want to be just a student, that I have plans, dreams,
ambitions, and that the road to their fulfilment would only be
barred to me here?'

When I brought up the most disputed question between us—
that if she must go to Palestine, why to agricultural school, why

not to the university where, according to her talents and capabilities, she actually belonged, and where she would certainly prove more useful and productive than in something so completely alien to her as farm work—I received an answer that had, by then, become customary: 'There are already far too many intellectuals in Palestine; the great need is for workers who can help build the country. Who can do the work if not we, the youth?'

At the beginning of September, the time of her expected departure, World War II broke out, and for the moment all roads leading to Palestine were apparently closed. I resigned myself to this new situation, but not she. She ran to various travel agencies, to the official representative of Palestine, to the Jewish Social Aid office—wherever she thought there was a glimmer of hope. Finally she succeeded in attaching herself to a group of Palestine-bound Slovaks, and we rushed to the Jewish Social Aid office to arrange her papers. Towards evening we were standing in one of the outer rooms when an official motioned us to follow him to his office. 'For whom shall I do this, if not for the daughter of Bela Senesh?' he said. 'He was one of my father's favourite pupils. I'm the son of Chief Rabbi Miksa Weiss.' After making out the required papers he informed us that departure would be at noon the next day from the East Railway station.

I felt as though ice were flowing through my veins. 'Tomorrow? But she has to get ready, to pack.' 'Madame, I've done my share,' he replied. 'The rest is up to you.'

Grandmother Senesh, the closest relatives, a few good friends were told, and came to say goodbye. Hannah and I packed all night. Next morning she still had to run to travel agents and consulates for visas.

On September 13, 1939, at one o'clock, we stepped through the gate of our little house. We both tried to control our emotions, but at the last moment, as she put her arms around our faithful Rosika, Hannah began sobbing and said, 'Rosi, take care of Mama.'

At the station one of my sisters saw to the customs and luggage, and we all took final leave of Hannah. Standing at the train window it required all her strength to choke back the sobs. The tensions of the last weeks, the excitement, were overshadowed by the parting, the final break, and the total uncertainty of the future. As the train inched out a great cloud seemed to fall over the entire station. When I arrived home in the early dusk of that September afternoon, the melancholy mood of *Rosh Hashana* (the Jewish New Year) had already settled over the empty house, and the flickering candles seemed to magnify my feelings. Fate had relentlessly intruded upon our lives, torn our little family apart, scattered us in three directions.

THE DIARY

'There are stars whose radiance is visible on earth though they have long been extinct. There are people whose brilliance continues to light the world though they are no longer among the living. These lights are particularly bright when the night is dark. They light the way for Mankind'—

HANNAH SENESH

Budapest
September 7, 1934

This morning we visited Daddy's grave. How sad that we had to become acquainted with the cemetery so early in life. But I feel that even from beyond the grave Daddy is helping us, if in no other way than with his name. I don't think he could have left us a greater legacy.

September 12, 1934

Today was the first day of school. Once again a year has passed. Everything seems so strange now; new teachers, and most important, a new form mistress. I shall miss Aunt Ilona* an awful lot, and even though Aunt Boriska seems nice, one can't form an opinion so soon. Our new teacher of Hungarian literature is marvellous, and a distinguished poet as well. His name is Lajos Jekely, but he writes under the name of Lajos Aprily. It is a joy to attend his classes.

October 7, 1934

Yesterday, and today, Sunday, no school. This morning there was a lovely celebration, and this afternoon I went to synagogue. Those afternoon services are so odd; it seems one does everything but pray. The girls talk and look down at the boys, and the boys talk and look up at the girls**—this is what the entire thing consists of.

I'm glad I've grown lately. I'm now five feet tall, and weigh just over seven stone. I don't believe people think me a particularly pretty girl, but I hope I'll improve.

* Hungarian children customarily call all adults, including teachers, uncle and aunt.
** In Orthodox synagogues men sit downstairs, women in the balcony.

October 14, 1934

Today I finally reached an agreement with Maria's mother. I'm to coach Maria six hours a week. I will be paid fifteen *pengö* per month*. It's not as much as I was paid by Mrs. Erdy, but I am happy about it just the same. I don't think any other girl in my class earns as much. Now I can pay for dancing and skating lessons with my own money. Perhaps I'll even buy a season ticket for the ice rink.

October 20, 1934

Yesterday morning Dalmady, whose father recently died, came back to school. The poor girl is very sad, naturally. But at least she did have her father for thirteen years.

Something very touching happened during physics. Dalmady, of course, had not prepared the lesson, and she wanted to explain why to the teacher. However, you have to stay at your desk during class, and if you want to say anything you have to do so from there. The poor dear began crying the moment she stood up. She remained standing for a few moments, uncertain what to do, then suddenly walked up to the teacher and whispered that her father had died. There followed a beautiful scene in which the old teacher shook hands with the little·girl. Written down this way it isn't moving, but almost the entire class wept.

November 18, 1934

I have not been able to write for a long time as I've been extremely busy. George found my diary not long ago, and read the entire thing. I was furious because he constantly teased me about it. But last night he took a solemn oath never to mention it again.

Friday was the fifteenth anniversary of Horthy's** election.

* Approximately £2.50 or $6.25.

** In the spring of 1919 a small 'national army' was raised under the command of Admiral Miklos Horthy, one-time Commander-in-Chief of the Austro-Hungarian Imperial and Royal Adriatic Fleet, to counteract the Communist-inspired uprising of Bela Kun. In November of that year, with the blessing of the Allies, Horthy was elected Regent of Hungary, and remained the head of the government until October 16, 1944, when he was forced to resign by the Nazis.

We went down to the *Vérmezö* and saw the whole celebration.
As I stood there watching all those soldiers, I somehow thought
that seeing them on parade was beautiful. But what would
become of them in a war? Mother says that the present atmosphere is very warlike. It's a good thing George is still so young.
Even so, God protect us from war. Why, the whole world would
be practically wiped out.

But at the moment I have more immediate problems: report
time is approaching. It's possible I'll have a bad mark for neatness, but we'll hope for the best. Otherwise I think I'll be all
right.

November 27, 1934

All my marks were good, including neatness. But I must improve
in French. It's nice to think that in less than a month the
Christmas holidays will be here!

December 25, 1934

Sunday we went to the Opera to hear *The Barber of Seville*. It
was a beautiful performance with an exceptionally fine cast. This
long holiday is wonderful—from December 22nd to January 7th.
I received a lot of presents too. From Mother tickets to the
Opera, from Fini Mama* two pairs of stockings, from my other
grandmother a lovely little brooch, from Aunt Ilus material for a
sweet little summer dress, from Aunt Irma handkerchiefs and
ski socks. Besides all this, three handsome books.

I embroidered a book-mark for Mama, I gave Fini Mama
stationery, and George a little savings bank.

January 13, 1935

It's Sunday, so I have time to write. I can't go ice skating
because I have a cold. This year I like to skate because I belong
to the Ice Skating Club, and all my friends go there.

The Dance Circle will be held on the 26th. I am rather jittery
about it, and wonder what it will be like. I have a lovely pink
dress for the occasion.

---

* Her maternal grandmother.

April 7, 1935

Evi* is arriving at lunchtime and will stay for a few days. I'm looking forward to seeing her. It's possible that she may come to my school next year, because its standards are much higher than those in Dombovár. I put up a big fight to get her to transfer, even though this would mean a great responsibility for me. I hope we won't quarrel—though I am a little worried about this. And we will have to be very careful not to become rivals. That would disrupt the peace.

April 27, 1935

We got our class reunion rings today. We'll meet on May 1, 1945. Ten years from now! What a long time! How many things can happen before then.

May 31, 1935

We are going to have a celebration at school and give a performance of Madách's *The Tragedy of Man*. I'm going to take the part of the Angel Michael. It was rumoured that boys would be invited and that after the performance there would be a dance. But the rumours proved false. I'm sorry because I do so like to dance.

Things at school look very good apart from French. I'm really ashamed of myself for having such difficulty improving in the only subject with which I have any trouble. This has nothing to do with grades—I actually got an A in French—but with my lack of self-confidence in the subject. My only consolation is that all the others in my class are being coached at home so they have a decided advantage.

Judy has invited me to their home on Lake Balaton for a holiday this summer. I will probably go there straight after the exams.

Aged fourteen   *August 29, 1935*

I didn't take my diary along this summer because I didn't expect to have time to write, and also because I was afraid someone

---

* Her cousin, eventually killed at Auschwitz.

might find it. Not that I have any secrets. Even so, I don't think I would like anyone to read it. So I'll have to write everything in retrospect.

School ended on June 15 (my report was all A's, as I expected —with the exception of French), and at two o'clock the same afternoon I was on the train. We met Judy and her family at the station, and I said goodbye to Mother.

I spent seventeen days at Lake Balaton. Considering everything, I must say I enjoyed myself, though I certainly did not feel as much at home, as, for example, at Dombovár. Nor did I achieve a truly warm friendship with Judy. Her little sister was the one, I think, who really was fond of me.

Aunt Ella and Uncle Egon were very nice, and what really made the two weeks most interesting and meaningful were all the new things I heard from Uncle Egon. He opened a whole new world to me, though there are a good many things in that world I don't quite believe in—like whether there really are elves and fairies. However, I think that in astrology, spiritualism, and the development of the soul, there is a lot in which I can believe.

During the summer I read Maeterlinck's *Blue Bird,* and found in it things of great value, such as I've found in no other book I have read so far. For instance, the premise that there are no dead because the dead can be resurrected through memories. I felt in sympathy with this great truth because just by thinking of Daddy I seem able to bring back that time when he was alive. I can't describe exactly what I feel, but one thing is certain: one must be careful with whom one talks about such things because most people just laugh and poke fun.

From Balaton I went to Dombovár on July 3. The first few days I missed Balaton a little, it's really wonderfully beautiful. But in Dombovár I joined in so many interesting and amusing activities that it amply compensated for not having the lake. I got along well with Evi. In fact we hit it off so perfectly that I felt horrible about her not being accepted by my school. Actually I got the news of her rejection while I was at the lake, and felt so badly about it I went to my room and cried.

Now I'm going to give myself the answer to a question George has repeatedly asked: Do boys interest me? Well, yes, they interest me more than before, but only in general because I didn't see a single boy I really liked the entire summer. True, I didn't meet very many. This is my idea of the ideal boy: he should be attractive and well dressed, but not a fop; he should be a good sportsman, but interested in other things besides sports; he should be cultured and intelligent, but good-humoured, and not arrogant; and he should not chase after girls. And so far I have not met a single boy like this.

I wrote only two poems during the entire summer. One is for Mama's birthday, the other I've told no one about. This is the poem:

> *Life is a brief and hurtling day,*
> *Pain and striving fill every page.*
> *Just time enough to glance around,*
> *Register a face or sound*
> *and—life's been around.*

This morning we went to the cemetery. As far as I'm concerned, I can see no point in going such a very long way merely to stand before Daddy's grave for a few moments when I'm actually with him in thought every evening, asking whether he is satisfied with me, whether my behaviour pleases him. I can hardly remember Daddy (his face) but just the same I love him very much, and always feel he is with me. I would like to be worthy of him as a writer, too. I know I have a little talent, but I don't think it's more than that. Although the desire to write is constantly alive within me, I still don't consider writing my life's goal or ambition, but rather a way of making myself and those around me happy. Perhaps, through writing, I will be able to contribute something towards human happiness. This, in itself, is a fairly ambitious task, and outside of it I don't really know what I would like to do or be. On the whole, I would say I would like to be a teacher, but this, I know, is difficult.

I am reading Harsanyi's *Ecce Homo*. It's very interesting.

September 16, 1935

Mama asked whether I would like to take piano lessons again this year, and I said yes. So I had my first lesson today. Although I know I haven't got a very good ear, and that I could never consider music as a profession, I still like to play the piano very

much, and really do enjoy music. Sometimes when Mama plays
Chopin I feel like crying. It is so inexplicably beautiful and
enjoyable.

October 4, 1935

Horrible! Yesterday war broke out between Italy and Abyssinia.
Almost everyone is frightened the British will intervene and that
as a result there will be war in Europe. Just thinking about it is
terrible. The papers are already listing the dead. I can't understand people; how quickly they forget. Don't they know that the
whole world is still groaning from the curse of the last World
War? Why this killing? Why must youth be sacrificed on a
bloody scaffold when it could give so much that is good and
beautiful to the world if it could just be allowed to tread peaceful roads.

Now there is nothing left to do but pray that this war will
remain a local one, and end as quickly as possible. I can understand Mussolini wanting to acquire colonies for Italy, but, after
all, the British ought to be satisfied with owning a third of the
world—they don't need all of it. It is said, however, that they
are frightened of losing their route to India. Truly, the ugliest
thing in the world is politics.

But to talk of more specific things: One of George's friends is
courting me. He is also in the 5th Form, like me. He was bold
enough to ask whether I would go walking with him next Sunday. I said I would, if George went along. If everything he told
me is true then I feel very sorry for him; evidently he doesn't
have a decent family life. There is something wrong there, that's
for sure.

October 25, 1935

Tuesday, the 22nd, was the première of a film based on Daddy's
play, *Terminal*. The leading role is played quite charmingly by
Paul Horbiger, and his co-star is Maria Andergast. The entire
film is rather delightful. I was very nervous about it. I don't
quite know why, because it would not have been Daddy's fault

if it had been a poor film. But the play was so good—and the material side doesn't interest me at all.

I have a new pupil, besides Marika. I can't say she's a great brain, but if she were she wouldn't need me! I asked twelve *pengö* a month to coach her, and they accepted without a murmur.

November 1, 1935

It's All Saints' Day. Though actually it's a Christian holiday, on such a day one does think more about one's dead. This afternoon we're going to visit the graves of Lorika and Uncle Roby. Goodness, how ungrateful I am! It's nearly a year since I was there. However, I don't think it pleases them at all, or that they even know whether I've been there or not. But I feel more at peace with myself if, in gratitude for the goodness and kindness they always showed me, I make the small sacrifice of going to the cemetery.

Last night George and I went to the Indoor Swimming Pool to see the match between America and Hungary. It was very interesting, and they broke the world record for the backstroke. (Kiefer won it for America.) However, I find today's enormous enthusiasm for sport a bit exaggerated (particularly as displayed by George).

Oh, I almost forgot to mention that we saw the *Scarlet Pimpernel*, which I had read in English. It was a very good film, one of the best I've ever seen. It starred Leslie Howard, who was marvellous.

December 22, 1935

I'm in bed. Ever since the serious attack of pleurisy I had two years ago, they are always afraid I'll develop something critical. Actually there has been absolutely nothing wrong with me since then. However, such an illness has a few advantages along with its enormous disadvantages! One has time to read, and to meditate. I'm now planning that when I'm older, about twenty, I'll have a children's summer camp at Lake Balaton. I spend my evenings working out plans for it, and have already drawn up an entire day's schedule.

January 16, 1936

I'm in bed with a slight cold. First of all, I want to write about last Saturday—not because it was so pleasant, but because I hope that after I've written about it I'll think about it less. I was invited to an afternoon dance at Zoya's house, and, but for me, everyone knew everyone else. The only person I knew was Zoya, who certainly did not prove to be the best hostess because all they talked about—at least in the beginning—were things that interested themselves only. This very boring situation lasted from 5 until 7, after which we had tea, and then the dancing began.

Frankly, I felt rather bad because I noticed how reluctantly most of the boys asked me to dance, and that they left me immediately the dance was over. As a matter of fact, only one or two of the boys were anything less than rude. It seems boys think all girls are so stupid that they don't even know that the music doesn't end in the middle of a record! However, I don't really mind the fact that I went, because at least it taught me a lesson: I'll never again go where I don't know anyone. The rudest of all was a girl who got up and moved away when I sat down next to her, taking everyone with her, and leaving me stranded. People are really strange!

But I want to write a longer account about a lot of far more interesting and enjoyable things. I went to a Furtwängler concert. It was fabulous! The *Manfred Overture* by Schumann, the Schumann *Spring Symphony in B Major*, and the *7th Symphony* of Beethoven. It was all simply magnificent!

Yesterday I had a little incident with Mama. I was reading something and Mama took it out of my hand, saying it was not a proper thing for me to read. This hurt me very much as it was a letter from school addressed to Mama, and I felt I could read it too. Later I thought about it, and wondered what I would do if the same thing happened with a child of mine. I decided that if she already had the letter in her hand I would not take it away, but would, instead, be careful not to leave such a letter lying about. Of course I don't know if I'll still think this way when I'm grown-up.

February 8, 1936

We've bought a house! This has been Mother's greatest wish, but now that it's fulfilled she is all doubts, wondering whether she made a wise decision. As far as I'm concerned, I'm very happy about it. It's in a wonderful position, and has a beautiful big garden.

April 19, 1936

Today was my first opening. My play is called *Bella Gerant Alii, Tu, Felix Austria, Nube.** We performed it for Aunt B. I wrote and directed it, and it was really an awful lot of work. But I don't feel Aunt B. is capable of properly assessing its worth. They say the play is quite good, but certainly not good enough to lead to anything. As far as a profession is concerned, I still think I ought to attend a school for hoteliers. A more serious and interesting profession which tempts me is one that has to do with children—such as running a boarding school on the lines of a British Public School, or something like that.

May 9, 1936

We're here in our new home already. It is such a wonderful feeling to be in our own house. Every day we discover something good and beautiful about it. Of course there is still a great deal to be done, but after all, we only moved in five days ago!

I'm invited out tonight. I hope it will be pleasant. George is coming too. Now he is rather interested in girls, and he would like me to introduce him to some of my classmates.

I must say George was very dear and decent yesterday. One of the boys said he couldn't understand what Gaby saw in me, whereupon George said I was very intelligent, and that even though I never study, all my grades were excellent. Hearing this his friend said, 'Well, that's something.' But I think that from a boy's point of view this is really not important. A girl has to have certain other attractions. This is very evident in Thackeray's *Vanity Fair*. I like the book very much; one is constantly

* Loosely translated: 'What others gain in battle, Austria gains in wedlock!' It refers to the fact that all the Habsburgs married for political expediency rather than for love.

reminded of oneself while reading it, or of one's friends. It is quite witty, as well.

May 31, 1936

The Gaby affair continues: yesterday he 'confessed' his love, in the literal sense of the word. True, only in writing. I suppose it's my fate to have boys of my own age confessing their love in writing. We were trying to do our physics assignment together, when suddenly Gaby wrote his 'confession' in the notebook. I didn't know what to say, and quickly closed the notebook. Later he asked if I had anything to say about it. I said I had not. Gaby is really very silly. A fifteen-year-old boy can't write such things to a girl his own age. It's too ridiculous. I don't think I really like him much, except as a sort of chum.

June 15, 1936

I have had such strange thoughts lately. I would like to be a writer. For the time being I just laugh at myself; I've no idea whether I have any talent. I've been inspired by the success of *Bella Gerant*—everyone likes it. But even so, I don't think I would write plays. I would rather write novels.

June 18, 1936

I got up at six this morning. It's such beautiful weather that I've no desire to stay in bed. And as Mother is away for a few days I can get up when I like. Since the 15th I've been living like a fish in water. I go swimming every day and play tennis (though I don't know whether fish play tennis!). I'm not going to Dombovár until the end of the month.

When I began keeping a diary I decided I would write only about beautiful and serious things, and under no circumstances constantly about boys, as most girls do. But it looks as if it's not possible to exclude boys from the life of a fifteen-year-old girl, and for the sake of accuracy I must record the development of the Gaby matter.

He was not satisfied with my afore-mentioned answer, but put into a book I borrowed from him (which, incidentally, is very

good and titled *Mirthful Thoughts*) a picture of himself auto-
graphed 'With Love Forever, Gaby'. I didn't say a word about
the picture. Ever since, whenever I see him (quite often) he
showers me with compliments, which I try to brush off.

Well, a few days ago he was here, and we played ping-pong. I
don't even know how we came to discuss it (in any event it was
my fault things went as far as they did), but I told him I had
already had two proposals of marriage. Of course I presented the
entire thing in a sort of jocular way, and even mentioned how
terribly embarrassed I was.

In answer to this the 'old man' said he would like to see me
get embarrassed, and what would I say if ten years from now he
would ask me to marry him, etc., etc. I told him not to be such
a baby, that this sort of thing made absolutely no sense since we
were both only fifteen, and let's just remain good friends.

Well, now my diary has become like that of any fifteen-year-
old girl, with nothing serious in it, and without any individuality.

                                                        Dombovár
Aged fifteen   *July 17, 1936*
As of today I'm a vegetarian. I am completely in agreement with
the Bircher-Benner concept, and will try to convince Mother too.
For the time being I am going to give it a six-month trial, and if
my views don't change during that time, I think I'll remain a
vegetarian.

                                                    August 3, 1936
I still long to be a writer. It's my constant wish. I don't know
whether it's simply a desire for praise and fame, but I do know it
is such a marvellous feeling to write something well that I think
it is worth struggling to become a writer. On the whole, the
above-average man suffers more, but his joys are greater too, and
I would rather be an unusual person than just average. I am not
even thinking now of the writing profession, because when I
think of an above-average man I don't necessarily think of a
famous man, but of a great soul . . . a great human being. And I
would like to be a great soul. If God will permit!

August 4, 1936

As I re-read my last entry I became quite angry with myself. What I wrote seems so terribly conceited. Big Soul! I am so far from anything like that. I'm just a struggling fifteen-year-old girl whose principal preoccupation is coping with herself. And this is the most difficult battle. But even this sounds contrived. Whatever I think and feel, however beautiful my thoughts, they sound so different in black and white. For this reason I would rather not write anything.

Budapest
August 31, 1936

Not long ago I wrote a letter to Dr. Bircher-Benner to ask him a few questions concerning the vegetarian diet. I received a meaningless reply from his secretary. So I think I'll eat meat a couple of times a week this winter after all; besides, Mother won't allow me to be a vegetarian all the time. George returned from his summer holiday. We're very good friends now, and I hope we'll stay this way.

September 18, 1936

It's the second day of the Jewish New Year. Yesterday and today we went to synagogue. I am not quite clear just how I stand: synagogue, religion, the question of God. About the last and most difficult question I am the least disturbed. I believe in God—even if I can't express just how. Actually I'm relatively clear on the subject of religion too, because the Jewish fits in best with my way of thinking. But the trouble with the synagogue is that I don't find it at all important, and I don't feel it to be a spiritual necessity; I can pray equally well at home.

September 27, 1936

I'm the treasurer of the Stenographic Circle, and secretary of the Bible Society. I'm pleased to be an officer in both, even though it does mean a lot of work. The Bible Society is going to have a celebration on December 12. Our 6th Form will be in charge of organizing things. I hope it will be a success. I'm already making ambitious plans.

Miki is coming again today, but it's a bit too much for me. We don't have enough in common, and I find him rather shallow. I'd like to meet a really nice boy because the old ones bore me. Gaby is teaching me to play bridge. It's an interesting game, but of course I still have only a vague idea how to play.

So this book is filled now. When I started it I thought I would never be able to fill it.

October 10, 1936

This morning we went to Grandma's and from her window saw the funeral of Prime Minister Gömbös. George and I did not go very willingly. This sort of military pageantry doesn't interest me much. They say I am too blasé, but I don't think it's that at all. After all, the most interesting things were the flowers, and some of the notables, i.e., Goering, Mussolini's son-in-law (Ciano), Austrian Chancellor Schuschnigg. And they don't interest me in the least bit.

This afternoon we went to synagogue. One of George's class-mates spoke, and he was quite good. I think it is an excellent idea to have a different boy speaking on each occasion.

October 19, 1936

I am reading *War and Peace* but nearing the end, and can now understand Tolstoy's ideas quite clearly. This book is among the very best I have ever read. The plot itself is tremendously interesting, but even more fascinating are Tolstoy's views on the historical facts which led to the winter campaign of the War of 1812 and other events, and the way he examines and passes judgements on those events. It is obvious he does not think the roles played by individuals in the enactment of history were nearly as important or decisive as one generally believes. This is particularly so in the case of his principal characters. The part I am reading now is most interesting: he discusses the question of power. That is to say, what exactly prompts or induces the mob to place itself under the domination of a single man, and then turn against that man and drive him to the scaffold? So far Tolstoy has not answered this question, but is content with merely throwing the out-dated concepts of historical writers on the rubbish heap. I am curious to see whether, in the end, he will answer it.

October 20, 1936

I finished *War and Peace*. Of course Tolstoy finally did answer
the question, but to be honest, I didn't quite understand the
answer. I must also confess that towards the end I was counting
pages, reading out of duty rather than for pleasure, and eager to
finish. Anyway, I'll re-read the epilogue—the part that is a
remembrance of the past—because it is almost impossible to
understand it completely after one reading.

October 25, 1936

I'm so happy! I read one of my poems, *The Ice-Cream Man,* to
Mother, and she liked it very much. Perhaps I can still hope to
become a writer. But so many people write!

November 4, 1936

My happiness was premature. Yesterday there was a conference
to discuss the holiday activities for Hanukah.* I read my play,
Marriage Proposal in 2036 (I wrote it specifically for school),
which I thought might be suitable for the celebration. But
judging by the icy silence which followed my reading I could
see they didn't like it at all. I think my face must have been
very red—at least it was burning—but I think I behaved well
enough. Now I'm nervous about having to read it in class
tomorrow, and I'm afraid it won't have much success there,
either. But in spite of everything I'm going to recite one of my
new poems at the Debating and Literary Society. I'll call it
Evening Mood, or *Twilight,* or something like that.

November 14, 1936

I read the play in class a while back, and it went down well. I've
written another poem. Its title is *The Tear.* It came out of a

* The Feast of Lights, commemorating the victory of the Maccabees over
the Greeks.

personal experience. I am going to enter it, and *Evening,* in the
Literary Society competition.

November 24, 1936

I have a pupil, from today, in arithmetic. I've already given her
the first lesson. She's a nice little girl, and I'm so glad I finally
have a pupil this year. I'm in such a great mood I actually sang
on my way home from school. It's really not because I'm earn-
ing money that I'm so happy, but because my wish has been
fulfilled.

January 10, 1937

Evi spent the greater part of her Christmas holiday here, and
left for home on Wednesday. She had a very good time here,
and it was hard for her to leave. The day before she went we
had a little party. I invited two girls and six boys, so there were
ten of us, including Evi and myself.

School has started, and the term has begun well. I was particularly pleased with my Hungarian essay, which was highly
praised by the principal. Yesterday afternoon I went to a literary
meeting, mainly to hear the principal's poems. I liked them quite
a lot, though I understand them better when I read them.

February 14, 1937

Except for drawing, I had all A's in my report. Meanwhile, an
important event: I got my first long party dress! It's blue
taffeta, and everyone says I look very pretty in it. So far I've
worn it only to the Hubermann concert, which was more note-
worthy than my dress! The programme consisted of Beethoven's
Spring Sonata, the Bach *Sonata,* Brahms and Schubert.

February 25, 1937

I just got back from the Literary Society, where I read *The Ice-
Cream Man,* which the Society considered good. But I thought
Agi's two poems were much better, particularly the first one,
Death of a Teacher, which I thought excellent. It somehow des-

troyed my confidence and interest in my own poems. Up till now I thought I was quite talented, but Agi is definitely more gifted. Perhaps I have greater potential as a writer of prose. I don't know. In a way I'm afraid to become too involved in writing, and in the idea that I am really talented. On the other hand, I can't stop writing, nor do I want to. I just sent two of my poems, *The Tear* and *Dance of the Moments,* to a magazine. The second of the two is new, and the best poem I've ever written. At least that's what I think. Now I constantly wonder whether my poems are as good as Agi's. Goodness, it would be wonderful to be truly talented.

March 21, 1937

The first act of what Mother terms a three-act comedy, is Zoltan; the second act, Peter, has already ended. The first act was much more pleasant than I expected. I didn't find the protagonist either stupid or arrogant, as I had been told by ill-intentioned critics he would be. He may be difficult with others, but he behaved very well with me. I don't find him particularly attractive, but I very much enjoy being with him.

The opening of the second act (Peter) was a trifle delayed. Instead of arriving at 11.30 a.m., he turned up at 12.30, as he couldn't find his way here. He was not all I had anticipated, perhaps because the wait was so long, or perhaps because I expected more than he had to offer. Not that Peter isn't a nice boy. In fact I liked him quite a lot, though I don't know if he feels the same way about me. He read my poems and liked them very much.

March 28, 1937

Meanwhile the third act (Johnny). He is an intelligent boy; one can really have a conversation with him. But now I'm going to put an end to this great adventuring with boys (!) . . .

April 15, 1937

For days I've been experiencing a general dissatisfaction with myself, and I don't know what's causing it. Because actually nothing unusual has happened to me. And I've certainly done nothing wrong. I can't understand myself. Possibly I'm just tired; I've been very busy. I'm doing all sorts of things, and I'm rather sorry I undertook so many school activities. The only thing I don't regret, even for a moment, is the coaching I do.

I'm bored with the boy situation too. They just keep coming, and I don't really know how I stand with them. I'm afraid I'm a little disappointed in Peter. He is too complicated, a bit pompous, and his manner of speaking is not entirely straight-forward. Perhaps after a few more meetings I'll have a more positive opinion of him.

Meanwhile Agi gave me her new poem to read. I am now less impressed by her.

May 1, 1937

For the first time in my life I've been paid for writing. Aunt Judith asked me to write something for her school's tenth anniversary celebration. So, as she was extremely pleased with the poem I wrote, she sent me a bankbook with a twenty *pengö* deposit. Of course I'm delighted about this.

I recently finished reading Zweig's *Fouché*. It's unusually interesting; I liked it enormously. At the same time I scanned Erich Kästner's *Lyrische Hausapotheke*, a really charming, first-rate book of poems. I'm absolutely delighted by his style and subjects, and find his interpretations completely original and artistic. I was sad to discover, however, that he has used certain ideas I, too, have had, which only proves that often what one thinks is a completely original idea has already been used by someone else.

Unfortunately there are problems with my pupils. Both T and M got relatively poor grades in math, and I feel so embarrassed I'd like the earth to swallow me.

May 15, 1937

The other morning there was some discussion concerning the election for the secretary of the Literary Society. Aunt Boriska reminded us that we had to keep certain factors in mind, among them that the person elected must be Protestant. This is certainly understandable in a Protestant school, but even so, it's very depressing. Of course it is not certain I would be worthy of the office, but this way I am already excluded from the competition. Now I don't know how to behave towards the Literary Society. Should I put myself out and work for the improvement of the Society's standards, even though I am now aware of the spirit that motivates it, or should I drop the whole thing? But if I drop it then I am going against the interests of my class. It is extremely difficult to find a way that is not demeaning, proud or isolationist, and also not forward. One has to be extremely careful before making any kind of move because one individual's faults can be generalized about. To my way of thinking, you have to be someone exceptional to fight anti-Semitism, which is the most difficult kind of fight. Only now am I beginning to see what it really means to be a Jew in a Christian society. But I don't mind at all. It is because we have to struggle, because it is more difficult for us to reach our goal, that we develop outstanding qualities.

Had I been born a Christian, every profession would be open to me. I would become a teacher, and that would be the end of it. As it is, perhaps I'll succeed in getting into the profession for which, according to my abilities, I am best suited.

Under no circumstances would I ever convert to Christianity, not only because of myself, but also because of the children I hope one day to have. I would never force them into the ignoble position of having to deny or be ashamed of their origin. Nor would I rob them of their religion, which is what happens to the children of converted parents.

I think religion means a great deal in life, and I find the modern concept—that faith in God is only a crutch for the weak —ridiculous. It's exactly that faith which makes one strong, and because of it one does not depend upon other things for support.

June 15, 1937

Today was the last day of school. I got A's in everything, but what I'm happiest about is that my poem, *Dance of the Moments,* was awarded ten points.

Saturday I went to the Berzsenyi ball. It was very pleasant and I danced a great deal.

En Route to Italy
I am writing this on the train.   *June 18, 1937*

I left South Station at 8.30 this morning. Mother was extremely nervous, and entrusted me to the care of a lady sitting opposite, who is very nice. In fact we have spent so much time chatting I've barely had time to read, particularly as we reached Lake Balaton meanwhile. Each time I see it it seems to me more beautiful. I stood in the corridor for a while in order to have a better view of the great, fabulous, sparkling inland sea.

A boy of about seventeen came out of the neighbouring compartment and with studied carelessness lit a cigarette, while watching my reaction out of the corner of his eye. I laughed to myself.

We are now leaving the principal lake resorts, Siofok, Földvár, etc. Meanwhile I've become quite friendly with my travelling companion.

Just before reaching the border there was currency control. I was simply asked how much money I had; it all went very smoothly.

At the moment we are at the border station of Murakeresztur, and there are a great many customs officers on board. Since I am only passing through they had little to do with me.

This Yugoslav part is very beautiful. We are passing through wonderful areas, the landscape entirely different from that of Hungary. The Drava River runs through relatively high mountains, and little stone houses cling to the sides of the hills, or are wedged between them. Now we're travelling through Laibach (Ljubljana). It's a rather large, attractive city with a lovely residential section. I particularly noted a green tram, and a lovely Greek Orthodox church.

In the meantime the lady in my compartment left, but I was not to enjoy my solitude for long. Before leaving she entrusted me to the care of the people in the neighbouring compartment, who immediately moved into mine: a lady with a good-natured seventeen-year-old son, and a young man who turned out to be the brother of one of my classmates. He has a letter of introduction to my relatives in Milan! I'm astonished how small the world is!

We arrived in Trieste at nine in the evening, and I broke my promise to Mother about not getting off the train. We spent an hour of the two-hour wait sightseeing. Trieste is quite a large city, but without any Italian characteristics. There are a great many sailors and cafés, and we went to one of the latter and drank a 'cappuccino', a sort of warm café au lait. We left Trieste at about eleven, and bedded down for the night in the compartment.

I slept for about an hour in all. We arrived at Venice at one in the morning, and of course I looked out of the window; even though I didn't see much, it was interesting to enter a station that was practically in the middle of the sea. We arrived in Ravenna at 3 a.m. and from then on I stood in the corridor and watched the countryside slip by.

We cleaned up a bit, and arrived in Milan a few minutes before seven. Géza was waiting for me with the car, and in a few minutes we were home in their adorable little flat, which is very near to where Klara and her family live.

Milan
June 20, 1937

This morning we went to Menaggio. There was ample room in the car—the three women in the back, the three men in front, including little Giorgio. The drive was most interesting, the first part because of the houses, all displaying Mussolini's proclamations, the second because of the magnificent landscape, which included Lake Como and its environs. It is truly a remarkable sight, the lake now green, now blue, surrounded by snow-capped mountains. The picture will, I believe, remain deeply engraved in my memory forever.

Menaggio itself, on the shore of Lake Como, is a dear little place. It has a splendid beach, wide lawns, swings, tennis courts, and above all, sun, water, mountains. In one word: magnificent. We bathed, sunbathed, played tennis for an hour and a half, and did not leave for home until after six in the evening.

June 21, 1937

The big event of the day was the *Duomo*. I had seen many pictures of it, knew it was built of white stone, that it had small pinnacles for every day of the week, and great pinnacles for holidays, plus a hundred to spare, that it was decorated with innumerable statues. In fact I saw it in my mind's eye. And yet, when I stood in the vast cathedral square opposite the resplendent, glittering structure, I stared, dumbfounded at the story-book cathedral. Then I walked towards it, and stepped through the embossed bronze portal.

The first few moments in the semi-darkness I saw only the huge pillared outline, and the brilliantly coloured, huge stained-glass windows. Then slowly my eyes reached the vaulted Gothic ceiling, and the tops of the statue-ornamented pillars. There, in the vastness, fluttered the countless lives of human beings whose hopes, fears, dreams and sorrows had been poured into those statues and pillars and wonderful frets.

I walked around the vast cathedral. Sacrificial candles burned on the altars, and the sun poured through some of the stained-glass windows. Suddenly the interior was both overpowering and exalting, and at the same time beautiful and meaningful. Even so, it was not that which most impressed me.

The hour I spent atop the dome—that, I shall never forget.

When I stepped out of the lift, which took me up several hundred feet, my breath caught in my throat. I was dazzled. I moved forward towards the lacy, supple Gothic arches, pinnacles and pillars, thinking, if this were music it would be trills played on the highest notes of violins. The white marble sparkled under the blue sky, and the entire scene reminded me of half-forgotten childhood fancies. This was how I had imagined fairyland to be: blue sky, white throne, white angels and tiny windows through which one could look down upon Earth. How distant the feverish commercial city, the noise of cars and trams from up there, how ridiculous the glitter of the shop windows looked compared to the great brilliance of that majestic height.

I reached the bottom of the tower and began climbing the narrow spiral staircase leading to the summit. A new vista at every turn, another statue, another lacy crenellation—like some sort of frost flower, or something equally diaphanous. I stood on the top step for a long while, feeling as if I had climbed there on Jacob's ladder, in a dream.

I looked at my watch. I had to turn back. I said goodbye at every step. It hurt so to leave the brilliance, the height, the peacefulness. I could take none of it with me. But as I walked down I suddenly knew I was actually taking an everlasting memory —a memory of a great longing for light, for height, for peace.

June 26, 1937

Tonight we attended an outdoor performance. The tickets cost four *lire*, which is very inexpensive. It is greatly to the credit of Fascism that such performances are arranged for, and placed within the means of, the people. The greater part of the audience of 5,000 appeared to be from the lower stratum of society, but despite this they had a better knowledge of music than the elegant audiences that generally attend the monstrously expensive concerts in Budapest.

June 27, 1937

This afternoon we went by car on a wonderful excursion in the direction of Certosa and Pavia. We spent more than an hour in Certosa, where we visited a magnificent church* and monastery. The enormous cloister was actually built for the use of just twenty-four people, and there are always twenty-four monks in residence. They live in separate cells, each decorated with frescoes, inlaid marble or embossed altars, icons and other priceless art treasures. A carved ivory polyptych of intricate workmanship was particularly beautiful.

Each monk has his own quarters. The cells are whitewashed, the workshop and dining room are downstairs, the bedrooms upstairs, and each monk has his own little garden to tend. They live out their lives there without ever talking to anyone, except for one hour each Sunday when they eat together and converse. I can't imagine that this sort of escape from reality is of any benefit to themselves, or to mankind.

July 1, 1937

We visited the famous cemetery of Milan. Somehow I felt it irreverent to tour a cemetery still in use, merely out of curiosity and armed with a camera. But this seems to be the accepted practice here. A group of Hindus visited it when we did, and they were taking one picture after the other.

---

* Undoubtedly the Certosa di Pavia, also known as the Carthusian Monastery.

The entrance to the cemetery is very beautiful too: arcades with crypts leading into them. The entire cemetery is looked after meticulously, and there are many handsome monuments. I recognized the three important ones myself, without the guide having to call my attention to them, which pleased me. The first represents a winding procession of the Calvary; the second consists of three masks: mockery, satire, pain; the third is a huge sculpture symbolizing man's labours and depicts a farmer ploughing with two yoked oxen. I was also impressed by a group composed of a nude, and in the background two nuns with bent heads. Opposite were a few atrocious figures in 19th-century dress, artless and ugly. But then they can't all be great works of art.

July 10, 1937

This afternoon we drove all over Milan. We visited the museum that is part of the Scala, and the most interesting thing in it— I think—is Rossini's spinet. After that we went into the Opera to see the stage and auditorium. Both are enormous, but of course during its summer slumber in mothballs and under covers it is not particularly impressive, apart from its size. It is interesting to note that the stage slopes, and there is a dome-shaped vault at the back which, when properly lighted, creates an impression of immensity. We saw all the percussion instruments used to create sound effects such as thunder, rain and wind, also the great bells, and the huge organ.

After the Scala we went to visit two churches. The second was Sant' Ambrogio, which we learned about in school, and I was pleased to be able to see it. It is plain, simple, Romanesque, with an excellent square courtyard. Built in two different periods, the steeple differs from the church proper.

We also went to Santa Maria del Fiore* where Leonardo da Vinci's *Last Supper* is hung. It had deteriorated badly, but not as badly as I had expected from what I have heard and read. The faces are still very distinct, and I enjoyed it very much, the more so since not long ago I read Merezhkovski's book, and thus felt closer to the spirit of the painting. The convent itself, the image of the one at Certosa, is inferior.

* Probably Santa Maria delle Grazie, where the *Last Supper* is hung in the adjacent Dominican Convent of Cenacolo Vinciano.

We saw the *Well of St. Francis,* a handsome statue so lifelike it seems to move. We merely passed by the War Memorial, the Lido, the City Park, the Municipal Stadium and the monumental stock exchange building with all its bas-reliefs. But we did stop and visit the great fairground that is in use only two weeks of the year. The rest of the time it is boarded up, its many buildings standing empty. It's a veritable labyrinth, with real, sturdy houses that do not have to be rebuilt every year, the way they are in the fairgrounds of Budapest.

July 12, 1937

I'm in a bad mood today, for the first time since I've been here —and not without reason. I wanted very much to go to Florence for a few days, but Mother won't allow me to. I found the news when we returned from Menaggio last night, and it ruined the wonderful mood I had been in all day. It was such a magnificent day, though very windy, and consequently the lake was really rough. But it's a wonderful sensation to swim in a lake with waves in it. I lay on a sort of wooden platform for a long time, while it was tossed about by the waves. We could clearly see the mountains, even snow-capped Mt. Rosa. All the way home we were in a fabulous mood, singing, laughing, wonderfully happy. And then Mother's letter with the news that Florence is out. What can I do about it? Of course I'll go straight home, but I now plan to stop in Venice and see it for myself. There is no time now to ask Mother's permission, but perhaps it's just as well because she might forbid me to do that too.

July 13, 1937

Last night we went to hear *La Bohème* in the courtyard of the Sforza Palace. The enormous quadrangle was filled with grandstands to accommodate an audience of 10,000, and the stage was equally impressive, both in size and decor. The performance started at nine, but we got there well in advance so as to find good seats. The birds fluttered overhead, and it all made a beautiful picture. At nine the audience began applauding, and soon the performance began. There was no curtain, only a blinding glare at the base of the darkened stage, which shone into the eyes of the audience whenever the sets were changed. It was a fine performance, the part of Mimi beautifully interpreted by the soprano. It was 12.30 by the time the opera ended.

On Board the Train
July 15, 1937

It is seven o'clock, and I have had a great day. When I got off the train at Venice this morning I left my luggage at the station and then, revelling in my independence, took a *vaporetto*. Of course I was already familiar with the Grand Canal from pictures, but even so, it was really interesting to see the steps of the palazzos leading directly into the water. I looked at the various famous buildings, blindingly white, reflected in the water. They are very old, and had they not been restored they would surely have crumbled long ago. It is mainly the foundations that are crumbling.

The *vaporetto* stopped near the Frari Monastery*. I got off, and after some searching finally found the Franciscan church. Because of my short-sleeved dress, I had to hire some sort of red shawl before I was permitted to enter. There are four world-famed masterpieces there: Titian's *The Assumption*, two Madonnas by Bellini, and the tomb of Canova. I was probably most impressed by the last. The frescoes are nearly all valuable works too. I spent approximately three-quarters of an hour there.

I took the vaporetto again, and arriving in St. Mark's Square went immediately to a restaurant. I ate, wrote a few postcards and paid. At about one I went to the Doges' Palace and across, through the ornate gate, to the courtyard. I looked at the two fountains, took some photos and walked up the giant staircase. Then I bought a ticket and set out to see the rooms. There are a great many frescoes by Tintoretto, Veronese, Titian and others. Of course it is impossible to look at everything carefully in such a short time, or even to make mental notes. In the arsenal I saw implements of torture, cannons and suits of armour. I found Tintoretto's *Paradiso* in the *Sala de Gran Consiglio* the most beautiful of all the paintings. It is at the end of an enormous room, and as one looks at it from the opposite side one is over-

* Santa Maria Gloriosa dei Frari.

whelmed by the swirling, writhing mass of figures. But taken one by one, and carefully examined, the figures separate and the painting is truly glorious.

I continued through the Palace, and on into St. Mark's Cathedral, with time only to glance at the wonders. I even managed to see the Tintoretto exhibition, and finished sightseeing at 4.30. Then I had an orangeade, and walked all the way back to the station. I am so glad I stopped in Venice, even if on the run. I saw so many remarkably beautiful things.

Now it is eleven o'clock at night, and since the Yugoslav border I've been sharing the compartment with a lady, the two of us alone. It's extremely pleasant.

Dombovár
Aged sixteen   *July 19, 1937*

I'm in Dombovár. Undoubtedly many things are different here, and of course I am more tied down. There I did almost everything the way it suited me, whereas here I am once again under Mother's wing. The meals are entirely different too. I am no longer used to the filling Hungarian diet.

At first the beach seemed tiny after the swimming pool at Milan, but I enjoy not having to sit alone with a book. I have so many girl friends here with whom I can go bathing. On the other hand, it's already quite clear that there will be no boys this summer. There are a great many non-Jewish boys, but the segregation here is so sharply defined one can't possibly think of mixing, or imagine that a Christian boy would even go near a Jewish girl. This segregation often seems comical, but actually it is a very sad and disquieting sign.

July 22, 1937

I'm writing on an empty stomach as I've been supposedly ill all day. I write supposedly because actually I'm as healthy as a horse. But they are forever trying to put me on a fattening diet, so I feigned a little indisposition as a counter-measure. The idea occurred to me because Evi was actually ill with an upset stomach, and so was Fini Mama. So I decided upon this little hoax. I had a difficult time convincing myself to do it, as it is, after all, a lie. But then I console myself that I am hurting no one and it's really good for the stomach to fast once in a while.

This morning Mother decided my tongue was coated (!) so I had to drink some bitter water. Of course I laughed to myself when she reached this conclusion. My luck is amazing because Aunt Eliz and Uncle Steve complained about a stomach upset too. So now they think we must all have eaten something upsetting. I must admit I'm a surprisingly good liar, but I really don't like to lie—it gives one a most unpleasant feeling.

Yesterday I finished a very charming and interesting book by Ernst Lothar, *Romance in F Major*. I could hardly put it down. It's the diary of a fifteen-year-old girl, and is very like mine, in both content and style. Now I am reading Nyiro's *In God's Yoke*, which I rather like. But I would never write that way myself, even if I could. Both language and environment are so foreign to me.

July 26, 1937

Good lord! I was interviewed! Mr. Szabo, the lawyer, told me yesterday that Mr. A., a journalist connected with the *Tolnamegyei News*, would like to meet me so that he could write an article about the 'poetess who is now holidaying in our town.' We said there was no point in this, whereupon Mr. A. arrived and proceeded to interview me very thoroughly. He asked a few trite questions. i.e., who is my favourite writer, favourite poet, etc. He then asked for some of my poems, and I read *Dance of the Moments*, and gave him *The Tear* to take away. Now I am waiting anxiously to see what he will write about me.

July 28, 1937

The paper appeared, and in the beginning of the article he wrote about Daddy, then about me. It's quite a good article, and everything would be fine but for one thing: he included the principal of my school in the piece, saying what a high opinion he has of me, or some such. This worries me a great deal, even though it is most unlikely this little paper will ever fall into the hands of the principal. But as this statement is not true, it is embarrassing.

Fini Mama is in bed; she has a severe cold, feels very weak, and is suffering a lot.

July 30, 1937

Fini Mama died last night. Sepsis, or some such, the doctor said. But it makes so little difference what it was. The fact is that for two days she suffered tremendously, and now she is gone. The closeness of death last night, when the doctor told us there was no hope, was so horrible that we all sobbed, and were incapable of saying anything. Mama is completely shattered, and I can do absolutely nothing to comfort her. I could only promise to do everything possible for her, to stay near her, as she will be so alone without Fini Mama. Daddy's death is constantly in my mind. I don't believe I have yet been able to grasp Fini Mama's death. Today I can't even cry. I have a continual feeling of strangulation, but otherwise I am quite calm.

Darling Fini Mama. I am happy now for every moment I was good to her, for the times I showed my love, and I think even if I hurt her once in a while, she loved me very much and was never really upset or angry with me.

July 31, 1937

I couldn't continue yesterday as Evi and I had to run around, helping as much as we could. Mother and Aunt Eliz are incapable of doing anything at all. Mother has been in bed all day, and I'm afraid now of how things will be when we return home. Aunt Manci arrived last night, and I see she has great self-control. I was told, however, that she was up all night, walking, and she, too, has been very much affected by the sudden blow.

I'm so tired. I've been getting up at *six* every morning, not because it's necessary, but because I can't sleep. I feel well enough in spirits, but extremely worried and fearful about Mama. I can understand how difficult life at home will be for her now. I also realize what silly conceit it was for me to think, even for a moment, that I could replace Fini Mama. But just the same, if George feels as I do, between us we can make things much easier for Mama. I am going to write to him now in Paris, but Mother doesn't want me to tell him about Fini Mama's death as he can't return on his own anyway; he must remain with his group.

August 1, 1937

We buried Fini Mama at two o'clock this afternoon. Many relatives came from all over, which meant a great deal of work, of course, so Evi and I were busy all day. The funeral was a little late starting. The entire thing was so awful. The catafalque was in the courtyard, and the rabbi spoke there. Then we accompanied the coffin to the cemetery on foot. It all seems so distant now. S.L., who remained here longer than the others because his train left later, laughed heartily at his own stories, and without wanting to we instinctively laughed with him. Life remains the same regardless. Only Fini Mama has gone. Poor Mama, how will she be once we return home?

There has been considerable discussion as to whether Fini Mama should have been buried in Jánosháza, next to Grandpa, but we finally decided it would be best to bury her here. I was in agreement with this, for after all, the entire ritual is more for the living, so they can occasionally visit the grave. If there is a soul which lives on, it can meet its loved ones anyway; and the body, which quickly disintegrates, doesn't care whether it rests beside the dust of a loved one, or beside that of a stranger.

Budapest
August 22, 1937

George returned on the 20th, and Frank and his guest from Belgium arrived on the same day. We were extremely eager to see George, who looks very well, and had a great deal to tell us before the others arrived. But since then we've had absolutely no time to talk. There is a lot to do, and sometimes the boys are away all day sightseeing, coming home only to eat and sleep. Even so, they cause a lot of extra work.

August 25, 1937

The boys left. The last day I guided them through Parliament and other places. Since they've gone there is considerably less work, but even so, thanks to my clumsiness I've broken a beautiful hand-engraved glass, and two lovely plates. And besides all that, today I put too much salt in the spinach. In connection with this last incident the usual remarks were made, of course*.

I can see Mother is convinced I'm in love with Peter, even though I'm now positive I'm not. Pity, because he is a very nice boy, and I am not indifferent to him. But even though I've now known him for six months we're still so distant, so remote, that it's difficult to imagine we could ever be really good friends. We talk about books and related subjects, but of other matters—not necessarily sentimental ones—such as plans for the future, dreams, hopes, doubts, there is rarely any mention.

August 30, 1937

School starts in a few days. I can't say I made the most of my last days of the holiday. As far as sports are concerned, I had little time for them. The time I did have I devoted to reading and to putting photographs and reproductions in order. (I already have five albums full.) Yesterday I went to the cinema, the first time I've been since Fini Mama's death. Saw Greta Garbo in *Camille*, and thought it superb. It's a sad film but beautiful, and Garbo gives a brilliant performance, as does her partner, Robert Taylor.

This afternoon three of my girl friends were here. I told them about my trip to Italy, and showed them pictures and souvenirs.

September 5, 1937

It's the Jewish New Year and I wondered whether or not to write on this day. But to my way of thinking this is a prohibition impossible to obey. Religion, in the truest sense, does not consist of such things.

School has started, and everything is much the same except that I've dropped Latin. I already thought about doing that last year, since it takes so much time, and I know I'll never have any use for it because I have no intention of going to the university.

---

* Old Hungarian axiom: too much salt indicates the cook is passionately in love.

September 16, 1937

A lot of things happened today, among them one that is very unpleasant. At the statutory meeting of the Literary Society I was nominated for office, along with several of my classmates. I was elected. The Literary Society generally accepts officers elected by the class, but in this case they called for a new election, and nominated two other girls to stand with me as candidates. This clearly indicated that they did not want a Jew—me, that is—to become an officer, which hurts me very much. Had I not been elected I would not have said a word, but this way it was a decided insult. Now I don't want to take part in, or have anything to do with the work of the Society, and don't care about it any more.

Fortunately, pleasant things happened as well. I began coaching Irma today. I am to give her two one-hour lessons a week, for which I will be paid twenty *pengö*. This is really very good. And she invited me to a party at her house next Saturday. There will be some really interesting people there.

Peter telephoned too, and asked whether he could come and see me. We arranged it for Sunday morning.

October 1, 1937

I'm just finishing Daddy's book, *The Eleventh Commandment*, and am completely captivated by it. Thanks to this book Daddy seems so close, even closer than before. I know a novel has little to do with real life, but just the same, it portrays Daddy's youth —with a bit of exaggeration—and his and Mother's love. It is so dear and charming. I want to read Daddy's other books now. It's really about time!

October 6, 1937

Peter was here this afternoon, and we went for a walk. We talked about all sorts of things that belong in a diary. After a good deal of tactful preamble he gave me to understand that he loves me. I listened quietly to his declaration—which did not surprise me. Yesterday we went to the cinema, together with Irma and another boy, and Peter kept looking at me in the dark in such a way that what he said today did not catch me unawares. Besides,

I thought he probably cared because he wanted to see me today after we had been together just yesterday. He also insisted, at all costs, that we go for a walk.

I was nice to him, too, even though I did not say I loved him, because had I said it it might well have been untrue. Anyway, I'm happy, as this was the first time I was pleased to hear such a declaration. (I can't say I was ever displeased to hear such a thing, but I certainly had no reciprocal feelings before.) In connection with this we then talked about a lot of things, and thus immediately felt much closer.

I don't know whether I'll tell Mama, though I think I will.

It's not very nice of me to have anything to do with any other boy now, considering how Peter feels about me. But the fact is, not long ago Sandor was here again, and we passed the time quite pleasantly. On another day János came. He is a bit shy, but an intelligent fellow. His parents are good friends of Mama, and he came with them.

October 23, 1937

What a long time since I've written! There's not much news, but one can always find little things to note. Since then Peter has been here only once. But we're meeting again this afternoon at the home of a friend.

Life at school is rather dull. I am not really working. At the moment I'm most interested in English. I read Pearl Buck's *East Wind, West Wind* not long ago, and now I'm reading *The Good Earth*. I received a letter from my English pen-friend and answered immediately.

At the moment, George and I are on good terms. He is very ambitious and having studied French arduously is now devoting himself to English. He is teaching me French once a week, and I'm teaching him English. I am also attending English courses at the Foreign Affairs Society, where they teach foreign languages comprehensively.

November 15, 1937

Oh, how wonderful it was yesterday, Sunday! We had planned an excursion in the morning with the usual crowd, but there was such a fabulous snowfall in the early morning that naturally I immediately thought of going skiing. I didn't know how the others would feel, whether I would find anyone to go with, and thought of giving up the whole idea, when first János, then Peter telephoned, both suggesting that we go skiing. I gathered together my ski things, and by eleven we were up at Schwab Hill. We didn't get back until five, though János and his sister left a little earlier. I stayed on for a little while with Peter and Danny, who had joined us. In the end I was quite tired, but it was really marvellous. I skied quite well, compared to last year.

Today's news: I'm going to coach two more of my classmates.

January 14, 1938

As I leafed through my diary, reading bits and pieces, I noticed that events concerning the Peter affair are not clear. In short, I was already a little bored with him, and he expected a greater response from me. I'm afraid I was not particularly nice to him, and he noticed my indifference. That was that! I wasn't a bit sorry.

At present my school life is quite satisfactory, and I have several interesting assignments. I also have a new pupil. On the whole, I'm very satisfied with things.

January 28, 1938

I've not mentioned Marianne's party before. I should really call it a Big Affair rather than a party; it was truly a large-scale, brilliant evening, the entire atmosphere delightful and gay. Between dancing and good conversation, the hours literally flew. I didn't get home until four in the morning. It's a good thing Paul is here from Dombovár so we can go out together, and I have no need of an escort.

Mary, my English pen-friend, wrote about my proposed trip to England this summer, but I'm afraid it probably won't be possible for me to go until next year, though I would much rather go now as times are so uncertain.

Saturday afternoon Náday was here again. I really can talk to him; he's such an intelligent, attractive fellow. We ended up discussing differential and integral calculus, but naturally we don't generally talk about such things!

Saturday night we spent in a most delightful manner: we read aloud the letters Daddy wrote Mama. They are such humorous, dear letters that it's a joy to read them. I can imagine how much they meant to Mama. We haven't finished reading all of them. Perhaps we'll continue tonight.

March 13, 1938

Today I want to write about two things: political events, and last night. And as in time and importance the political situation is foremost, I'll begin with that.

Not long ago, just before Hitler's annual progress report to the Reichstag (February 20) the Austrian Chancellor, Dr. Kurt von Schuschnigg, went to Germany at the invitation of Hitler. Ostensibly they had a most cordial conference, and we heard little about the question of *Anschluss*. Arthur Seyss-Inquart, a lawyer and Nazi politician, became a member of the re-organized Austrian cabinet (Minister of Security), but there were no other visible signs of Hitler's influence. Thus, understandably, there was an uproar when Schuschnigg—on Wednesday, if I correctly recall—ordered a plebiscite for Sunday, March 13, for the question of *Anschluss*—Yes or No. The sudden decision naturally surprised everyone, including those outside Austria, but we all calmly awaited the results, confident the vote would be in favour of independence. This was the situation on Friday.

That evening we happened to turn on the radio, and were appalled to hear the following: 'The plebiscite has been postponed. Germany has given an ultimatum demanding the resignation of Schuschnigg. Compelled to submit to force, Schuschnigg bade farewell to Austria in a radio address, and Seyss-Inquart seized controlling power of Austria. In the interest of establishing peace and order in Austria he urgently requested German troops.'

Saturday morning (March 12) the occupation of Austria began, troops were on the march, and at this moment Austria is entirely under Nazi control.

These events have caused indescribable tension in Hungary too. In school, on the street, even at parties, it is the main topic of discussion. The lives of many people here are closely affected by these events. But even those not immediately involved are awaiting the mobilization of Czechoslovakia with deep concern and interest, wondering whether she will take steps to insure the safety of the Sudeten Germans. There is also speculation concerning the next moves of England and France (there is a political crisis in the latter), and whom Italy will side with. And not least, what will happen to us in the shadow of an eastward-expanding nation of seventy million?

Hitler is arriving in Vienna today. Setting aside all antipathy, one must admit he accomplished things extremely cleverly and boldly. At the moment everything is at a standstill, and everyone is awaiting developments, apprehensive of the future.

A gayer and lovelier event was the affair last night at Lily's house, where about forty of us were invited. After the usual leisurely beginning, we danced, had a buffet supper, sang, and the atmosphere became delightful and relaxed. I danced a lot, and had a fabulous time.

April 4, 1938

I'm ashamed not to have written anything about today's depressed, tense, agitated world, and even now I'm writing only to sum up the happenings of Saturday evening. But one talks and hears so much about events in Austria, and one is so nervous about the local situation, that by the time it comes to writing about things, one feels too depressed and discouraged. Of course George won't go to Austria next year, as planned, but perhaps to France—for good. Thus we'll be torn apart, scattered.

But to get back to Saturday night. We were at Vera's and I really enjoyed myself. The atmosphere was superb. We danced a lot, and Vera improvised a charming little bar. As usual, the company was wonderful.

I spent most of the evening with George Revai. I don't believe I've mentioned him before, though I've met him several times. When we first met we danced together only occasionally, but lately much more often. He's a wonderful dancer, and a rather nice fellow. He told me, among other things, how much my behaviour, manner of speaking, etc., etc., appeal to him. He said he would like his sister to be like me, and 'consoled' me with the assurance that, even if I didn't have as many admirers as some of the other 'types', I would always have greater success than they with boys who are really worthwhile. It's interesting that Marianne's cousin said exactly the same thing about me not long ago.

Of course I danced with a good many other boys besides Revai, and it was daylight by the time the party broke up.

Dombovár
April 24, 1938

It's been such a long time again since I wrote. Meanwhile really a lot has happened. I've been in Dombovár a week. Left Budapest Tuesday, and had an exciting adventure on the train. Well, adventure is an exaggeration; let's just call it an encounter. When I got on the train a young man helped me with my bag, sat beside me, and I immediately noticed he wanted to get acquainted. So I got out my book, *The Moon and Sixpence* by Somerset Maugham—a wonderful novel which actually deserves a separate paragraph—and started reading.

'Will it bother you if I smoke?' 'Are you going to Dombovár?' (The conductor had mentioned it when he took my ticket.) 'Do you know . . . there?' I answered his questions rather laconically. But when I started pulling at the window and he got up and vigorously helped me yank it down, I couldn't do anything but answer his questions. It turned out he is a Presbyterian theologian, and when he tried to convince me that I ought to attend divinity classes, I gave him to understand this would be impossible because. . . .

This did not deter him from asking further questions. On the contrary. He insisted upon knowing my name. However, I did not tell him, whereupon he stated it was evident that we Jews stubbornly withdrew from all possible social contact and integration. We discussed matters in connection with this question, and I assured him that this was certainly not why I wouldn't tell him my name. Whereupon he pretended he was very upset and vowed he would wait for me one day after school. I asked him not to do that, and thus the matter ended.

The debate on the Jewish Bill* is now in progress. There has

* On March 11, 1938, as a result of the Austrian Anschluss, anti-Semitism increased in Hungary, and a debate on the 'Jewish Question' was opened in the Hungarian Parliament. This resulted in the 'Jewish Bill', which became the first 'Jewish Law', and reduced the ratio of Jewish representation in the economic field to twenty per cent. It was also stated that 'the expansion of the Jews is as detrimental to the nation as it is dangerous; we must take steps to defend ourselves against their propagation. Their relegation to the background is a national duty.'

been, and continues to be, terrible tension about it, and conjecture as to whether there will be a law concerning this Bill. People are talking about it everywhere. Commerce, industry, the theatre, cafés—everything is at a standstill while this matter is under discussion in Parliament. I wonder how all this will end?

Budapest
April 28, 1938

School has started again. There isn't much news. All in all, the atmosphere is tense and restless. There are great problems about what it would be best for George to do after graduation, which is drawing close. I've written very little lately. My 'novel' is progressing rather slowly. I can work only when there is no one at home. I wrote an historical poem as a school project, which I like, as do others who have heard it.

May 7, 1938

George's graduation ceremony took place this morning, and this afternoon there was a farewell gathering at the synagogue in honour of the graduates. This has been customary for years, but this year it had a special significance, and was a much sadder occasion than usual. Boys of this year's class will be scattered and can look forward only to an uncertain future. Ivan spoke, and attempted to make his message strong and hopeful, but even so it was such a hopeless and resigned speech. True, one can hardly feel otherwise these days. At any rate, it was a sad affair, and particularly so for me because of George. It was only then that I actually realized what it means to have him leaving home immediately after graduation, without knowing what will become of him, when he will be able to return. How awful it must be for Mother.

Among George's classmates there are a few Arrow-Crossers* and he asked them to look after Mother and me if there should be any trouble. It's horrible how everyone takes it so much for granted that there will be trouble, and very naïve to think these boys would do anything for us if the need arose. At any rate, it was dear of George to speak to them.

After the services at the synagogue I went to play tennis— the fourth time this season—and it went very well.

* Hungarian Nazis.

May 30, 1938

I'm writing this after another 'night of revelry'. I try to convince myself that my diary is not concerned only with such events, but at any rate I've only remembered to make an entry about it now.

We were at Mary's house. I went with Peter, and wore my new dress—the muslin de soie over blue taffeta, with a pink flower in the belt. It's really adorable. I did my own hair, and was a bit nervous it wouldn't turn out right. But it looked quite good.

I ought to mention, as a preliminary, that I was somewhat dubious about going to Mary's party as the family have only recently converted to Christianity, and I very much condemn this. But my desire for a night of fun conquered my reluctance. We got there at 10.15, the last to arrive. They had just begun serving supper. I sat at a small table with a very pleasant group. After supper we danced, and it was a most enjoyable affair.

I have some big news: the Virags have invited me to spend the summer at Lelle where I will help a bit in their guest house. I'm delighted as this sort of work interests me greatly. My trip to England is out of the question anyway, so this will be very nice.

I've written a new poem. It's called *Blue*. I like it very much.

June 15, 1938

Today was the last day of school. I got A's in everything, and won second prize in the photography competition. This year it was the only activity in which I competed. I haven't participated in the Literary Society since the incident last Autumn. On the whole, I was rather lax the entire term. Next term I'll work harder.

I think a worthy manner in which to close today is to note that I just finished reading *Crime and Punishment*. I was enormously impressed by the characterization and somehow—subconsciously—felt there was considerable similarity in family traits and characteristics between the family portrayed in the book and ours. Of course only in certain particulars.

This diary has also come to an end. I think it will belong among my most cherished mementoes.

June 23, 1938

I'm starting a new diary once again. This will be my third, and I'm beginning it with considerable emotion. I'm reminded of the words of Mr. Toth, the schoolmaster at Dombovár who encouraged me to start my first diary four years ago. He told me it would be such a delightful memento that if ever a fire broke out in my house the diary would be the first thing I would think of saving! Perhaps he was right.

I can only write a few lines now. I'm in the midst of feverish packing and general commotion as I'm leaving for Lelle this afternoon. It will be very difficult to say goodbye to George.

Lelle
June 28, 1938

I'm going home. I am terribly ashamed at not being able to adapt myself to the principles of Lisbeth's mother. The only real pastime here is bathing in the Balaton, but near the shore the water is so shallow it's only possible to wade and splash about. I was given to understand that Lisbeth's mother would not permit us to swim beyond the point where we could touch the bottom, so I swam out to about shoulder-depth. This, however, is relatively far out, so it's difficult to see a white bathing cap in the distance. Today, when Lisbeth's mother came to the beach and saw how 'terribly far' I had swum, she had palpitations, and became extremely upset. When I begged her pardon she declared she was not disposed to be upset by me, etc., etc. I gathered she thought it would be best if I went home. I remained relatively calm and spoke politely, but felt near to breaking point and began crying, so ran to my room. I locked the door, and cried for a long time. Meanwhile I began writing in my diary.

I was infinitely hurt by the entire thing, and am ashamed to think I'm going home under these circumstances. . . . I was sitting like this, crying, when Lisbeth and her mother came to the door. Lisbeth's mother was very kind then and asked me to believe she was only concerned about my safety and welfare, and that she realized she had been hasty. In other words, she had cooled down. She asked me not to let the same thing happen again, kissed me, and entreated me to stop crying. Of course this is easier said than done. Now I must stop writing as I have to go down to lunch. I hope my eyes aren't too red.

It's now afternoon. The storm is over, everything has calmed down, and seems to be all right. But it has left a deep impression on me. If I stay on, even if I try to convince myself it was all due only to tension, worry and basic good will followed by kind words, I think I'll still have difficulty forgetting this morning's scene. I could still cry if I weren't making a considerable effort to contain myself. I don't think I'll stay beyond the middle of July, unless there is more work, things to see and learn that would fill my days. In other words, I'll see how things go.

July 2, 1938

I've already forgotten the incident of the other day. Since then everything has been going very nicely. These last two days we've spent a lot of time boating, and I've even learned to row, which I've enjoyed tremendously. What we do, Lisbeth and I, is take the rowing boat out, sit in it, sunbathe, read, and watch the *D-22*, a beautiful big sailing boat which circles around us a good deal . . . of course not empty, but with its three masters. This is the only interesting boy situation, as the young chap at the guest house really doesn't count. If he comes down in the afternoon and stretches out in a hammock near us, I immediately start reading *The Village Notary**, and laugh when he wonders how I can read this 'required' reading matter during my holidays.

Matters concerning George's emigration, i.e., foreign currency, documents, etc., have been settled, thank God, and he'll soon be leaving. I am so glad everything is finally in order for his departure, regardless of how my heart aches at his going. If his train passes through Lelle we're going to the station to see him. Poor Mother; I'm so sorry for her. I know she's crushed, but I'm sure this is best for George—as far as anyone can tell these days.

July 10, 1938

I see I've neglected to report that we boarded George's train according to plan, and managed to exchange a few words with him. I don't know when I'll see the 'old man' again. The farewell

---

* A Hungarian novel by Baron Joseph Eötvös, once compulsory reading in all Hungarian schools.

itself wasn't really emotional since we confined our conversation to all sorts of banalities, such as a new tennis racket, my Italian lessons, my suntan, mutual friends and so on. The train had already begun moving when I told him the length of the swimming pool in Milan. But behind it all was the fact that he is starting out in life on his own. It must be very difficult for poor Mother, home alone. She writes that fortunately she has a lot to do. I would like her to have a holiday too this year, without fail. She's the one who has the greatest need of a bit of rest and peace.

Today the weather is ugly, stormy. But Lake Balaton is perhaps most beautiful at such times, though the colours and vistas are so wonderful most mornings and evenings that it's impossible to say when it's loveliest.

I wrote this poem, *Farewell*, for George's departure:

Farewell*

You left. We waved a long while.
Porters clattered behind.
We watched and you disappeared.

Life took you. You were happy.
Maybe your heart had songs within.
Our tears were well hidden.

Wordless, we went home
Watching the sky, pale and blue,
And our soul, unseen and secretly
Is waving still to you.

July 14, 1938

Mother wrote to say that she showed some of my poems to Alkalay, a journalist and translator, and that he was surprised and favourably impressed by them. I'll hear all the particulars when I get home. He mentioned someone to whom I could take the poems, and I shall do so. I now need honest and serious criticism, not just the praise of family and close friends.

I feel that writing isn't difficult for me, and if something turns

* Translated from the Hungarian by Peter Hay.

out well it gives one such a great feeling. The other day, in a
weak moment, I recited for Lisbeth the farewell poem I wrote
for George. I think it's good because of its simplicity and
informality. Whereupon she remarked how nice it is when a
person can write a poem when he wants to, and that she wrote
her last poem when she was twelve, but since then hasn't felt
like writing poems. I could have used greater discrimination in
my choice of audience, but sometimes the overwhelming need to
share and confide gets the best of one.

A while ago I had a great adventure: for 60 fillér I found
out about my future. A gypsy read my left palm. I need not say
what a disappointment such a thing can be. When I'm eighteen
I am going to be a bride, my husband is going to own a car. . . .
Later she said that he won't be rich but that we're going to have
a very happy and satisfying life together. I am going to have
only one son. She couldn't tell me much about the rest of this
year, but for 1939 she predicted a lot of happiness.

Aged seventeen

Budapest
July 21, 1938

I finally arrived home on Tuesday night. The last days at Lelle
were quite pleasant. Gaby came on Saturday. It was good to be
able to talk to him. Saturday evening a rather large group of us
went out and celebrated my birthday—my seventeenth. At mid-
night we drank to my health, danced a bit, and at about two in
the morning went home. Sunday morning a lot of people con-
gratulated me, Gaby sent flowers. In the morning we went
swimming, rowing, and played ping-pong. The lake was a bit
rough, which I enjoyed tremendously.

That afternoon I said goodbye to everyone, and left. Arrived
back at nine in the evening, and am wonderfully happy to be home
again. Mother and I were so delighted to see each other, but
we're already discussing the possibility of my going away, somewhere in the mountains.

July 25, 1938

It's been settled. I'm going to Biela-Voda, near Tatralomnic.
They say it's a very beautiful and pleasant place. I'm very happy

now about the idea, though at first I really didn't have much desire to go. I'm leaving on the 30th, and staying until August 20th, just three weeks. It will cost two hundred and twenty *pengö* plus the fare, which is expensive. But somehow everyone has now lost the value of money, wondering whether what has happened in Vienna will happen here. If it does, it will make really very little difference how much one has left for them to confiscate. Perhaps one should not take this attitude, but we're so thoroughly prepared for the worst and feel it's really only a matter of time. It's a good thing George has got out, and our only consolation and comfort.

July 28, 1938

Yesterday I went to see Piroska Reichardt, one of the journalists on *The Nyugat**. I have long been wanting the opinion of a professional, and believe I got exactly that from her. She received me by saying the poems surprised her, and she thinks I'm talented. She said they are definitely better than average, and thinks I will become a writer, though not necessarily a poet. Judging by the poems, she doesn't consider me entirely lyrical. She then told me what the faults are: they are apt to be long, and she feels I compromise the form for the sake of content. She also feels that sometimes my manner of expression is still rather immature. But on the whole she finds me talented. I was terribly pleased. Somehow, one has more confidence after professional criticism.

Day after tomorrow I leave for Biela-Voda. It's near Teplic, and I believe it will be very nice. Evi and I are going together; she's arriving today from Dombovár and I'm meeting her at the station. I have an awful lot to do, packing, shopping for a few things, and so on.

I still have to mention the Danny affair. Not long ago I received a letter from him in which, among other things, he wrote that he has been in love with me for years. He claims he made such an enormous effort to do well at school only to please me, and feels he could eventually go quite far—for my sake. He asks me to answer yes or no.

I was tremendously surprised by this letter. I didn't consider

* The foremost Hungarian literary magazine of that era.

THE MORRIS AND DOROTHY HIRSCH
RESEARCH LIBRARY OF
HOLOCAUST AND GENOCIDE STUDIES

Danny an idealist, one who silently struggles and suffers (he
claims he suffered too!). At any rate, the entire affair was quite
uncomfortable, but I answered at once because if what he writes
is true, then he actually does take the whole thing most seriously,
and I don't want to keep him waiting for my answer. I was very
kind but firm in my refusal. I am not saying he's not a very
decent fellow, but he has certain characteristics which preclude
my taking his proposal seriously even for a moment.

Biela-Voda
July 31, 1938

We arrived in Biela-Voda yesterday. The road up was lovely,
particularly the second half, after we reached the mountains and
pine forests. We got off at Poprad, where Aunt Magda and a
few girls were waiting for us. We came up by car along a
magnificent road. Biela-Voda itself is fabulous. The house is very
attractive, the mountains glorious. There is a forest, and paths
for walking right in the heart of it. It's truly wonderful. I don't
have much time to write now.

The company is absolutely delightful. Last night we went for
a walk, and this morning I got up at five and went for a walk
again. It was marvellous. I was all alone, the air was heavenly,
the view superb. I saw the sunrise, sang, picked strawberries,
and some other edible berry, looked for a four-leaf clover (didn't
find one), carved the map of Hungary on a bench and the letters
N.N.S.*, then sat on a tree stump and marvelled at the view.
Stupendous!

August 4, 1938

Last night we had a jolly evening, for which we prepared all day
Wednesday. Evi and I performed *The Proposal* in four different
ages, and presented it the way we once did at school. I have a
right to copy the production as it was my idea to begin with.
The four scenes consisted of 1,000 B.C., the time of the
Crusades, the age of our grandmothers, and the future. Evi and
I performed them all. We managed to assemble some excellent

* No, No, Never! The Hungarian slogan meaning they never would give
up the fight to regain the ceded Territories.

costumes, and everyone thought this was the highlight of the evening.

Afterwards there was a dance. Not that there is a single boy worth writing about, but all the girls are very nice.

August 12, 1938

Again several days have gone by. Mother has arrived too, but I don't know whether it will suit her. I feel wonderful here. Since I last wrote we made an excursion to Moses Springs, from where the view is breath-taking, even frightening. Then we went back to Steinbach Sea and descended along a rather long road to Gemse where there is a perfectly situated hostel. On the most beautiful section of this road there is a magnificent foaming-white waterfall which springs from an extremely precipitous cliff. It's really an extravagant sight. From there we hiked down to Lomnic, and that evening arrived home dead tired.

Now ping-pong is in full force, and I won the championship. Such simple pleasures still exist in this world.

Budapest
August 30, 1938

This summer, as all the others, has gone by so quickly. School starts on the 3rd. In times past I was always glad to return to classes, but this year I await the opening with mixed emotions. I am partially prepared for serious work, on the other hand I feel some concern about the Literary Society, and the likelihood of similar unpleasantnesses cropping up—and they probably will. And then the knowledge that this is my last year of school is so strange. At home we're already beginning to discuss the choice of a career. I never imagined it would be as difficult for me to choose as it is for most others.

At the moment we're considering hotel management, but in the background there is always the possibility of writing pro-fessionally—and whatever I do, the biggest question is *where*? Here, or somewhere abroad? It's not easy to find a job any-where. It can't be said we were born into an easy world, my generation.

Now everyone is again talking about war, but this doesn't

even interest me anymore because for the past six months the situation has been vacillating from dangerous to less dangerous. I'm trying not to be too concerned with things because I know I'll have great need of good, steady nerves in the near future, and it would be a pity to ruin them now.

September 9, 1938

It's three o'clock and I've already finished all my homework. Susie and Manci, and a boy named Bela, whom I met yesterday quite by chance, are coming later this afternoon.

Mother's old piano teacher came to town, and Mother went to visit her. As the place she is staying in is close to the tennis courts, Mother convinced me that I ought to go up after my game and meet her. So I went, and quite by chance there was this boy from Kolozsvár in town for just a few days. When we left he immediately asked when he could see me again, but I gave him an evasive answer. Whereupon he telephoned at lunchtime and asked 'When and where?' So I asked him to come over this afternoon as some friends were coming to play ping-pong.

September 17, 1938

We're living through indescribably tense days. The question is: Will there be war? The mobilization going on in various countries doesn't fill one with a great deal of confidence. No recent news concerning the discussions of Hitler and Chamberlain. The entire world is united in fearful suspense. I, for one, feel a numbing indifference because of all this waiting. The situation changes from minute to minute. Even the *idea* there may be war is abominable enough.

From my point of view, I'm glad George is in France, though Mother is extremely worried about him. Of course this is understandable. The devil take the Sudeten Germans and all the other Germans, along with their Führer. One feels better saying these things. Why is it necessary to ruin the world, turn it topsy-turvy, when everything could be so pleasant? Or is that impossible? Is it contrary to the nature of man? Gaby sees the war entirely differently. Materialistically. To him the annihilation of mankind is unimportant. And he is able to defend his point of

view so ingeniously that one can hardly stand up to him with a
counter-argument.

September 27, 1938

Ten days have passed since my last entry, and the situation
remains unchanged. Negotiations, Mussolini's and Hitler's
speeches, Chamberlain's flights back and forth, news bulletins
concerning mobilization, denials. There have been practice air-
raid alerts and the situation remains unchanged. One wonders,
will there be war, or won't there? Though the atmosphere is
explosive I still believe there will be peace, perhaps only because
I just can't possibly imagine war.

Under these circumstances one can't look forward to the
Jewish New Year holidays as a time of renewed hope and peace.
For us Jews the situation is doubly serious, and it's difficult to
imagine how all this will be solved. I am going to the synagogue
now, though not with any great enthusiasm. There will be some
sort of youth service, though the situation doesn't arouse much
feeling of devotion in one. But I'm going just the same.

September 29, 1938

I think one can safely state that the excitement and tension have
reached a peak. Hitler's ultimatum* runs out tomorrow, and
peace is only possible if Czechoslovakia hands over the territories Hitler demands—free of Czech nationals. This is impossible. Today, at the last moment, Chamberlain, Hitler, Daladier
and Mussolini are making a final attempt to save the peace.
Though until now I believed in the possibility of maintaining
the peace, I am now beginning to have doubts. Mobilization has
started everywhere. Perhaps George has already left France. I
feel so sorry that the poor boy has to make such difficult decisions alone. Perhaps he'll return home, perhaps he'll be lucky
and manage to get to Switzerland. Mother's tension is understandable; but everyone has something or someone to worry
about.

Now an entirely different subject: I recently had a letter from
Bela. It went even further than Danny's. I don't know how to

* The Godesberg memorandum to Czechoslovakia.

answer him. It's a difficult business. And my usual luck—I don't like him the tiniest bit.

October 1, 1938

It is the Saturday before the Day of Atonement. I should have gone to synagogue, but instead I wrote a poem, and now I would rather attempt some self-analysis in my diary.

I don't quite know where to begin. That I made many errors this past year (though I don't feel I actually sinned) I know. Errors against God, righteousness, people, and above all, against Mother, and even against myself. I know I have many mistakes to answer for, and see them all clearly in my mind's eye. But I find myself incapable of enumerating them, of writing them all down. Perhaps deep down I'm afraid that someday someone might read what I have written. And I am really incapable of 'confessing'.

I would like to be as good as possible to Mother, to wear my Jewishness with pride, to be well thought of in my class at school, and I would very much like always to be able to believe and trust in God. There are times I cannot, and at such times I attempt to force myself to believe completely, firmly, with total certainty.

October 16, 1938

I see I write only when there is something wrong. I constantly lamented the danger of war, but I did not comment upon the Four-Power Conference* and the easing of the situation. True, too much rejoicing would be precipitate since so far only the demands of Germany and Poland have been satisfied. Our [Hungarian] territories have not yet been returned. So far we have been given only two small areas. Other than that they wanted to give us barely anything, and the Hungarian-Czechoslovak conferences were recently discontinued.

There has been a resumption of the draft. New age groups are currently being called up, and there are other signs that if things can't be peacefully settled they will resort to arms. But

---

* Undoubtedly a reference to the Munich Agreement of September 29, 1938, signed in the early morning of September 30.

nevertheless we're all hopeful that a settlement will be reached—without war.

October 27, 1938

I don't know whether I've already mentioned that I've become a Zionist. This word stands for a tremendous number of things. To me it means, in short, that I now consciously and strongly feel I am a Jew, and am proud of it. My primary aim is to go to Palestine, to work for it. Of course this did not develop from one day to the next; it was a somewhat gradual development. There was first talk of it about three years ago, and at that time I vehemently attacked the Zionist Movement. Since then people, events, times, have all brought me closer to the idea, and I am immeasurably happy that I've found this ideal, that I now feel firm ground under my feet, and can see a definite goal towards which it is really worth striving. I am going to start learning Hebrew, and I'll attend one of the youth groups. In short, I'm really going to knuckle down properly. I've become a different person, and it's a very good feeling.

One needs something to believe in, something for which one can have whole-hearted enthusiasm. One needs to feel that one's life has meaning, that one is needed in this world. Zionism fulfils all this for me. One hears a good many arguments against the Movement, but this doesn't matter. I believe in it, and that's the important thing.

I'm convinced Zionism is Jewry's solution to its problems, and that the outstanding work being done in Palestine is not in vain.

November 12, 1938

I have so much to write about I don't even know where to begin. We have got back the Upper part of Northern Hungary*. From the 2nd of November until the 10th the joyous and enthusiastic entry of Hungarian troops took place from Komarom to Kassa. We had no school, and thanks to the radio we too felt involved

* Following the Munich Agreement, Hungary was awarded 7,500 sq. miles of the Czechoslovak Highlands, with a population of 500,000 Hungarians and 272,000 Slovaks. This was originally part of Hungary and was lost in World War I.

in the entry. And this morning the four senior classes, in groups of ten, attended a special holiday sitting of Parliament which was very interesting. But I must honestly state that to me the road I am now following in the Zionist Movement means far more, both emotionally and spiritually.

I am learning Hebrew, reading about Palestine, and am also reading Szechenyi's *Peoples of the East,* a brilliant book which gives fundamental facts concerning the lives of all the people of the world. On the whole, I'm reading considerably more, and about far more serious subjects than hitherto.

I am determinedly and purposefully preparing for life in Palestine. And although I confess that in many respects it's painful to tear myself from my Hungarian sentiments, I must do so in my own interest, and the interests of Jewry. Our two-thousand-year history justifies us, the present compels us, the future gives us confidence. Whoever is aware of his Jewishness cannot continue with his eyes shut. As yet, our aims are not entirely definite nor am I sure what profession I'll choose. But I don't want to work only for myself and in my own interests, but for the mutual good of Jewish aims. Perhaps these are but the vague and confused thoughts and fantasies of youth, but I think I will have the fortitude, strength and ability to realize these dreams.

Mother is having difficulty accepting the idea that I will eventually emigrate, but because she is completely unselfish she won't place obstacles in my way. Naturally I would be so happy if she came too. The three of us must not be torn apart, must not go three different ways.

George is well, and we are always eagerly awaiting news from him. Recently he won a ping-pong tournament in Lyon; his picture was even in the papers there. We were so pleased for him.

November 20, 1938

The thought that now occupies my every waking moment is Palestine. Everything in connection with it interests me, everything else is entirely secondary. Even school has lost some of its meaning, and the only thing I am studying hard is Hebrew. I already know a little . . . a few words. Eva Beregi is teaching me. She is remarkably kind, and won't accept any money from me, so I'm racking my brains to find some possible way of reciprocating. I have also joined a correspondence course. They send lessons, and it's quite good.

I'm almost positive I'll choose some sort of profession connected with agriculture. I'll probably study dairy farming and cheese production. A woman who was in Palestine, and enchanted by it, gave me the idea. She also told me all sorts of wonderful things about the Land. Listening to her was a joy. Everything that is beautiful, cheerful, and of some consolation to the Jews stems from Palestine.

Here the situation is constantly deteriorating. A new Jewish Law* is soon to be proclaimed. It will be the 'most urgent' thus far. They are going to 'solve' Land Reform by distributing the land at present in Jewish hands—and only that. The truly great estates won't be touched. But of course this was to be expected.

December 11, 1938

It's nine o'clock in the morning but I'm the only one up—surrounded by paper streamers and an untidy mess. Yesterday I finally had my 'evening'—or whatever one can call it, as it was 6.30 in the morning by the time I got to bed. Whether it was a successful party I can't say. I would be pleased to state it was, but to me the entire thing was, somehow, a disappointment. Perhaps one of the contributing factors was that I, personally, didn't enjoy myself very much. By this I mean there was no one with whom I spent any great length of time, or who really interested me. But there is something else: the times. And above all, my ideological point of view has so vastly changed since last year that I could not help but consider the affair frivolous, empty, and in a certain measure quite unnecessary at a time such as we're now going through.

There were nearly thirty people here, and only a few among them seriously interested me. I kept thinking how nice it would have been to have put all the money the party cost into the collection box of the Keren Kayemet**. Oh, dear, I would like

---

* Four to five per cent of the land was in Jewish hands when the law of 1939 authorized the Government to order the sale of Jewish agricultural properties.
** Jewish National Fund.

best of all to go to Palestine now. I would be glad to forfeit my
graduation, everything. I don't know what has happened to me,
but I just can't live here any longer, can't stand my old group
of friends, studying, or any of the things with which I've been
familiar up till now.

I don't know how I'm going to bear the next half year. I
would never have believed that I would spend my senior year
this way. I see I haven't written anything at all about the party,
but I just can't. A ship is leaving today with a great many
Hungarian Jews aboard. I so wish I could have gone with them.
I don't understand how I could have lived this way for so long.

I've just read what I've written. It's so pathetic. I see how
greatly I've been influenced by Szechenyi's diary—his style is
very noticeable in my own. But I can't help it. I think the sadness comes from deep within me, and I also like Szechenyi's work
very much.

January 26, 1939

But for the date I probably could not even tell when I last wrote
in my diary. I have so much to do. Three private pupils a week,
each for two hours. Then my Hebrew and English lessons, Bible
Circle, the Maccabee Society (a Zionist organization I attend
from time to time), etc., etc. The only thing I spend little time
on is my homework. It's been a week since I opened a book.
But in times like these one doesn't feel like studying.

February 6, 1939

I've been ill for several days, and I'm not going to school today
either. I would like to write a few words about the book I
finished yesterday: Ludwig Lewisohn's *The Island Within*. I
liked it enormously. Perhaps now that I am so immersed in
Jewishness I understood and enjoyed this book doubly. More
so, certainly, than if I had read it perhaps a year ago. He
chronicles the lives of four generations of Jews, from the ghetto
to New York, from belief and unity to complete spiritual and
emotional insecurity and family disunity. He relates the struggles
of the rootless fourth generation, and its recognition of the
essence of Jewishness. In other words, he presents all these deep

and burning problems incisively, and with clarity. I would like to give everyone who wonders why he is a Jew (and there are a tremendous number of such people) this book to read. It's a must!

Meanwhile I've leafed back through my diary and see I mentioned Bela. I must finish that story. While he was in town he was here a couple of times, then when he returned to Kolozsvár (Cluj) he wrote me very warm letters—which I answered, though with considerably less warmth.

When the first Jewish Bill* was introduced I received a letter from him in which he wrote that now he understood why I was so reserved: I must have thought that he, a Gentile, would be disturbed by the fact I am Jewish, whereas, etc., etc. When I read this I instantly sat down and replied that evidently he could not believe a Jewish girl still had pride and self-respect. I told him that if he felt I was an 'exception to the rule' (that Jews are inferior), I did not want to be considered as such (exceptional) and to please remember that he can safely include Jews among those about whom he can safely say something good.

This is a paper I read at a meeting of the Bible Society:

ROOTS OF ZIONISM OR
THE FUNDAMENTALS OF ZIONISM

When anyone in Hungary spoke of Zionism five or even two years ago, Jewish public opinion condemned him as a traitor to Hungary, laughed at him, considered him a mad visionary, and under no circumstances heard him out.

Today, due perhaps in large measure to the recent blows suffered, Hungarian Jews are beginning to concern themselves with Zionism. At least so it seems when they ask, 'How big is Palestine? How many people can it accommodate?' and 'Is there room for me in the expanding country?' Often the answers to these questions decide whether or not the questioner will become a Zionist.

* March 1938 (see page 50). The second Jewish Law was announced in 1939. The number of Jews in intellectual life was to be reduced to six per cent, in commerce and in industry to twelve per cent. A Jew could no longer be a member of Parliament, or a judge, teacher, lawyer, etc. On February 3, 1939, a bomb was thrown into the largest synagogue in Budapest during the Friday evening service. Many were injured, some fatally.

But the question least frequently voiced is, 'What is the purpose of Zionism, its basic aim?'

It is exactly with this seldom-voiced question I would like to deal, because I believe it to be the most important of all questions. When one understands and feels this and applies it to oneself, one will become a Zionist, regardless of how many can emigrate to Palestine today or tomorrow, whether conditions here will improve or deteriorate, whether or not there are possibilities of emigrating to other countries.

Thus, without relating it to the times and circumstances under which we are now living—in fact apart from all pertinent circumstances and situations—I would like to summarize absolute Zionism.

If we had to define Zionism briefly perhaps we could best do so in the words of Nachum Sokolov*: 'Zionism is the movement of the Jewish people for its revival'.

Perhaps many are at this very moment mentally vetoing this with the thought that Jews do not constitute a people. But how is a nation created out of a community? From a common origin, a common past, present and future, common laws, a common language and a native land.

In ancient Palestine these motives were united and formed a complete background. Then the native land ceased to exist, and gradually the language link to the ancient land weakened. But the consciousness of the people was saved by the *Torah***, that invisible but all-powerful mobile State.

It is, however, inconceivable that in the stateless world of the Middle Ages, when religion was the focal point of life, the self-assurance of the ghetto-bound Jew could have become so strengthened that he could have expressed his longing for a nation, or the restoration of his own way of life, or that he would have thought of rebuilding his own country. Yet the yearning expressed in the holiday greeting 'Next Year in Jerusalem' is absolute proof that the hope of regaining the Homeland never died within the Jew.

* Nachum Sokolov, 1861-1936, Zionist leader and Hebrew journalist; President of the World Zionist Organization and Jewish Agency, 1931-35.
** The Five Books of Moses.

Then came the Human Rights Laws of the 19th century and with them new ideas and concepts of national values. From the peoples of the greatest countries to those in the smallest Balkan enclaves, all attempted to find themselves and their rights. It was the time of decision. Did a Jewish people still exist, and if so, would it be influenced by the strength of the spirit of the New Movement?

The greater part of Jewry asked only for human rights, happily accepting the goodwill of the people among whom it lived, and in exchange casting off individuality and ancient characteristics. But a few hundred inspired zealots, young men from Russia, started off towards Zion, and shortly thereafter Herzl* wrote the *Judenstaat*. Thousands upon thousands endorsed the concept and ideals of Zionism, and suddenly there was a Jewish nation. He who feels there is not, let him speak for himself, but let him not forget those to whom Jewishness means more than the vital statistics on a birth certificate.

One of the fundamentals of Zionism is the realization that anti-Semitism is an illness which can neither be fought against with words, nor cured with superficial treatment. On the contrary, it must be treated and healed at its very roots.

Jewry is living under unnatural conditions, unable to realize its noble characteristics, to utilize its natural talents and capabilities. Thus it cannot cultivate its natural and immortal attributes or fulfil its destiny.

It is not true that during the Dispersion we have become teachers of the people, leaders. On the contrary, we have turned into imitators, servants, become the whipping boys for the sins and errors of those among whom we live. We have lost our individuality and renounced the most fundamental conditions of life.

How many great Jewish ideas and ideals died behind the walls of ghettoes during the Middle Ages even before seeing the light of day, or behind the invisible ghetto walls of modern Jewry?

If we compare the accomplishments of the 500,000 Jews

* Theodor Herzl, 1860–1904, founder of modern Zionism, devoted his life to the creation of a Jewish state.

now living in Palestine with the same number of Jews living in Hungary today, perhaps we will no longer voice the opinion that we can reach our aims only in the Diaspora. Thus Dispersion cannot be our aim, and certainly the sufferings of the Jews must be alleviated.

We don't want charity. We want only our lawful property and rights, and our freedom, for which we have struggled with our own labours. It is our human and national duty to demand these rights. We want to create a Homeland for the Jewish spirit and the Jewish people. The solution seems so very clear: we need a Jewish State.

'The Jewish State has become a universal necessity, thus it will become a reality', stated Herzl. Those Jews who want it, will create it, and they will have earned it, and deserved it. If we renounce Zionism, we renounce tradition, honour, truth, the right of man to live.

We cannot renounce a single one of our rights, not even if the ridiculous accusation were true—that Zionism breeds anti-Semitism. Anti-Semitism is not the result of Zionism, but of Dispersion.

But even if this were not so, woe to the individual who attempts to ingratiate himself with the enemy instead of following his own route. We can't renounce Zionism even if it does strengthen anti-Semitism. But amazingly enough, Zionism is the least attacked in this area. On the contrary, the only hope of lessening or ending anti-Semitism is to realize the ideals of Zionism. Then Jewry can live its own life peacefully, alongside other nations. For only Zionism and the establishment of a Jewish State could ever bring about the possibility of the Jews in the Diaspora being able to make manifest their love for their Homeland. Because then they could choose to be part of the Homeland—not from necessity, but by free will and free choice.

When the possibility of a new Homeland came up for discussion, the general Zionist opinion unanimously opted for Palestine. By so doing it gave assurance that its aim was not only to create a homeland, or haven for persecuted Jews in any spot on earth, but that it definitely wanted a Homeland, and that it wanted to create that Homeland on the very ground to which its history and religious heritage binds it.

I don't want to talk about the work which has been going on in Palestine for several decades, because that has nothing to do with the ideals of Zionism. That is, instead, a part of the realization of the Homeland. But one thing must be said at this time: that reality—that which is happening in Palestine—has justified and verified many times over the concepts and ideals of Zionism. The Jew has proved his will to live, his love of work, his ability to establish a state; and he has shown that the name of Palestine is so powerful that it is capable of gathering in Jews from any and all parts of the world.

This tiny piece of land on the shores of the Mediterranean which, after 2,000 years, the Jew can again feel to be his own, is big enough to enable the new Jewish life and modern Jewish culture to be attached to its ancient, fundamental ways, and flourish.

Even today, in its mutilated form, Palestine is big enough to be an island in the sea of seemingly hopeless Jewish destiny, an island upon which we can peacefully build a lighthouse to beam its light into the darkness, a light of everlasting human values, the light of the one God.

March 10, 1939

Perhaps I don't exaggerate if I write that the only thing I'm committed to, in which I believe, is Zionism. Everything connected with it, no matter how remotely, interests me. I can barely think of anything else. I am not afraid of being one-sided. Until now I have had to cast my sights in many directions. Now I have the right to look only in one direction—the direction of Jewry, Palestine and our future.

The Round Table Conference*, predictably, will end without achieving any particular results. I think that the *Yishuv*** is ready for anything, even battle, if they don't find a reasonable solution to the question.

I am sending off my application to the Nahalal Girls' Farm. If only they'll accept me!

* A reference to the London Conference, which was to be followed by the British White Paper of 1939, restricting Jewish immigration to Palestine. Until 1948, Britain was the Mandatory Power in Palestine.
** The Jewish Community in Palestine.

Graduation is fairly close, but it leaves me completely cold, and I'm not studying. What possible use will Hungarian history, geography, or history of art be to me? And as far as German is concerned, it only brings horrible things to mind. I'll have no use for French in Palestine, which leaves algebra and physics, and of course Hebrew. Unfortunately this last is not taught in my school. Instead, we are discussing the Jewish Question in connection with the 19th century, and the subject is presented in the most malicious way possible.

A copy of the letter I sent to the Girls' Agricultural School at Nahalal, Palestine. I wrote it in Hebrew:

> To the Management:
> Attached to my application is my *curriculum vitae*.
> My name: Hannah Senesh. Mother's name: Katalin, maiden name, Salzberger, widow of Bela Senesh, writer. I was born July 17, 1921, in Budapest. I am a Hungarian citizen. I completed my elementary schooling in a state school. Since 1931 I have been a student at a High School for girls. I will graduate at the end of this term. So far I have completed all my studies with honours.
> Apart from French and German—the languages I learned in school—I also speak English.
> Even before the tragic turn of events concerning our people in my native land, I longed to live in Palestine, and for the way of life there.
> I decided to learn this profession so that I could take an active part in the creation of the state and the cultivation of the land.
> Following this decision I have learned a fair amount of Hebrew and am continuing to improve my knowledge of it, in the hope that I will have no language difficulties when I am there.
> May I request a favourable decision? An acceptance to the school would give me great joy and happiness. It would be the first step towards the realization of my life's ambition.
> With cordial Zionist greetings,
>   Hannah Senesh

April 22, 1939

We were in Lyon for ten days to see George. We have already been back a week—and so far I've not written a single word about it. Yet it was all so delightful, so nice. The trip itself was wonderful, even though I had already seen it all—except for the stretch after Milan. The most beautiful part is the landscape before and after the Franco-Italian border, the snow-capped rocky mountains, the valley, the precipices, waterfalls, streams, little houses crammed one next to the other, carefully guarded and cared-for strips of land, enormous power stations, sparkling-white winding roads, viaducts, tunnels.

But the outstanding beauty and wonder of the countryside were dwarfed by the joy and importance of seeing George again. He doesn't want to remain in France, but wants to go to Palestine too. He has also become an ardent Zionist, and it was wonderful to talk to him about these things, and to discover how alike our thinking is about such matters. He showed us his school. It's a handsome, modern, richly appointed institute, and I think he likes his profession.

Oh, dear, I could write so much more about George and how perfect it was to see him again.

June 18, 1939

I don't want to do any more studying before tomorrow's final examinations and I'm in the mood to write in my diary. Perhaps I'm just a tiny bit nervous, even though the question of *praeclara** is entirely a matter of vanity and means absolutely nothing otherwise.

At first I thought it would not interest me even this much, but now, on the eve of graduation, I would very much like to do well. I don't have the results of the written examinations as yet. In Hungarian Literature I wrote a paper on *The Hungarian Peasant's Tragic Role in our Literature.* I hope it's good. My German assignment was a Hungarian-German translation. I had an appointment at 67 Andrássy Boulevard for an interview concerning my application to the Agriculture School at Nahalal, so I handed in my paper before eleven. I must admit I rather dashed it off. There was an examination in French translation

* *Summa cum laude.*

too. I'll see tomorrow whether my grade was below that of
my class grade (which was A). If it is, then I'll have to take
an oral in French.

Of late I've been going regularly to the Zionist Organization.
I like being there, and feel comfortable with the members. We
have a great many problems in common, and there are always
a lot of intelligent people there to talk to. It's so comforting
to feel that despite their many faults these are our people.
Judging by the sort of faults they have I dare say that, for
the most, they are the results of years of exile, of living in
Diaspora. It's possible, however, that their many qualities are
due to the exile as well. But perhaps in Palestine we'll succeed,
at least in part, in throwing off the faults, and retaining the
advantages. Immediately after graduation I want to busy myself
with Hebrew and Zionism*.

I want to read the Bible in Hebrew. I know it will be very
difficult, but it is the true language and the most beautiful; in
it is the spirit of our people. I am now writing this without a
dictionary, alone, and—certainly—with many mistakes, but this
makes me happy for I see that I'll be able to learn Hebrew
quickly. I want to write some more: about George, my brother.
He's also learning Hebrew and, at the end of one of his letters,
he wrote: 'It's good to die for our land'. Recently that sentence
has taken on real meaning, for these are difficult times in
Palestine. The British have concocted a White Paper of awful
content and, understandably, the entire Jewish community
decries this betrayal.

July 11, 1939

As of today, I shall keep my diary in Hebrew. I had intended
doing so once before, but I think this time it will 'click'.

I still haven't written about my matriculation examination. I
really wasn't nervous. Well, perhaps just a little on the last
morning. The first test was in German. I was given a selection
from Grillparzer to translate, and then I had to discuss *Sappho*,
a drama by Grillparzer. After the German oral, I left the class-
room—that's the procedure in our school. I returned ten minutes

---

* Up to this point, the diary was kept in Hungarian. From here on she
alternated between Hungarian and Hebrew.

later and found the question in Hungarian Literature on my desk. I was given two subjects. For a moment I was dejected, but then I saw I knew what to reply, and walked up to the examiner light-heartedly. (He is really a wise and pleasant man; it was delightful being questioned by him.) I spoke for a long time, but even so didn't say half of what I wanted to. Then he told me he was sorry, but it was impossible to hear me out. I answered the second question too, and saw my teacher was very pleased.

The third test was in History. When I got to my seat and saw the questions I had no idea how I would manage. I was supposed to speak on the subject of Reform Parliaments. I didn't really know much about when they were called and what happened in them. The second subject was better: the French Revolution—its forerunners, its course, its accomplishments. I prayed he would ask me this one first and handed the Director the two questions, with the 'Revolution' on top. I was lucky; he asked that one first. Without boasting—I knew it perfectly. And he didn't ask the second question.

I wasn't afraid of algebra or physics. During the recess, which lasted half an hour, I 'phoned home, and ate lunch. I wasn't at all nervous. But when I saw the algebra problem, my high spirits sank. It was the easiest subject in the entire syllabus, but that was exactly why I hadn't studied it. I finally worked out what to say. Physics was the last subject, and the questions were all beauties—I knew them, and received 'excellent'.

I haven't time to continue today, but hope I'll soon be able to write more smoothly in Hebrew, and more about Zionism. I'm studying very hard.

Tomorrow we are going to Dombovár.

Aged eighteen

Dombovár
July 17, 1939

Today is my birthday. I am eighteen. It is so hard for me to see myself as such an 'old lady'. But I know these are the most beautiful years of my life, and I enjoy my young ideas, my youth. I am happy with my life, with everything that surrounds me. I believe in the future. My ideal fills my entire being, and I hope I'll be able to realize it without disappointment. The

reaction of friends and many relatives is that I will be
disappointed in *Eretz**. But I think I have a good grasp of the
situation; I know the people living there make mistakes too.
What I love about it is the opportunity to create an outstanding
and beautiful Jewish state, and the future depends on this. I
want to do everything within my power to bring this dream closer
to reality—or the reverse, to bring reality close to the dream.
I am writing in Hebrew all the time now, and though I write
less than if I were writing in Hungarian, I do better thinking
a bit in Hebrew than a lot in Hungarian. Perhaps in a few
more months I'll write less awkwardly, with less difficulty.

July 21, 1939

I've got it, I've got it—the certificate! I'm filled with joy and
happiness! I don't know what to write; I can't believe it. I read
and re-read the letter bearing the good news, now I can't find
words to express what I feel. I have no feeling other than overwhelming happiness. But I can understand that Mother can't
see the matter as I do; she is filled with conflicting emotions,
and is really very brave. I won't ever forget her sacrifice. Not
many mothers would behave as she is behaving.

I have to be in Palestine by the end of September. I still
don't know when I'll leave. I won't write any more now, but
there is one more thing I would like to say to everyone, to all
those who helped me, to God, to my mother: Thank you!

Yesterday we went to Pécs. It was a beautiful day, very
pleasant. But I can't write about the trip because it is nothing
compared to what happened today.

July 22, 1939

I spent all day reading an interesting book, *The Singing Valley*
by Shalom Asch. Everything takes place in the Emek Valley**
at the time of the difficult beginning in Palestine. I was very
happy to find this book and finished it in a day and a half. I
read another book, and went to copy a selection from it into
my diary so that I won't forget it. The book is a translation of

---

* The Land (Palestine).
** The Valley of Jezreel, usually called *Emek* which in Hebrew means
'valley'.

Lion Feuchtwanger's *The Jew of Rome*. I'll try to translate the thought into Hebrew. 'Jewish history is the history of this war, in which the spirit must battle the anti-spiritual tendencies, and what is common to Jewish history is common to the spirit, too'. This sentence appeals to me; I feel it is true.

That I'm happy is self-evident.

Budapest
August 2, 1939

I'm back home now. I didn't have the patience to stay in Dombovár any longer. There are so many things to arrange that I really have no time to write. But I must copy the poem by my father which my mother gave me today. It is called *Night Game*.

August 14, 1939

I don't know how to begin. It's so dreadful. I'm afraid I'm not well. I still haven't been to see a doctor, I still haven't told my mother, and I don't want to believe it yet. I pray it's not true, that it will pass. The fact is I feel a small pain in my heart, day after day, even now as I write. I'm close to tears because if my heart is not well at this early age it is the worst possible thing that could happen to me. But my father had a sick heart from the age of eighteen, and lived with the knowledge. If fate so wills it, I shall also be able to bear the knowledge. But that's not the worst of it. For me the important thing is *Aliyah**. I'll be going to an agricultural school; that means I'll have to undergo considerable physical labour. I'm going where I most longed to go, where so many girls long to go. But if I'm really ill and now give my place to someone else, I'll never again have the opportunity of emigration to Palestine, and that will be the end of my great good fortune, of my life's goal. But if I go to Palestine as I am, ill, and wait for them to discover I'm not fit for work, in the eyes of the Zionists I'll be an irresponsible, supremely reckless girl.

What shall I do? I can't discuss this with Mother. I must decide alone. At the most difficult moments in life everyone is alone. I want to see a doctor. My God, my God, let this be just a bad dream.

* The immigration of Jews to Israel.

August 21, 1939

I went to the doctor with Mother. First I telephoned and told him what it was all about. But I told Mother I merely wanted him to check to see if there was any post-operative problem concerning my tonsils. The doctor examined me thoroughly, checked me through the fluoroscope, and the result is—I can work. There is nothing wrong with my heart, or anything else, beyond a nervous tension which is causing the pain.

August 22, 1939

I happened to open my diary at the place where I wrote nearly a year ago about the excitement concerning the possibility of war. If I want to, I could discuss this now as the danger of war is again imminent. In times of such crises we humans are like animals about to go to the slaughter. Just today I read in the newspaper about a sudden and dreadful thing: the Germans have concluded an agreement with Russia. In terms of German politics this is an extremely inconsistent step, since only a few months ago the Anti-Comintern Pact was formed solely as a protection against Russia—and the one who spoke the loudest at that time was, of course, Germany. And certainly what was then said on Russian radio about 'the brown dog' was not exactly friendly.

September 8, 1939

Much has happened, but I have had neither the time nor the desire to write about it. The war we feared has begun. It broke out over the matter of Danzig and the Polish Corridor. Danzig itself is a small place, and while its population is actually German, all of Poland—and finally all Europe—is in danger. If they had really wanted to they could have preserved the peace. But they didn't want to—so there is now war between Germany and Poland. The Germans have already captured a large part of Poland, and France and England, Poland's allies, have entered the war. There is nothing they can do as yet to be of any real help, but they're standing by, arms at the ready. Italy is still neutral, as are Hungary and many other countries. They are all aware that war nowadays will cause more destruction than ever before, and they are doing everything to prevent it. That is politics.

As for our private lives, George is in France, and Mother doesn't know whether he should return to Hungary, or stay there. We are still at peace, and France is at war. But who knows whether Hungary will participate or not; to be a Hungarian soldier now is not a particularly pleasant thing. And who knows what will happen to foreigners in France? Our situation is difficult, and we can't decide.

And now for myself. I received the certificate, and yesterday I also received the visa. I long to leave already, even though a sea journey now is not particularly safe.

The following two letters to her mother are included with her Diary, rather than her Letters, since they form a transitional link between Hungary and Palestine.

Mezötúr

Dearest Mother, *September 13, 1939*

So both of us can enjoy the advantage of this fabulous little typewriter as quickly as possible, I am starting a letter to you here, on the train, at 4.45 p.m., which I can perhaps send even before reaching the border. After that I shall get used to using postcards and telegrams.

Truly, Mother dear, that moment when the train started and I could not control myself, was extremely difficult. Regardless of the fact I was so overjoyed about the journey, I forgot all my dreams, plans, and hopes, and at that moment felt only the pain of parting with you for a very long time.

The other farewells weren't difficult. Yes, when we left our little house—that was painful too. After all, it is more or less the symbol of my life so far. But even so, it was the easiest part of the farewell. How I felt about leaving you—what purpose does it serve to write about it in detail? You surely must know.

Certainly we won't be spending the Jewish holidays in the happiest of circumstances, and I'm afraid, Mother dear, these will be very sad days for you too. No matter how preoccupied I am with my plans and the journey itself, my thoughts are

constantly with you, and I shall spend this New Year holiday
with you in spirit.

Don't be upset, Mother, that this letter is so empty. When
one has a great deal to say one can't find words—beyond these
two: dearest Mother.

On Board the Bessarabia
Dearest Mother,   *September 17, 1939*
Our ship is anchored in Constantinople, and I am on deck, my
typewriter on my knees. I hope you received my telegram from
Constanta and have not been at all worried about me. There
really has been no cause for any concern. Everything went
perfectly. I saw very little of Constanta as the train went straight
to the docks. From on board ship I was able to glance around a
bit, but by then it was already evening, so only the illuminated
Casino was visible.

I can see a trifle more of Constantinople, since we will be
tied up in the harbour for about three hours; but of course we
are not permitted to leave the ship. Nevertheless I can see
mosques, towers, narrow streets, watermelon carts, stevedores,
a coffee bazaar, and on the hillside quite modern and attractive
buildings. On the other hand, there are horribly run-down
shacks too, so there must be great contrasts here.

Life aboard ship is extremely pleasant, and the cabin is quite
comfortable. I asked for an upper berth, and it's right next
to the porthole, so it's nice and airy. I slept wonderfully well;
perhaps being tired had a lot to do with it! My cabin mates are
congenial people—women, that is—Polish and Palestinian, so we
speak a lot of Hebrew, and my French has been useful as well.

This morning I got up at six because I couldn't stand staying
in bed when I saw how beautiful the sunrise was. I walked about
the ship, all over the decks, and though I'm already quite familiar
with it, there are times when I still can't find my cabin in the
maze.

The majority of the Jewish passengers are from Palestine,
returning from visits to relatives. But there are a great many
Poles and Czechs as well, and a lot of children from Palestine
who are adorable and speak only Hebrew. There are opportunities
to practise my Hebrew with them, and as there are a great many

people who speak Hebrew as a general rule, I grab every opportunity to accustom myself to speaking the language.

Don't be angry, but I can't write more now. The view is so beautiful that it's a pity to miss a single moment of it. I think we'll soon be in Athens.

Nahalal Agricultural School
Palestine
September 23, 1939

Today I must write in Hungarian as there are such an endless number of things to write about, so many impressions to record, that I can't possibly cope with them all in Hebrew as yet.

I would like to be able to clearly express today, on *Yom Kippur,* the Day of Atonement, all that I want to say. I would like to be able to record what these first days in Palestine mean to me. Because I have been here four days.

A little *Sabra** is climbing up the olive tree directly behind me; in front of me are cypress trees, cacti, the Emek Valley.

I am in Nahalal, in Eretz. I am home.

The being 'home' does not refer to school. After all, I have been here only two days, and haven't become a part of the regular life yet. But the entire country's atmosphere, the people—all of them so friendly—one feels as if one had always lived here. And in a way this is true since, after all, I've always lived among Jews. But not among such free, industrious, calm, and, I think, contented Jews. I know I still see things idealistically, and I know there will be difficult days.

Yesterday, on Yom Kippur Eve, I was very low. I mean spiritually. I made an accounting of what I had left behind, and what I had found here, and I didn't know whether the move would prove worthwhile. For a moment I lost sight of the goal. I deliberately let myself go because once in a while one must completely relax from all one's tensions and from being constantly on guard. It felt good to let go, to cry for once. But even behind the tears I felt I had done the right thing. This is where my life's ambition—I might even say my vocation—binds me; because I would like to feel that by being here I am fulfilling a mission, not just vegetating. Here almost every life is the fulfilment of a mission.

* The name given to Jews born in the Land.

To write a stage-by-stage account of the two-day, exciting train journey, the five-day voyage on the *Bessarabia* (a Roumanian ship), of the inexplicably pleasant experience of disembarking in Tel-Aviv and Haifa and of being among Jewish porters and officials, and what this means to a person . . . to write about Haifa, Beth Olim, the Krausz family, where I went on the recommendation of Art Thieben, and where I found a most warm welcome . . . to write of the drive by bus to the Emek and of the arrival at the school . . . somehow or other I can not write any of this now. But everything is beautiful, everything is good, and I am happy that I'm able to be here. I would like George to come as soon as possible. And then Mother.

November 2, 1939

I haven't written for a long while. It's true I'm working hard, but there are other reasons. My new surroundings interest me so much that I cannot focus on personal matters.

There is much I could write about my life here. I do simple work in the laundry, and frankly I must admit it has little educational value. I've learned to launder and iron a bit . . . I'm learning somewhat more in the courses, both in content and in terms of language. This month they devote more time to working than to studying farming or a craft; this is the programme for all first-year students. I don't mind. Just that I sometimes think I could use this year for more important studies.

I'd like to continue in Hungarian because I feel I'm not writing exactly what I would like to express. At the same time, however, I want to overcome this difficulty and will continue in Hebrew. I *must* get accustomed to it.

*Shabbat** here is very nice. I've already got to know some people and sometimes I even have visitors. I read, play ping-pong, or visit the *kibbutzim*** and other neighbouring places. Thus there is some variation. Mother writes regularly, but I didn't get a letter from her last week. A postcard came today, however. She writes that all is well with her, and that George is able to continue his studies in Lyon.

The girls occasionally ask whether I'm homesick; I always

---

* Sabbath (Saturday).
** Kibbutz (*plural: kibbutzim*): Collective settlement.

answer, No, and it's the truth. The atmosphere of home, and the general environment, I really don't miss. But I do miss Mother and George very much. If I could at least see George. I haven't seen him for so long. Mother I saw only a month ago. But we're so far from each other. That's the only hard part. The only one? I think so. All the rest is nothing compared to it.

I love the Land. Rather, I *want* to love it, but don't know it well enough yet to say how it impresses me. Of course, the great difference between the Diaspora and the Land is something I feel every day in the school and everywhere else. The liberty, the humaneness . . . oh, it's so difficult as yet for me to say all I want to . . .

December 16, 1939

I'm now working in the dairy. I was very happy to be assigned to dairy work because I once wanted to choose it. For the first three weeks I'll be cleaning up, but that's all right.

What has been happening to me during this long interval? Well, there was the Hanukah holiday—my first in the Land— and I visited the Krausz family in Haifa, where I spent two pleasant days. I also went to some parties, danced and sang a lot. I saw city life and was again convinced it won't be difficult to do without it. I am very content in the country, in Nahalal, even at school.

Since I'm keeping a diary, and it is proper to confide to a diary about boys, I'll give the news on that front briefly. Miki and Ben wrote to me from Hungary and each proposed. It's funny. They both write as if it were a very serious matter. I answered them. I didn't have to think for a moment what the answer should be. That was really simple because they don't interest me. I've got to know some boys here too. They come to Nahalal for an evening . . . to stroll, to converse a bit. At first I was happy to spend some time with them, but then I realized it wasn't really worthwhile. We'll see . . .

During my holiday I didn't just dance and sing, I also saw something of life in the Land. I saw hardship and mistakes, but I also saw those interesting people, the first *chalutzim* [pioneers], who have been living here many years. But I still lack the vocabulary to write about all this. I lack fluency in the language, and besides that, I don't have time. In a few minutes we'll be going to the *Oneg Shabbat**, so I must stop.

January 1, 1940

I'll write again now, if only to enter the new date in my diary: 1940. It's incredible and frightening how time flies. Though this day is not considered a holiday here, it will do no harm to make a little accounting, as I used to at home. After all, the past year —1939—brought so many changes in my way of life—and within me. It was a year filled with constant tension, excitement, fear, and last autumn World War II began. The year also contained the anxiety of the Jewish Laws, the crisis in the internal politics of Hungary, and what was of even greater concern to me (even though still so distant) the riots here in the Land, and the excitement of the conferences. Due to these outer pressures, plus my personal leanings and abilities, I became a Zionist, and a real Jew.

I need not comment to what extent emigration has changed me. And now when I look back upon the past year I see how very eventful and difficult it was, what an emotional struggle. It was a year which ended one of my life's chapters, and began another. A year filled with tension and excitement, yes. But, withal, it was a very rewarding year in which I became aware of, and sensitive to, many things.

What do I expect of 1940? For myself, work, study, progress in Hebrew, and if I succeed, to draw closer to, and become familiar with, the life and the people here. And if God intends this year to be a very beautiful one for me, then perhaps I'll see George here too, and even Mother. And for Eretz perhaps this year will bring a bit of prosperity, which it could use so very, very much. I think in the 'outside world' this year will be no calmer, no more peaceful than the last was.

February 17, 1940

Several days ago my interest was caught by two things: a postcard from Budapest in which Eva describes a friend's party, and then how, after reading it, my gaze, unintentionally, wandered

* Friday night gathering of friends for social or discussion purposes.

to my work-scarred hands. Suddenly I asked myself, Wasn't it foolhardy romanticism, against my instincts, to leave the easy life, to choose a life of hard work, virtually that of a labourer? But I was immediately reassured, since I'm absolutely convinced I couldn't possibly live in the Diaspora again. My place is here in the Land.

The only question is, did I choose the best way? But I believe I did. I don't think I'll remain an ordinary labourer. I have the drive and strength of will to develop, to improve, and hope eventually I shall also have the necessary know-how. Yesterday a minor occurrence again proved to me I have organizational ability. We dedicated the reading room here. I organized everything, and it was so gratifying to see how the girls suddenly began showing interest in the project, pitched in and worked, and how extremely enthusiastic they were. I think it exceedingly important, particularly here in Eretz, to strengthen the intellectual interest of the people, to influence their spiritual and emotional moods and states, as nearly everyone has problems and faces hardships.

It is so very difficult to write about all this in Hebrew. And difficult, in general, to write clearly about matters that are not yet entirely clear to me.

March 6, 1940

What can I write when there is such a tremendous number of things which I can't clarify even to myself? Recently the stringent laws decreed by the British White Paper have been strengthened. There is great bitterness and opposition in the entire land. There have been demonstrations in the cities, victims, curfew, and a seemingly hopeless situation.

War against the British rule—it seems that is the desperate, bitter public opinion, and the country's leaders incline in the same direction. I don't know what it is within me—love for the land and the people, or horror of all wars, or perhaps a point of view which belongs in another world—but I still condemn any step which leads to hopeless, unnecessary bloodshed.

As far as I'm concerned, I think they ought to build with greatly renewed energy within the designated areas, and then, when the existing lands are irrevocably in our hands, and if the

British political situation does not change meanwhile—*then* if
we still must fight, we can do so with guns. But bloody
encounters, or more exactly fighting in the cities just so we can
show 'the world' that we protest—would be a meaningless waste
of blood and life. This is what my common sense tells me. But
the majority judge and see things differently, and it is possible
they are right.

National manifestations—force, guns—are undoubtedly the
implements of today. But not in our hands—at least not yet.
Perhaps despair will supplant what we lack in number. It would
be so good and so simple if with a prayer such as, 'My Lord,
help Your people . . . our people', one could trust and believe,
and not pry into, or dwell upon, the possibilities of the future.

Are these just words that get lost in the rat-a-tat-tat of gun-
fire? Who can answer these questions? I feel very much alone.
Sometimes I feel as if I am thinking of important things in a
dream, making decisions about my life, and not understanding
what it is all about.

April 10, 1940

My thoughts are generally motivated by existing conditions and
return to 'idealism'. For example, while sorting grapefruit in the
storeroom, selecting the beautiful, good ones, and putting them
at the bottom, the battered weak ones on top, the comparison ran
through my mind that this is the way God arranged our people.
He piled the strong at the bottom so they could bear the pressure
which represented the weight of a developing country, while the
battered remain for the top. And within me a request was born:
My Lord, may our people be like wholesome, faultless, stainless
fruit so Your hand won't have to search among those which will
bear the weight and those which are weak. Or, if possible, let
there not be a lower and an upper level, but rather a great, wide
shelf upon which everyone is placed side by side. But I can't
really believe in this.

Lately we have been learning primarily about root cells, which
are the first to penetrate into the earth, prepare the way for the
entire root. Meanwhile, they die. My teacher used the comparison: these cells are the pioneers of the plants.

I think the words flew over the heads of the other pupils; but

here, in Nahalal, if one examines the lined faces of the farmers—
who are young in years—one can't help but be struck by the
strong imprint left by their battle with the soil, and this is not
difficult to understand. They were the cells that perished so they
could penetrate the soil and help to create roots for every plant.
Shall our generation become such root cells too? Is this the fate
of the farmers of all nations? These questions are of far greater
interest to me than the study of botany.

Hebrew has become part of me. I write it easily now (though
incorrectly), but lines which came to mind this morning during
my walk in the meadow came in Hungarian*. I don't think I
shall ever be able to write poetry in Hebrew.

April 20, 1940

I would now like to write about the boy question, though it's
really not worth going into detail; in fact it's best to generalize.
Since I've been here, five or six boys have tried to approach me.
Now and then I go walking with them of an evening, but
generally break off quite abruptly. I can clarify the reason to
myself: I would love to have someone who loved me, and I
would like to really love someone. That's why when I meet
someone the thought immediately arises, perhaps this will be the
real one. But when I see I have been wrong I prefer breaking
off completely because I can no longer go on with these little
courtships. I feel that it must be a serious friendship—or let's
just be forthright and say, I need a real love affair—or nothing.
It's fine to talk a bit, to take walks, but the boys, for the most,
are not satisfied with just this; and I, too, begrudge the time
wasted on this sort of thing.

Day after tomorrow I am going to Jerusalem. I have a lot of
friends there, particularly Alex, who is waiting for me, and who
proves he often thinks of me by doing delightful, thoughtful
little things to please me. And several people have told me that
he finds me attractive. I don't know him very well yet, so don't
want to pass judgement. But deep in my heart I already feel it's
no. And I am sorry because I would so like it to be yes, at
last.

* The reference is to the poem entitled *Harvest*.

May 14, 1940

I was sitting, studying a notebook on general agriculture, when
suddenly I was struck by the realization of how cut off I am
from the world. How can I have the patience to study and prepare for an exam while the greatest war in history is raging in
Europe? We are witnessing, in general, times which will determine the fate of man. The European war is engulfing vast areas,
and fear that it will spread to our land is understandable. The
entire world is gripped by tension. Germany grows mightier
daily. And with the entire world on the edge of an abyss it is
difficult to deal with minor problems, even more difficult to
believe that personal problems are of any importance.

May 18, 1940

There are so many things I don't understand, least of all myself.
I would like to know who and what I really am but I can only
ask the questions, not answer them. Either I have changed a lot,
or the world around me has changed. Or have the eyes with
which I see myself changed?

I feel uncertain, undecided, positive and negative at one and
the same time. I'm attracted and repelled, I feel selfish and
cooperative, and above all, I feel so superficial that I'm ashamed
to admit it even to myself. Perhaps I feel this way only compared to Miryam because she knows her direction and her judgement is more positive than mine; she can penetrate more deeply
to the heart of things. Or is it because she is two years older
than I? I'm already making excuses for myself, afraid to face
facts. I say it's being optimistic to see the good side of everything. This is an easy attitude, but it doesn't lead very far.

My behaviour towards others is so unnatural, so distant. Boys?
I am really searching for someone, but I don't want second best.
I'm kind, perhaps from habit—until I'm bored with being kind.
I'm capricious, fickle, supercilious; perhaps I'm rough. Is this
my nature? I want to believe it is not. But then why . . .?

Today I listened to music. Sound after sound melts into
harmony, each in itself but a delicate touch, empty, colourless,
pointless, but all together—music. One tone soft, one loud,
staccato or long, resonant, melodious, vibrant. What am I? How

do the many tones within me sound all together? Are they harmonious?

May 26, 1940

I must now record that I am reading some wonderful books. The poems of Rachel, and a book in German by Martin Buber entitled *Talks on Judaism.* In Rachel I *feel* many things. In Buber I *understand* many things about Judaism and about myself that I didn't know before. In the sense Buber interprets Judaism, I am a true Jewess. Reading this makes me happy.

I took my exams in general agriculture and in dairy production. I hope I passed. Yesterday I visited Kfar Avoda, an educational institution for problem children. I found it very interesting. But it is difficult to study the most interesting aspects of the school in such a superficial manner. I hope I'll have another opportunity of studying the institution and the children more closely.

June 4, 1940

Budapest—Lyon—Nahalal

Between these three points my thoughts flash with lightning speed. Meanwhile the cities are becoming more constricted, confining, and the thought of Mother, George, and myself is all that remains to me of the cities and countries. Through this I feel all the tensions of these nerve-racking days. All tensions? I know this is a lie. I can't feel a thousandth part of what Mother must now be living through. She is suffering for our plans, dreams, which perhaps in this world holocaust will turn to ashes. If at least George were already here. But I'm so afraid that it's already too late. And if it is, it's due to my recklessness. It's all my fault.

The sky is a brilliant blue, peace and fertility encompass the Land. I would like to shout into the radio, 'It isn't true! It's a lie! It's a fraud that there are a million dead and countless injured, bombings, cities destroyed!' Who could have wanted this? Who can understand the historic mission of this butchery? To lay Europe waste and then, upon its ruins, build a new world? But who will build it, for whom and why? Only so there will be a new Europe to destroy? 'Struggle Man, and trustingly

trust'*. But why struggle? I won't write the second question. I
want to believe.

June 17, 1940

The Germans are on the threshold of Paris. Perhaps today the
city will fall. Paris and France, and the entire world. What is
going to become of us? All I ask is, how long? Because that
Hitler must fall, I don't doubt. But how long has he been given?
Fifteen years, like Napoleon? How history repeats itself.
Napoleon's career, life, battles; but a 20th-century German ver-
sion turns everything into inexpressible horror.

Italy has also 'stepped into the war', one hears a thousand
times over. Due to this the immediate danger has increased here
also. We are preparing as much as possible. If we are still alive
10–15 years from now perhaps we will know why this is happening. Or perhaps it will take a hundred years before this life
becomes history.

June 29, 1940

France, George, my mother . . .? It's difficult to say what hurts
most as the days pass. France has negotiated a shameful peace.
It has actually ceased to exist.

Communications with George have been cut off completely.
His certificate arrived too late. I've no idea where he is now.
But I'm still hopeful; perhaps he'll still come; perhaps he'll still
be able to leave. I study the face of every young man, secretly
hopeful. . . . Oh, how awful it is to feel that I'm to blame, that
I'm responsible for matters, in so far as they concern George.
On the other hand, I know that in times like these, during a war,
no one is to blame. It is impossible to judge, to decide whether
it is best to be here or elsewhere.

And Mother . . . I can imagine her spending sleepless nights,
getting up in the morning worried, searching the newspapers,
waiting for the post, locking all her worries and sadness in her
heart because she is much too noble to burden others with her
worries. And I, thousands of miles away, cannot sit beside her,
smooth her creased brow, calm her, share the worries.

* From a poem by Madách, the great Hungarian poet.

I'm working in the field, gathering hay, reaching—or imagining I'm reaching—my goals. And my goals are, I think, worthy—even beautiful. But does one have the right to long for what is distant, and give up what is close at hand? The only possible way I can answer this question is by saying that I would not have been able to continue living the life I led in Hungary. I would have been miserable. Each of us must find his own way, his own place and calling, even though the entire world is on fire, even though everything is in turmoil. No, I can't look for explanations, reasons. The 'aye' and the 'nay' storm within me, the one contradicting the other.

Kfar Gil'adi
July 3, 1940

I'm at Kfar Gil'adi. Miryam and I set out this morning and we're headed for Metulla, in the extreme north. We took a wonderful route: the Kinneret*, then the hills, cliffs, isolated settlements. And now—Kfar Gil'adi. Winds, hills, quiet. Perhaps in Hungarian I could write about the distant blue hills, about the sky, the trees, the people. This is the first day of our excursion. I hope it will all be as nice as this.

In the Land
Aged nineteen   *July 5–26, 1940*

How shall I begin? I have seen and felt so much during these past days. At the moment we're in a eucalyptus grove near Kfar Gil'adi. Miryam is carving her name on a tree, and I'm trying to record everything before a car comes along to take us further.

Early Saturday morning I climbed the hills facing Kfar Gil'adi. Wonderful scenery. And in the brilliance of the beautiful morning I understood why Moses received the Torah on a mountain top. Only on the mountains is it possible to receive orders from above, when one sees how small is man yet feels secure in the nearness of God. From there one's horizons broaden in every respect, and the order of things becomes more understandable. In the mountains one can believe—and must believe. In the mountains one involuntarily hears the query:

* Yam Kinneret (The Sea of Galilee).

'*Whom shall I send*?' And the answer, '*Send me to serve the beautiful and the good!*' Will I succeed? Will I be able to fulfil God's command?

In the morning we went on an excursion with several members of the kibbutz. We rode up to Metulla in a kibbutz truck, and from there, along beautiful paths, to Tannur. We returned around noon, and immediately got a ride as far as Dan.

What else can I say about Kfar Gil'adi? It's a large, pleasant, orderly, well-developed kibbutz. Among its members I particularly want to remember Gershon, a kind, charming man. We got to know him on the road, and he took particular care of us. A real pioneer, a man of goodwill; I was delighted to meet him.

Another spot we visited was Dan. It's a little settlement, an island in the heart of a luxuriant region. Its members, mostly Transylvanian immigrants, received us warmly. One of them took particularly devoted care of us. He guided us to Tel-El-Kadi, the source of the River Dan. It's an enchanting spring, next to it a primitive Arab mill. I must note how well, in general, the inhabitants of Dan get on with their Arab neighbours, and even with the Syrians who live across the border. Of course they can't depend entirely upon their goodwill, but the friendly relationship adds to their feeling of security.

We spent a night at Dan, and set out the next morning to tour the countryside. Sasa, Dafna, Sh'ar-Yashuv—new settlements whose situations are still difficult. The soil is good, water is abundant, but the land must be cleared of stones, and from a political point of view, carefully guarded. However, should their development remain unhampered by events, they can look forward to a happy future. They have all the requirements to develop into fertile agricultural settlements.

We also visited some of the girls who have graduated from the school at Nahalal. All of them are getting along well, and judging by this we concluded that the school has really prepared them properly, and given them a sound foundation.

The following day we waited at the roadside until evening, and nearly gave up. Towards nightfall we lost patience and agreed to wait only another fifteen minutes, though we certainly did not feel like returning to Kfar Gil'adi. Even Tel-Hai, which lay ahead, is more a symbol than a good place to spend the night. But finally a car came along. If Mother had seen me standing in the middle of the road, hitch-hiking! In fact, if she could have seen me at any time throughout the trip I wonder what she would have said!

We reached Hulata that very evening. It's a young collective with a charming group in a wonderful setting. Excellent opportunities to swim and row. It's superfluous to add that I enjoyed myself enormously.

We rowed on to the mouth of the Jordan, the place where it flows into Lake Huleh. The region is tropical, with papyrus reeds, water lilies, flamingoes, and the placid green waters reflect the surrounding beauty. Later we went rowing with two of the fishermen (twenty men from the collective are fishermen). One of them, Moshe, was 'mine', the other Miryam's. I saw he liked me, and I liked him a little too. He is really an attractive young man, strong, handsome, simple, likeable.

That evening we went out with the entire fishing fleet to watch them at work. It was a moonlit night. The lake was absolutely calm, and the night still. We could hear only the soft and monotonous splashing of the oars. The muscular bodies of the fishermen swayed left and right in the course of their work. They are familiar with the marshes, with the places where the fish teem, thus cast their nets with assurance. We returned to the collective at 10.30; the nets were left in the marshes until early morning.

When we reached home Moshe visited us for a while. He said he loved me, wanted to kiss me, but I wouldn't let him. He suggested we keep in touch but I said that although I had enjoyed the day we spent together, I saw no point in corresponding since we had so little in common, and in all honesty I was not that interested in him. I wanted to part with a handshake but he kissed my hand.

I thought about him after he left and realized I had actually been rather foolish, and even apprehensive. What harm would there have been in a kiss? Yet I could not. . . . I suppose it's ridiculous that I'm still 'waiting for the right one. . . .'

We went on early next morning, and reached Safed, the ancient city high in the hills. The scenery is beautiful, the types of people fascinating. We wandered about the town for hours, just looking. Then we turned back to Rosh Pina, and from there continued on to Ginosar, where we spent the night. It's a settle-

ment of young people who are struggling against great odds, and
are having considerable difficulty with the soil. We didn't have
time to see much of the kibbutz because we left early in the
morning so as to reach Afikim before noon.

If only I could describe it all: Lake Kinneret, the Yarmuk
River, the Jordan, the old and new kibbutzim, the delightful
people we met everywhere, the beautiful excursions we arranged
to places around Afikim, Ya'akov who 'sort of' fell in love with
me, the beautiful vineyards, the ride to Yarmuk on horseback,
the soft nights sitting on the grass, talking, discussing life. It
was all beautiful and I could fill an entire notebook describing
everything, particularly the way a kibbutz is run, managed. In
short, it was all wonderful, absolutely wonderful.

We spent about five days there, then finally left the Jordan
Valley by train for the Emek. We saw Bet-Alfa, Tel Amal, Ein-
Harod in the distance, and before we knew it our journey ended.
I spent the last day of my holiday with the Farkas family at
moshav* Merhavya. They were very friendly and hospitable,
and the warm family atmosphere was most welcome after so
many days of communal life in the various kibbutzim, and I was
happy to have the opportunity of comparing the two different
ways of life.

Beyond a doubt the kibbutz, economically speaking, is far
more rational, and from the point of view of working conditions,
simpler; and life, lived on a communal basis, is easier on the
kibbutz. But from a spiritual point of view village life has its
positive advantages. Certainly it's very obvious that not everyone
is suited to life on a kibbutz. I suppose in a matter of years a
middle-of-the-road way will be found, which may successfully
combine the advantages of both.

The entire holiday was glorious. I was so strongly aware of
the beauty of youth in everything I did and saw: in song, in
laughter, in boundless energy, in my overwhelming desire to see
and absorb everything, to enjoy all the wonders of the Land,
to glory in it. And certainly there was endless opportunity to
sample every phase of life in the Land, to see all its wonders.
This holiday strengthened my faith in the country, in myself,

* A moshav is an agricultural village whose inhabitants possess individual
homes and smallholdings but cooperate in the purchase of equipment, the
marketing of produce, etc.

and in our common future. For two weeks I forgot that there is a war raging, that it is so close to us. Haifa has been bombed twice, and on the second occasion there were a good many victims. Here, in Nahalal, life continues as before. At night, blackout; and when Haifa is bombed we hurry to our shelter.

My work consists of field work and housework. Four hours indoors, four hours outdoors.

The books I'm reading: Rachel's poems, which are beautiful. And Kautsky on socialism. This last is a fundamental explanation of Marx's *Das Kapital*. I wasn't acquainted with these works, but now I must familiarize myself with them as well.

Nahalal
September 6, 1940

It's been two years since I last saw my brother, except for the few days spent in Lyon, and I'm so afraid that by the time we meet again we'll be like strangers. The title of a book keeps ringing in my ears: *The Burnt-out Soul* by Lajos Zilahy. It's about two people who are separated for a long time, grow apart, and when they finally meet have nothing to talk about, no mutual interests, and stare at each other like strangers. Two years . . . and how many more? I'm still hopeful. I want to continue being hopeful.

October 11, 1940
Yom Kippur Eve

I want to record a poem I've attempted in Hebrew*.

> In the fires of war, in the flame, in the flare,
> In the eye-blinding, searing glare
> My little lantern I carry high
> To search, to search for true Man.
>
> In the glare, the light of my lantern burns dim,
> In the fire-glow my eye cannot see;
> How to look, to see, to discover, to know
> When he stands there facing me?

* This is her first poem in Hebrew. It is translated by Peter Hay.

Set a sign, O Lord, set a sign on his brow
That in heat, fire and burning I may
Know the pure, the eternal spark
Of what I seek: true Man.

November 2, 1940

I dream and plan as if there was nothing happening in the world, as if there was no war, no destruction, as if thousands upon thousands were not being killed daily; as if Germany, England, Italy, and Greece were not destroying each other. Only in our little country—which is also in danger and may yet find itself in the centre of hostilities—is there an illusion of peace and quiet. And I'm sitting here, thinking of the future. And what do I think about my personal future?

One of my most beautiful plans is to be a poultry farming instructor, to travel from one farm to another, to visit settlements, to advise and to assist, to organize, to introduce record-keeping, to develop this branch of the economy. In the evenings I would conduct brief seminars for kibbutz members, teach them the important facets of the trade. And at the same time I would get to know the people, their way of life, and would be able to travel about the country.

My other plan is to instruct (seems I only want to teach) children in some sort of school. Perhaps in the institute at Shfeya, or in a regional agricultural school. The old dream is to combine agricultural work with child guidance and teaching.

My third plan—a plan I consider only rarely—has nothing to do with agriculture or children, but with writing. (As I write this the *Unfinished Symphony* is being played on the radio downstairs.) I want to write books, or plays, or I don't know what. Sometimes I think I have talent, and that it's sinful to waste or neglect it. Sometimes I think that if I really do have talent I'll eventually write without worrying about it, that if I feel the need of self-expression, the urge to write, I'll write. The important thing is to have a command of the language. I've made considerable progress during this first year in the Land, but I must do better.

And I've yet another plan. I'd like to live on a kibbutz. This can, however, be in conjunction with the other plans. I'm quite sure I would fit in, if only the possibility of working at something that really interested me existed.

When I visited Merhavya during my holiday, I was able to imagine myself finding purpose and satisfaction in a moshav, but this way of life seems to me to be the least satisfactory. Generally speaking, it's difficult to discover what suits me best since I take easily to all conditions, environments, kinds of work.

I don't think I've written anything about my daily life. I haven't even mentioned my work in the chicken house, which I really like very much. Nor have I said anything about the Bible Society, nor about the end of term celebration. Yesterday was both Pnina's and Miryam's birthday, which I didn't mention either. Nor about my relationship with them, nor my feelings about the school, nor about my visit to the Vadash family in Kfar Baruch. They're really very nice people.

I haven't mentioned my horseback riding, one of my greatest pleasures and one in which, unfortunately, I can indulge only rarely. But that's all right . . . I don't mind leaving all these things out of my diary, but it's impossible for me not to write about a book I recently read. It's called *Jeremiah*, and was written by Kastein. This book made a tremendous impression on me. Considering the present situation of world Jewry, it is extremely timely. He penetrates and analyzes the basic questions of the Jewish religion through his characterization of the Prophet Jeremiah. It is impossible not to be impressed. It was doubly interesting to me since it gave expression to my own interpretation of religion.

Before I was familiar with the point of view of the prophets, and what, in general, the Jewish religion was about, I instinctively objected to empty religious forms, and searched for its true content and morality as expressed in deeds. Needless to say, I only searched but did not always find. Yet at least I tried. I was never able to pray in the usual manner, by rote, and even now neither can nor want to. But the dialogue man holds with his Creator, and about which the prophet preaches, is what I, too, have found. I see the sincere, inner link, even if it comes through struggle within myself, and through some doubt. But I cannot fit into a conventional mould which is, in part, dead, and which in part crystallizes thoughts which are so foreign to me. The book touched my heart because of its sharp expression of all this. In many respects I had the same feeling about Buber's book.

November 27, 1940

A ship filled with illegal immigrants reached the coast. The British would not allow them to disembark, for 'strategic reasons', and for fear there might be spies among them. The ship sank. Part of the passengers drowned, part were saved and taken to Atlit. I brood over this and ask, What is right? From a humane point of view there is no question, no doubt. One must cry out, Let them land! Haven't they endured enough, suffered enough? Do you want to send them far away until the end of the war? They came home; they want to rest; who has the right to prevent them from doing so? But from the point of view of the country . . . really, who knows? They come from German-occupied countries. Perhaps there are elements among them likely to endanger the peace of the Land, particularly at a time when the front is drawing closer.

We argued about these matters among ourselves today. I tried to take the side of the British, but didn't believe in my own argument. Perhaps this is born of our fear of objectively seeing our insoluble dilemma—a tiny country between two formidable adversaries: one the representative of anti-Semitism, the other author of the White Paper. Needless to say, we have but one road: to side with Britain against Germany. The British are taking advantage of our situation. We stand here powerless, awaiting events. We can do nothing else; we're forbidden to take action, though there is certainly a difference between passivity and inactivity.

They're putting out the lights. I don't have time to explain now. That's the way life goes on here. I don't have time to clarify these burning problems even to myself, to get any deep knowledge of the issues involved, and to reach a conclusion. I feel superficial and wanting, lacking in the years normally devoted to contemplation and dedication. I'm afraid those years will never come, not because of my age, but because of circumstances.

December 14, 1940

A ship of refugees sailed for New Zealand. The demonstrations and protests didn't help. The entire Jewish community unanimously demanded that they be allowed to remain in the Land. But the ship sailed during the night, stealthily leaving the coast and Haifa. What is there to add? What can we feel as human beings, as a people? And the question arises, 'How much longer?'

Today is the Sabbath. An empty Sabbath which offers only a part of the day's significance: a day of rest, but not a holiday, not a day of festivity. I read a bit of *The Mother* by Shalom Asch, and an article in a trade journal. There is an emptiness about me; I've no interest in reading any more. I would like to go riding, or to meet people. Perhaps this is a strange parallel, but it stems from the same source: I'd like to break out of my physical bounds, to fly across the fields and feel the wind in my face as I once did during a storm on my way back from the village. Running in the wind I want to cast off everyday shackles, to use words I don't use every day, to meet people I don't meet day after day.

January 2, 1941

I was ill for a few days. I had jaundice. I'm not yet completely recovered. But what worries me most is that I again have those stabbing pains in my heart. I'm terrified by the thought that there may be something wrong. I'm not only afraid of dying young (I really do love life) but also that this may prevent me from following my chosen path and from choosing the work I like best. I haven't spoken to the doctor yet; I postpone doing so from day to day. I want to reassure myself that it amounts to nothing at all. This is what is known as 'ostrich diplomacy'.

February 25, 1941

It's time I wrote about Alex. Even though it's more 'his' affair than something we share. Several things happened last month which I didn't write about, not only because I was busy working at the incubator, but also because I find it difficult to write about matters that aren't entirely clear to me, or about which I am undecided.

I've known Alex for about a year, but only recently have our meetings become more frequent. There is no question at all but that he is extremely fond of me, and that he is serious about me. But what I'm not sure about are my feelings towards him. He is honest, decent, good, and loves me. But I'm convinced we aren't suited. Our educational background, our interests, perspectives are too different. I could probably live a pleasant, simple life with him, but one which would not satisfy or fulfil me.

He recently told me he loves me, and asked me to marry him. I told him that although I respect and like him, I don't feel as he does. Nonetheless, I couldn't say this with absolute certainty, and the matter was left unresolved. He comes to see me as usual, but I asked him to wait a while before demanding a definite answer.

Why this hesitation? If I feel so certain the relationship ought to be discontinued, why continue it? Perhaps because I feel a certain responsibility towards him, and towards myself as well. I want to be as sure as possible before making a decision one way or the other.

But what about myself? This question raises many problems concerning my future, problems not too clear to me, and therefore difficult to solve. I think living on a kibbutz is likely to be an interesting experience for a year or two. But I can't see myself living out my entire life on a kibbutz. On the one hand I feel bound to some form of public service, yet everyone must have personal freedom, quiet, an opportunity for individual initiative and development.

Of course I am fully aware of the advantages of a working life, and of the opportunities it offers. I constantly have new ideas concerning my work, 'invent' things that are reasonably good and make the work easier. I'm now working on a plan connected with the automatic brooder, which is really keeping me busy. I have an idea (though still don't know whether it's feasible) which entails introducing coloured chalk, or some other colouring agent into the chicken, which would then mark every egg. Each hen would have its special marking. This sounds a bit strange and comical, but I don't think the idea is impossible, and want to pursue it further.

However, I think poultry farming, and agriculture in general, are relatively well organized here, or at least eventually will be

without any help from me! The agrarian economy is based on a
firm foundation, and is in good hands. The general problem
here is organizational. Political, educational, and social conditions
are very disorganized, though these are exactly the areas in which
our future and our fate are determined. I wonder whether I
wasn't really meant to lend a helping hand in government? I've
noticed at times that I have the ability to influence people, to
comfort and reassure them, or to inspire them. Have I the right
to waste this facility, hide it, ignore it, and to think about the
automatic brooder instead? I don't know whether it's a blessing
or a curse that everything I become involved with stimulates my
interest so that I instantly begin thinking of ways of repairing,
renovating, improving, developing whatever I come in contact
with, be it the filling of sacks with potatoes, or the problems of
mankind.

I'm not afraid of overestimating myself, and I'm not bragging
about my positive qualities. It's not to my credit that I have been
given these attributes; I didn't do anything to merit them.
They're talents I was born with, probably inherited. The joy is
in the knowledge I was granted them, and I think it's my duty
to utilize them. I wonder, will I be able to take advantage of
them? I wonder, is this way I've chosen the right one? Whatever my future, I won't regret these two years for an instant.
Wherever I am, these two years will make it possible for me to
understand everything, everyone better: the working man, and
all kinds of crafts and trades. These two years will bind me to
the Hebrew village, both in deed and spirit.

I started to write about Alex, and seem to have gone far
afield. But perhaps therein lies the answer. The problem I now
face is whether to marry a man 'just like that', to disrupt my
plans, give up my independence. Naturally, it's difficult not to
be impressed and flattered by the love of a man of character, a
man you respect and esteem. But this is still not love, and thus
there is really no reason to continue.

April 12, 1941

Why am I so lonely? Not long ago I strolled through the
moshav one evening. It was a fabulous, starry night. Small
lights glittered in the lanes, and in the middle of the wide road.

Sounds of music, songs, conversation, and laughter came from all around; and far, far in the distance I heard the barking of dogs. The houses seemed so distant; only the stars were near.

Suddenly I was gripped by fear. Where is life leading me? Will I always go on alone in the night, looking at the sparkling stars, thinking they are close? Will I be unable to hear the songs . . . the songs and the laughter around me? Will I fail to turn off the lonely road in order to enter the little houses? What must I choose? The weak lights, filtering through the chinks in the houses, or the distant light of the stars? Worst of all, when I'm among the stars I long for the small lights, and when I find my way into one of the little houses my soul yearns for the heavenly bodies. I'm filled with discontent, hesitancy, insecurity, anxiety, lack of confidence.

Sometimes I feel I am an emissary who has been entrusted with a mission. What this mission is—is not clear to me. (After all, everyone has a mission in life.) I feel I have a duty towards others, as if I were obligated to them. At times this appears to be all sheer nonsense, and I wonder why all this individual effort . . . and why particularly me?

April 23, 1941

Yugoslavia has fallen. In Greece the British and Greeks are retreating. The fighting in Libya is heavy, and the results still uncertain. And Palestine is deadlocked in weakness, misunderstanding and lack of purpose. Everyone is discussing politics; everyone is positive the front is getting closer. But no one dares ask; What will happen if the Germans come here? The words are meaningless—on paper. But if we close our eyes and listen only to our hearts, we hear the pounding of fear. I'm not afraid for my life. It's dear to me, but there are things I hold more dear. Whether I want to or not, I must imagine what the fate of the Land will be if it has to confront Germany. I'm afraid to look into the depth of the abyss, but I'm convinced that despite our lack of weapons and preparedness, we won't surrender without resisting strongly. Half a million people can face up to a force, no matter how greatly it is armed. And I'm sure Britain will help us—or, to be more exact—will do all it can on its own behalf. And I continue to believe in a British victory.

But will there still be an Eretz? Will it be able to survive? It's dreadful to contemplate the possibility of its end at close hand. And though everyone wants to be hopeful, to reassure himself, deep within is submerged the thought . . . perhaps . . . And no man has come along yet with the ability to unite the people and to stop, even for a moment, the inter-party conflicts. There is no one to say, 'Enough!' No one to whom they will listen. I feel a deep sense of responsibility: perhaps I ought to say the word! But this is not my job. I don't have the opportunity to do so, or the knowledge. But even if I had the courage to rise up and speak, they wouldn't listen to me. Who and what am I to assume such a task? I can't do this, of course. But to do nothing, merely to look on from afar—that I can't do either. As if in a nightmare, I would like to scream, but no voice comes from my throat; I'd like to run, but my legs lack the strength. I can't come to terms with the thought that everything must be lost, destroyed, without us having the slightest say or influence on the course of things.

I want to believe that the catastrophe won't come to pass. But if it does, I hope we'll face it with honour. And if we can't hold out, that we will fall honourably.

The words of Shneur ring in my ears: 'It's glorious to die the death of the saints, and to leave the world to the inglorious.' What is a heroic death? To consecrate God's name? Is it possible to consecrate God's name in a manner divorced from life itself? Is there anything more holy than life itself?

It's three o'clock. I must go to work.

May 17, 1941

There is a certain feeling of transition in our lives now. We plan something and add: 'If meanwhile . . .' and don't finish the sentence. Everyone understands. I don't think about dying, in any sense, though objectively speaking the possibility is very close. But I feel I still have a lot to do in this life, and that I cannot die before doing it all. Obviously everyone feels this way, particularly the young people who have already met death, and those who will yet meet it during this dreadful war. Our entire young country, filled with love and the will to live, feels this way.

June 14, 1941

Greece has fallen, and so has Crete. The war is now raging in Egypt and Syria. The British army marched into Syria three days ago, so the war is now virtually on our doorstep. Haifa was bombed for two nights. We went outside and listened to the bombs exploding, and the firing. Today we heard that Tel-Aviv was bombed last night too, leaving many dead and wounded. The city is defenceless, an easy prey. It looks now as if the war is starting here.

At times one wants to view things from a longer range, from an historical rather than a fatalistic point of view, to seek explanations for things that can't be explained.

Look, let me draw a picture of a fruit orchard: an orchard of people. Saplings and full-grown trees, good trees and bad trees. They have blossomed, yielded fruit; winter has come and their leaves have fallen. The gardener comes and sees their dry, stunted branches. He thinks of the spring, and mercilessly trims and prunes, thereby strengthening them.

An ancient tree stands in the middle of the orchard, its trunk thick, its roots and branches spreading over and under the orchard. Its branches have dried up, the earth's life-giving moisture is unable to reach it. The gardener's eye notes that its roots are still vigorous, its trunk healthy. It's a noble tree, still able to yield fruit. But it must be more carefully pruned and tended than the other trees. He unhesitatingly cuts off the thick branches, and the pruning hook leaves fresh, golden wounds.

Will the tree survive? Look! In place of the amputated branches new ones are budding. A small twig appears near the roots, with fresh, full buds containing the hope of renewed life. Does the pruning hook snip it off too? Is it possible the gardener will fail to recognize the new life under the grey bark? And should the unseeing hand trim it off . . . will the Tree of Israel ever blossom again?

July 9, 1941

They haven't started pruning yet. At least not for the time being. The pruning hook has turned towards Russia where the fiercest battles since the beginning of the war are now raging. Germany attacked Russia about two weeks ago, and swiftly captured

Russian Poland, as well as a good part of Finland, and has begun advancing towards the interior of Russia. According to newspaper and radio reports, the Nazis are now encountering strong Russian opposition. Everyone knows the results of this struggle will be decisive to the future of the world, thus the suspense is enormous. The bombings have become frequent here too, and it's a miracle there have been so few casualties.

Yesterday I received a telegram from Mother which came via Turkey, and I gather she is frightened and worried about me. It's awful to think that while I'm living a normal, comfortable, peaceful life Mother is worried sick, envisioning me in all sorts of frightful situations, allowing herself no peace. I'm conscious-stricken that I have it so good and easy here while others are suffering, and feel I ought to do something—something exerting, demanding—to justify my existence.

Aged twenty   *July 30, 1941*

We handed in our vocational theses today, and talked with Levine, one of our teachers. My marks were all 9's and 10's—the highest. Only one other girl did as well. Naturally I was enormously pleased and happy. The results of the other exams don't particularly interest me, and I'm impatiently awaiting the end of school.

And what comes next? First, excursions, making the rounds of the kibbutzim. It's difficult to imagine myself tied to one place. I feel as if all the land were mine, as if I belonged to the entire land. But to settle in one place, to give all my energies to it, to live there all my life . . . ?

We're about to begin a one-week seminar at Kibbutz Gesher in order to familiarize ourselves with one of the new projects of Working Youth. I'm eagerly looking forward to this. Though I'm not a member of Working Youth, I'm interested in its projects. Zionist Youth, Working Youth, Youth, and even the *Shomer Hatzair** are fighting over me to join it. Strangest of all was the invitation of the Hungarian founders of Kibbutz Dan. They made a special journey just to speak to me, though I don't know the reason for all this sudden attention. Perhaps I'll visit

* Socialist Youth Movement. All the others mentioned are also youth organizations.

them, but I have no intention of joining them since I have no
reason for doing so.

August 3, 1941

I'm completing this diary* the day before the school's annual
excursion, and think my stay at Nahalal will end at the same time.
It seems to me that a period of my life had ended—a twenty-year
period of preparation—and that now I must repay society what
it has invested in me. I think my first step towards life will be
the week to be spent at Gesher. Though it's hard to define that
specific 'life'. After all, didn't I breathe, eat, think, meet people,
laugh and cry, have ideas, thus far? Wasn't all that 'life'? But
all those actions lacked a certain sense of responsibility probably
due to a feeling of transition and insecurity connected with the
way of life. In this respect I probably won't feel any immediate
change in the kibbutz as the struggle for existence there is not
pronounced or noticeable. But I intend to write about everything
that lies ahead.

August 25, 1941

If I wanted to yield to symbolism I'd put off starting my new
diary until my departure from school, which is fast drawing to a
close. But after three weeks of holiday I have a lot to write about,
and won't postpone doing so for the sake of symbolism. I won't
have enough time now for everything since the work bell will
soon ring, but I'll take advantage of this bit of free time before
work to write a few paragraphs. I'll start with Gesher.

For the eight of us interested in joining the United Kibbutz,
or, to be more exact, a project of Working Youth, a seminar was
arranged to introduce us simultaneously to both the kibbutz
system and the new project. Behind this general plan lay the
special purpose of the seminar's organizer, Razi, to convince us
to join Kibbutz Gesher, which is greatly in need of additional
personnel.

We left for Gesher in the morning. We were really looking
forward to the days ahead, our first in a kibbutz, and were convinced beforehand we would enjoy ourselves.

* She ends her third notebook here.

A minor incident on our trip (we hitch-hiked, as usual) is worth mentioning. We were given a lift by three South African officers, two of them Jews. They had come up from Egypt on leave, and were touring the Jordan Valley, as well as the rest of the country. They were very decent chaps, especially one of them, named Roy, and were sincerely interested in everything that is happening here, and in the life in general. The kibbutz concept struck them as a bit odd. They asked a thousand questions, were very impressed by our answers, and liked everything we told them. They were not too eager to return to Egypt. I hate writing about this meeting so colourlessly and meaninglessly because at the time I was very taken by their behaviour, and by the interest they showed in all the questions of vital interest to me. We all went swimming in the Kinneret, travelled up to Daganya, and then they drove us over to Gesher. It was really a pity we had to say goodbye.

But to return to present matters. We reached Gesher, and the seminar started the following day. I'll sum it up: lectures, discussions, readings concerning the course of the Workers' Movements in the Land, the United Kibbutz Movement, Working Youth, economic problems, the organization of a kibbutz. We worked a few days too, and sat in on kibbutz meetings.

Considering the short time we spent there, I managed to learn a lot, familiarize myself with things, and was favourably impressed with the place. There are a number of outstanding people there with whom it would really be interesting to work, and the entire group made a good impression.

But there are two factors against my joining: first of all, the kibbutz is perhaps too young for me, though this is not a serious reason. The real crux of the matter is that the spot is two hundred meters below sea level, and the heat is awful; the place to be eventually chosen for the permanent settlement will most likely be in the same area. This, in itself, should not be decisive. But I'm hesitant because the doctor used to insist that I go to the mountains every summer because of my heart. Though concern for my health may be a justifiable excuse, I'm not being entirely honest. Actually, my convictions are not strong enough to renounce half my life. This probably sounds exaggerated, but it's true. During the summer, in such climate, doing hard work, one can't become involved or interested in anything else but the kibbutz. And I feel I would be giving up more than I want to.

Naturally, this isn't a decent excuse. After all, hundreds settle in the Negev Desert, in the Bet Shean Valley, and even down by the Dead Sea. I would too if I were linked with a group. But to choose such a spot of my own free will, knowing what it means, is too difficult a step for me. Nevertheless, the kibbutz's atmosphere tempts me, and I haven't completely decided against it.

From there I went on to visit the young group at Kinneret, composed of the Transylvanians who were in Afikim last year. They understood that my visit was not merely for fun, and made it possible for me, despite the brief three-day visit, to get to know something of the place and the people. My impression in brief: they are serious, well-educated intellectuals who enjoy human comforts (they're home-loving, which is in their favour), and are still partially tied to the Diaspora, particularly in language and culture.

On the basis of all this, it would seem they are really closest to my taste. But opposites attract, and thus I'm drawn to the settlements where the atmosphere is different. They, on the other hand, are considering the possibility of amalgamating with a Palestinian group, which would really be a good solution for them. But that's still in the future. At any rate, I'm not sure there is anything to be gained by my joining a specifically Transylvanian group, since our common origin would be of little advantage, and would only hamper my progress in Hebrew and Hebrew culture. That's why I left Kinneret feeling that although pleasant, it was not the answer for me. But at the same time . . . maybe—perhaps. It seems the more one sees, the more difficult it is to decide.

While at Gesher, I heard there would be a week's course given in Jerusalem on poultry ailments, and decided to attend. I returned to Nahalal, went on to Herzliya (where I spent a heavenly day on the beach), then to Petach Tikva, and finally on up to Jerusalem. Professor Fekete welcomed me cordially, as usual, and arranged for me to attend the course at the university.

The week was really interesting and pleasant. I went to the university daily, attended the lectures, participated in the laboratory work, i.e., microscopic investigations, and so on. In the evenings I met friends, went to the theatre, the cinema, had long talks, visited the Hadassah and university buildings, and the local branch of Working Youth. And in my spare time I read an excellent book, *Gone with the Wind*.

During this week I realized I'm not the same liberal, sociable girl I was two (or three) years ago, able to acknowledge and accept all strata of society, all modes of living. I can no longer pass the time, or chat 'just for fun', aimlessly. I can't help seeing shallowness, even though at times I know I carry my criticism and faultfinding too far. Involuntarily I find myself judging the far too many faults of society to such a degree that it spoils my fun. But I would be less than truthful were I to say I didn't enjoy the week in Jerusalem, despite the fact that my critical voice and scrutinizing glance were constantly active.

I'm back in Nahalal now, preparing for my final departure. Everyone asks what my plans are, and they're amazed I haven't made a decision yet. As far as I'm concerned, I'm in no hurry to make up my mind, and not in the least bit worried. I have a fatalistic attitude based on the conviction that I'll find the right answer when the time comes.

September 1, 1941

My farewell speech in the name of the class at Nahalal:

It seems such a short while since we stood on the Nahalal road for the first time, surrounded by the three agricultural school buildings. It is difficult to believe that the day has already come to make a farewell speech, to sum up, in the name of the class, two years of study and work.

I said 'two years of study and work'. But for the girls who are native-born, and come from settlements, this was a period for furthering their knowledge of practical husbandry, and for gaining a foundation in agricultural technology. For the majority of us, however, who came from countries in the Diaspora, the years spent here were far more comprehensive.

These were our first years in the Land, transitory years, years of fundamental changes, the sort of changes which decide a person's future. During these years our path has led from the Diaspora to *Eretz Yisrael*, from a foreign language and culture to Hebrew, from city life to village living, from our families to a new, strange environment, and from a life of leisure to hard agriculture work.

Our road was not an easy one. It was filled with obstacles, contradictions, misunderstandings. There were also differences of opinion. And we still don't know whether we've attained our goal. We haven't been put to the test yet. We still don't know how well we'll stand the rigours of a life of work, a life which will demand our best possible efforts, and all the knowledge and preparation we acquired here. If we can fulfil all the demands the working settlement will impose upon us we'll prove to the school and to ourselves that we really benefited from our two years here.

One thing we know already: we're going out to do peaceful battle, to work. And we're armed with a valuable weapon: a knowledge of agriculture.

We thank Hanna Meisel, director of our school, and all the teachers and counsellors who provided us with this important weapon. We thank the village and the entire region for unconsciously teaching us by the example of their daily lives and the Hebrew atmosphere they provided.

We thank the parents in the Land who understood the value of furthering agricultural knowledge, and who, for a period of two years, did without the help of their daughters in order to enable them to further their education.

And in our thoughts we thank our parents in the Diaspora who willingly, unselfishly, renounced us, their beloved children, so we could stand up in life with heads held high. Words alone cannot thank them. If our work and our lives prove a blessing to our surroundings, and satisfying to ourselves—that will be our thanks.

And finally I wish to salute the school: may its life be long, but may it remain young and flexible in spirit so that it can fulfil all the difficult and important tasks that fall upon it in these critical times, as well as in the future.

September 6, 1941

The last week, the last Sabbath, the last afternoon at Nahalal. The room is a mess. Miryam and I have been packing. I just finished, and will be leaving tomorrow morning. While packing I again realized how much unnecessary stuff I have. To be more exact, how many of the things I brought along will be superfluous to the kind of life I've chosen. At any rate, it's important that I have what I need; the surplus can't hurt.

I'm taking advantage of this last opportunity to talk to Miryam, to clarify matters, since we certainly won't have a great deal of time together in the future (apart from a brief excursion we've already planned). I think Miryam was my best friend. Whether I've got to know her well is difficult to say. There were times when I felt she was distant, that beneath the outer layer of self-control, which she acquired through self-discipline, she is entirely different, and that the 'two Miryams' are contradictory.

I don't think our friendship was as candid and genuine as it might have been, because our aims and dispositions are too much alike, which has always tended to create competition between us. We had many heated arguments, besides our long ideological discussions and differences. There were times when our wrangling ended abruptly and in anger, as one or the other would say, 'I don't want to discuss this with you any further,' or would suddenly end the argument in mid-sentence with, 'That's enough! I want to sleep!' These heated discussions generally took place at night, after ten o'clock, and more than once were so stormy that our neighbours yelled, 'Stop it!'

What did our friendship stem from? At first, shared experiences. We arrived at Nahalal at the same time; we were both newcomers; both of us knew little Hebrew, but were zealously determined and eager to learn it. We shared similar backgrounds, similar cultures, aspired towards similar goals, and had similar ideas; though there were vast differences in our outlook, in our ideological education and expression. We both wanted to give our surroundings everything we had to offer, and to receive from them whatever they had to give. We were both too tense, too avid for everything in the Land. We both had the same attitude to our work—a hazy, idealistic attitude. We both desperately wanted a new way of life.

What is most important is that I was able to turn to her with all my problems, tell her everything. I knew she understood me, was able to give me advice. I always valued her opinions. And she felt the same way about me, and sought my opinion and advice. This was of considerable help to both of us in overcoming both minor and major problems. But it wasn't only this. We also glanced at the world together, laughed together at its expense, poking fun at ourselves all the while, and at the people around us. We criticized the entire world, but in a constructive way. In short, it took but a glance, a single word, or even just a hint, and we understood each other.

We both laughed at boys, but both of us would have been happy to have found 'the' one—not just anyone. And because we didn't find that right one, we kept making fun of those who were interested in us, who came to court us.

Petach Tikva
September 8, 1941

As I expected, parting was not too difficult except from Miryam and Pnina. When the rounded outline of the village disappeared beyond the horizon, I felt myself bound to it, as well as to the entire surrounding valley, and I knew a chapter of my life entitled 'Studies and Preparations' had come to an end. This rather spoiled the pleasure of that happiness I had so long looked forward to—that moment of going out into the world and facing life on my own.

Today, on my way from Haifa to Petach Tikva, I travelled with a Revisionist* who tried to explain his and his friends' political views. I'm sad when I hear and see how great the political split is growing. However, the conversation was interesting, and I must admit my knowledge of party matters is very limited.

September 14, 1941

I'm writing a play**. I don't have proper working conditions because I can only write when it's quiet.

Everyone keeps asking what I'm writing . . . People generally think I'm bored when I'm alone.

Ness Tziyona
September 21, 1941

It's the eve of *Rosh Hashana*, the Jewish New Year. Two years have already passed since I left home. Two years away from my

---

* An extreme Zionist Party, founded in 1925 by Vladimir Jabotinsky, which opposed the 'moderation' of official Zionist policy.
** Called *The Violin*, it is based on kibbutz life, and popular with the youth in the kibbutzim.

mother, my home; from my brother I've been away three years; and I've lived two years in the Land. If I could, I would write a few words to my Mother. I have so much to tell her. It's hard to know what I'd talk to her about were we to meet now. I would tell her about these years, about my dreams, my plans, my anxieties. I would tell her how I felt yesterday: I was so desperately depressed that I cried. I felt I was faced with two possibilities: to seek personal happiness and shut my eyes to all the faults in my surroundings, or else to invest my efforts in the difficult and devastating war for the things I deem good and proper.

But I don't think the decision is up to me. I feel hidden traits within me will determine my course, even though all the hardship and suffering it will entail are clear to me. But I wonder whether I have the strength and the ability to achieve what I want. I also wonder if what I want will be the right thing?

Dear God, if You've kindled a fire in my heart, allow me to burn that which should be burned in my house—the House of Israel. And as You've given me an all-seeing eye, and an all-hearing ear, give me, as well, the strength to scourge, to caress, to uplift. And grant that these words be not empty phrases, but a credo for my life. Towards what am I aiming? Towards all that which is best in the world, and of which there is a spark within me.

So much for myself. Now what can I say about the world around me—the world that is virtually destroying itself? Or about the tens of thousands of people perishing daily? How shall I grieve for them on the Eve of Rosh Hashana? About the suffering, the pain; the injustice . . . what can I say, and to whom? *He* knows—thus there is nothing for me to say on this solemn evening.

Do I believe in God? I don't know. For me He is more a symbol and expression of the moral forces in which I believe. Despite everything, I believe the world was created for good.

Kiryat Hayim
September 28, 1941

On my last day in Ness Tziyona we went on a pleasant outing that included Givat Brenner, Kibbutz Schiller, and the Experi-

mental Station in Rehovot. We were particularly impressed by
the Experimental Station, where everything was completely and
interestingly explained to us. We saw Givat Brenner only
superficially.

On my way back from Ness Tziyona I stopped at the home
of Avigdor Hameiri, the author, in Ramat Gan. The first thing he
said was, 'You look exactly like your father'. He couldn't get
over how much I resembled him. It seems he knew Father well
as a young writer, and reminisced about their common past.
Then he discussed the trend of the theatre in Palestine and in
general, and its future possibilities. He said Father's plays,
deliciously humorous and entirely devoid of political or social
tendencies or implications, would be completely unacceptable to
the theatre here.

I then told him a 'friend of mine' had asked me to show him
some of her poems, and to ask for his opinion. I said my friend,
a twenty-year-old girl from a well-to-do family, had arrived in
the Land two years ago, and had learned Hebrew here. I read
him *Moment* and *To the Galil*. He listened attentively, and said
they were 'interesting examples, showed technique, facility of
expression, and simplicity.' In short, he considered my 'friend'
talented, and said he would like to send *To the Galil* to his newspaper for publication. I said I was not authorized to submit the
poem (because this isn't really important to me, but I was happy
to have the objective opinion of an expert). He asked me to send
him the poem, but I don't know whether I will. I don't think
this is the right time.

No news from home, or from my brother.

Yom Kippur Eve
September 30, 1941

This evening too—the Eve of Yom Kippur, the Day of Atonement—my thoughts are with them. What's happening to them?
Had I definitely known things would turn out like this would I
have left them? I think yes. After all, I knew even then that this
possibility existed, and perhaps only wanted to quieten my fears
with the futile hope my brother would join me in a year, my
mother in two years. That was probably the argument I gave
myself in order to ease my conscience about the irrevocable decision I had made to come to this land.

I'm not fasting because I don't feel the need. In my opinion, the only value of fasting is for the Jews in the Diaspora to express their solidarity. I feel I have other ways of expressing my ties with Judaism, and I'll forgo this one, which is completely alien to me. However, I'll observe the essence of the day by soul-searching and confessing.

I recall seeing a wonderful painting at the museum in Tel-Aviv called *Yom Kippur Prayer*. I was enormously impressed by its power, the force of expression in the faces, the hands, and the bodies of the men at prayer. And I saw something else that was beautiful: an Abel Penn exhibition in Tel-Aviv. Burning Jewish eyes, and depth and simplicity of expression such as I've never seen before in paintings.

The Hungarian radio is blaring in my ears. These days I speak a lot of Hungarian; I'm in a Hungarian atmosphere. It's time to go 'home' to the kibbutz, to *my* atmosphere. It's time for the first step—renewal at either Sdot-Yam or Ginosar.

October 7, 1941

I've been at Ilonka's for two weeks now, and tomorrow I'm going to Sdot-Yam, the kibbutz. I find it difficult to explain even to myself exactly why I chose Sdot-Yam. Naturally, I'm just going for a trial period now, but why did I choose this particular kibbutz in the first place?

I was looking for a group composed of young people my own age, attached to the Working Youth Movement, socially and politically alert and spirited. Besides, I'm very much attracted by their plans of settling in Caesarea*. The only difficulty lies in joining a group entirely new to me, not only as far as the individual members are concerned, but in its general structure. At least that's how I feel about it now; however, I don't want to make any decisions in advance. I'll see soon enough.

But I want to give myself a simple word of warning even before starting out, and which I want to repeat in the difficult moments that may lie ahead—a warning I don't want to forget: I don't feel as if I'm going into the kibbutz for the rest of my life. I can justify kibbutz life, and in so far as I've come to know it, I like it. It's the way of life I've chosen. Nevertheless, I feel

* An ancient Roman port, twenty-two miles south of Haifa.

it is merely the first stage on a long route. At the moment I'm all excited about the next few weeks, of course, and want to tell myself something 'for the road', something to remember at difficult moments, to remember I said it and thought it *before* I joined.

It's important to know whether the ideological basis of the kibbutz—a constructive socialist society in the Land—is correct. If it is, everything must be done to implement it, despite all the hardships. Its ideals look beautiful on paper and in books, but it is not easy to put them into practice and live by them. There is no need to follow the written word with one's eyes closed and meanwhile forget that the ideal must serve people, the individual. The basic function of the kibbutz is to afford satisfaction to all its members. No one is able to live long as a blind instrument used only to further a social aim. He will only be content if he himself moves towards his goal.

Even if a socialist slogan is placed on a mountain peak as a constant spur and incentive, we must not forget that if the members do not feel fresh air all around them when they reach the peak, if they do not sense a broader horizon, if they do not feel free—if they are considered only as working robots who blindly come and go—then all the efforts will have been wasted. For what is the use of a man reaching the mountain peak if he can't appreciate all the beauty around him because he is broken in body and spirit?

And another thing: I'll never say I'm disappointed with the kibbutz. I have nothing to be disappointed with, except myself. If I can't take that kind of life the fault lies within me, in my character. I'm afraid only of one thing: I may miss my solitude. Were I certain I'd find a quiet corner for myself now and then, I'd have no qualms whatever. But I'll see. Why conjecture? Why prophesy?

Sdot-Yam
October 12, 1941

I've already been here a few days. It's difficult to form impressions after only three or four days, but I feel kibbutz life suits me, and I'm enjoying it. The only question is whether *this* is the right kibbutz for me. The group is not particularly well-developed, or perhaps I haven't got to know them well enough yet. I'm mostly concerned about the girls, since the development of the character of the kibbutz is, to a considerable extent, in their hands.

As to the work: at the moment I'm working in the kitchen. There is no chance to do anything but indoor work since there is no agricultural development as yet. I may have to spend several years in 'service', which is a pity, and really a waste of my time and ability. I no longer have the patience to 'take turns' the way I did in Nahalal, where it was important to become familiar with every phase of farming, as well as with inside work. Now I feel the need of some sort of work to which I can give maximum effort. I would also like to be active in the Movement. Obviously there will be an opportunity for this while I'm here, but getting started is difficult. What attracts me to this place is that there is a great deal to do, and they have a beautiful plan for the settlement. The conditions are difficult, but not without hope and possibilities. The fundamental problem is the people. I must get to know them better.

October 18, 1941

Yesterday we attended the Water Festival at Caesarea. This was the first time I saw the spot Sdot-Yam has chosen for its settlement, its 'project'. It really is enchanting, and I felt like staying. Not only because of the beautiful scenery; I see something great in its inception, and would like to be a part of it. I'm also aware they need me in many ways, and would offer me a great deal in turn.

It's just that I'm uncertain about the group, though impressed by their dedication and devotion to a 'vision'—to the project. But this is almost the only force binding them as a group, and it takes more than that, I think. They're so far removed from me in education (not in knowledge, but in approach) and in their perspectives that it's somewhat frightening. The group's social ties are too lax because of the closeness of the city, and the work in the port. Still, their devotion to the vision is attractive.

I've only expressed superficial impressions, and don't really have the right to judge as yet. My old mistake. . . .

Ginosar
November 13, 1941

I left Sdot-Yam with favourable impressions, and many invitations to return. I really don't know if it's right to leave a group you enjoy in order to get to know a second, and a third group. Every place has its good and bad aspects, and in the end it makes it that much harder to decide.

I spent two days in Tel-Aviv, met Miryam there, and was glad to exchange impressions of everything that had happened to us both in the month since we parted. I saw two plays, *Alleys of Jerusalem* and *The Eternal Jew*. I wasn't particularly impressed by either, nor did I think the acting very good.

After Tel-Aviv I made the rounds: Petach Tikva, Nahalal, Merhavya (a beautiful place where I enjoyed the heartiness and simplicity of everyone), Balfouriya, Yagur. In Yagur I heard an interesting discussion at a general meeting on the subject of quarriers. And finally I returned to Ilonka in Kiryat Hayim.

I came to Ginosar with mixed feelings. On the one hand, I was curious and honestly eager to become acquainted with it, and on the other I knew in advance I wouldn't stay. Sdot-Yam still attracts me. I have some kind of aversion to joining a settlement which has got past its initial hardships and has begun to enjoy the fruits of its difficult years. I don't want anything 'ready-made'—though in the few days I've spent here I've come to realize that things aren't so 'ready' here either, that everything is still pretty much in a state of formation. Even so, my original reaction hasn't changed. The group's age suits me, as a matter of fact, and its composition also seems right for me. True, I don't know the people well enough to judge them, but meanwhile I'm simply staying on, working, and for the time being have no inclination to come to a final decision.

November 18, 1941

I've been in Ginosar for over a week now. Naturally, it's still difficult to decide. I can speak only according to first impressions. I've found a number of very intelligent people in the group here. I'm sure I'd find them interesting and become good friends with them. But the group, in its entirety, is not sufficiently alert. Nonetheless, they have made a good impression on me. To be more specific, it's a group composed of many fine individuals, but lacks the means of expressing itself in such a way as to form a common bond. This lack of expression is noticeable in every field of mutual endeavour, beginning with the reading room, all the way to the general assembly. I feel my sentence is murky, and not totally justified.

Regarding the work, I have no physical difficulties. I work wherever I'm assigned—in the garden, the laundry, the warehouse. But I feel as if there were a 'fire within me'. I don't feel I'm using all my abilities, but rather that I'm wasting myself. Throughout the Movement they complain of a lack of youth leaders, and a two-month leadership course is being started in the very near future. I may be wrong, but think (in fact I'm convinced) I could do very well in this kind of work. The only doubt I have is whether, with my limited knowledge, I can fulfil such an assignment. I'm quite confused about the issue—a thousand arguments, pro and con, race through my mind.

*Histadrut** elections will be held soon. Battles preceding the convention are already stormy. It's a good thing there's a spirit of sharp criticism, but here's hoping it won't undermine the Histadrut's prestige more than necessary, and weaken it instead of strengthening it.

Sdot-Yam
December 25, 1941

I'm back at Sdot-Yam, this time not as a guest but as a candidate. I'm firmly convinced that my ultimate decision is wise, and that this will be my permanent home.

But I'm still intrigued by that unconscious, hesitant voice that says, 'Perhaps you shouldn't . . .' And it finds expression in the minor—though major—fact that I didn't bring all my things with me.

January 2, 1942

I'll try to write a bit, though my hands are nearly frozen. Outside —a fearful storm. Five tents were blown down during the night. Ours didn't collapse, but the wind is howling around it on all

* Workers' Union.

sides, sand has covered everything, and my bed is rocking cease-
lessly with a monotonous beat.

Today is my Sabbath, my day off. I've wrapped one rag on
top of another around myself and am now in one of the rooms,
since it's impossible to remain in the tent. I want to write about
the past year. Without noticing, we stepped into 1942.

It is a grey, rainy day which depresses one's very soul, and
though the rain doesn't penetrate the room, it robs me of the
incentive to do anything.

It's difficult to believe this grey, dismal rain will ever stop—
and the same applies to the war. It doesn't touch us, yet locks us
in our rooms, denies us our peace of mind—though we do not
suffer from it the way the peoples of Europe are suffering. It's
hard to imagine that spring and sunshine will come again, and
difficult even in this little house to do anything, to clean it,
pretty it up a bit. One just doesn't have the desire to do anything. It's possible that the rain will come in, that there may be
leaks. But who wants to go out in the pouring rain to build, to
mend, to do?

January 7, 1942

It's difficult for me to write. My hands are nearly frozen after a
day of washing. I work in the laundry regularly, and even in this
work one can find some interest and satisfaction. But the days
are much too short. After a day's work I have neither the time
nor the strength to read, study, or pursue social contacts. There's
time for a little of everything, but not enough to do anything
thoroughly.

Yesterday a closed session was held on cultural matters. I was
invited too, and they wanted to elect me to be on the Committee
for Cultural Activities. I thought that at the beginning I would
not participate in any specific project or serve on committees. I
consider it a sign of weakness that they have no one for the job
other than a member who has been in the group only a very
short while. But at the same time I see there are not many who
are both willing and qualified to serve in this field, so perhaps I
had better accept the assignment.

As far as my social integration is concerned—it's too soon to
tell. I'm still almost a complete stranger here, meeting members

only at work or at meals. Of course a good deal depends upon me, but I want to use my free time to read and study.

I'm reading an excellent book by Maxim Gorky, *The Mother,* and I've begun Kant's *On Absolute Peace.* I've also got hold of a copy of *The Communist Manifesto,* but haven't finished it yet. No time.

Miryam visited me. We were delighted to see each other. It was good to talk to someone freely and in detail. She's the only person in the Land with whom I can discuss everything that concerns me, and who understands. Sometimes I look about me and realize how very alone I am among my colleagues and acquaintances. I wonder if everyone feels this way, or am I unique? I read my poem, *Ginosar,* to Miryam.

January 31, 1942

This afternoon we held memorial services for a member of the settlement who was drowned at sea a few days ago when his boat capsized in a storm. This was a warning for the future. The sea is a merciless, cruel tyrant, and demands, and will continue to demand, sacrifices from those who want to conquer her. This was simply expressed in the service today, and thus deeply moving.

I work in the laundry all the time; in fact one day I even worked outside the settlement doing laundry in a private home. Viewed from a distance (I worked there several days ago) it's difficult to describe my feelings. At first I felt some trepidation, simply because of the hard work entailed, and the responsibility. Then I felt strange because of the nature of the work, and also because I was serving in a private home—and as a laundress at that, the meanest of all forms of housework. I thought of Mother and my home, and felt a certain pride. Why? After all, I'm quite aware that thousands of girls have had to leave well-to-do homes and do hard work. But they were forced to do so by circumstances beyond their control, and constantly attempt to improve their situation. But we, at least, have the satisfaction (which may be entirely imaginary) of freedom of choice, idealistic justification, and a goal. At any rate, my fears were unfounded. Though it certainly wasn't an easy day's work—eight-and-a-half consecutive hours of washing–they were satisfied with my work and very kind, and paid me 35 *grush*. I was in a wonderful mood all the way home, singing and laughing. There was a feeling of enormous satisfaction in knowing that if I must I can do even that.

This evening I'm in charge of the children's building, thus have time to write in my diary, and perhaps to add a bit to my play, which is progressing slowly. During the day I sometimes think, How shall I cast Yehudit? What do I do on-stage while she's off-stage? But all this is pushed aside by workday pre-occupations.

February 4, 1942

I've just returned from a short visit to Caesarea. It was my second time there, and I was more impressed with the site than ever. The infinite horizon, the sea. . . . As one sits by the sea one thinks of the world's past, and contemplates its future; one's scope broadens, one's determination to achieve something great and beautiful strengthens. For various reasons the atmosphere of the group there is now much more intimate and unified.

In the morning I strolled among the ancient ruins, in the afternoon in our fields—or, to be more exact, where our fields will eventually be. And when I watched the waves storming the coast with foaming fury, and then saw how silent and placid they became when they broke on the beach, I thought, perhaps our enthusiasm and fumings are no different. When the waves pound in they are full of virility and vigour. When they reach the shore they are broken and tamed, and play in the golden sand like good little children.

February 9, 1942

I made a mistake. I spoke up at several general meetings and discussions. Now I'm very sorry. I'm sure most of the members see this as a desire to be conspicuous, which won't make my acceptance by the group any easier. It's always more difficult to mend fences than to break them.

It seems that estimations of my character pass through three phases: the first impression is very good, but entirely wrong. In this one I include all superficial acquaintanceships and unwanted

Bela and Catherine Senesh, Hannah's parents, in the early 1920's.

The young Hannah and George Senesh, interviewed by a journalist.

Hannah Senesh on her first day in Palestine (Haifa, September 19, 1939).

visitors. In the second phase the impression takes a turn for the worse; and in the third phase they get to know me as I really am. But not many get that far.

Here in the Land only Miryam really knows me. Here in the settlement I think I've reached the second phase. It's hard to explain the basis for my feelings, but I sense a coldness, and a lack of trust. The cause is obvious: either they think I'm very naïve, or take me for a chatterbox who arrogantly talks big about things she can never realize. They think my initial enthusiasm and activity will wane as I encounter reality. Naturally, no one has said any of this to me, but I'm sensitive enough to feel it. The words of Ady, the great Hungarian poet, ring in my ears, 'I'd love to be loved'. The second half of the line, 'to belong to someone'—there is no question of at all. I still don't see anyone.

Today I washed 150 pairs of socks. I thought I'd go mad. No, that's not really true. I didn't think of anything. I worked automatically, without any regard for time, without a thought in my head.

April 22, 1942

Yesterday I received a letter from home. It's so difficult.

I work at Yagur. I once began to note this and stopped. Briefly, work is from six to six; at six I return, shower, change. At seven we—a small group—read a chapter of the Old Testament, Isaiah; then, supper. Even if the rest of the evening is free, fatigue precludes any serious activity. The most important work I do in my free time is for the Movement, though I find this very difficult since I lack experience. But it does a lot for me, satisfies me. This is the first time I've had to deal with something that presents problems.

I've given considerable thought to enlistment. The entire country is being asked to mobilize for the war effort, as the war is coming closer. Although I have enlisted in the working front of the kibbutz, and know it is no less important or difficult than the recruitment of girls for the army, I nevertheless feel as if I'm failing to fulfil my duty. Perhaps the reason for this is that on the kibbutz the war effort has not yet reached its peak. In any case, many girls can't join the army. Those who can, who have no family ties, ought to join. I'm thinking of enlisting—

not in the British army, but in the Home Guard. Though army service is more interesting, what is important at the moment is the assurance that these guard units serve to protect the Land directly; the army can leave the country at any moment.

May 16, 1942

Since my last entry, a few changes have taken place concerning my status in the group. First, in connection with the draft: they've elected me to the group's Recruitment Committee. But even more important, I was proposed as a candidate for recruitment in the *Palmach**. Of course I proposed my own candidacy, but everyone was ready to agree to it in terms of my suitability. They objected only to the fact that I was so new to the settlement. Besides, they wanted me for another job.

After a long debate they elected me Supply Officer of the kibbutz as well. At first I objected strongly but in the end I had to agree, and they convinced me, to some extent, that I should at least try. I don't know myself whether I'm suited to this work, but I'll see. I'm starting together with another girl, and hope we'll make a go of it together. I discovered two things during the election: a) there is a lack of girls on the settlement, b) the decent behaviour of the settlement towards me, or, to be more exact, that the members trust me. This pleases me very much, of course.

Now I'll have more time. I'll continue working for the Movement too. I find the work very rewarding.

June 2, 1942

Just a sentence from *Broken Grindstones* by H. Hazaz: 'All the darkness can't extinguish a single candle, yet one candle can illuminate all its darkness.'

Aged twenty-one   *August 22, 1942*

'I'm well, only my hair has turned a bit grey,' Mother writes. It is obvious between the lines why her hair has turned grey. How

---

* The striking fist of the *Haganah,* the clandestine Jewish self-defence force in Palestine.

long will all this go on? The mask of comedy she wears, and those dear to her so far away? Sometimes I feel a need to recite the Yom Kippur confession: I have sinned, I have robbed, I have lied, I have offended—all these sins combined, and all against one person. I've never longed for her the way I long for her now. I'm so overwhelmed with this need for her at times, and with the constant fear that I'll never see her again. I wonder, can I bear it?

November 14, 1942

At the meeting of the Secretariat today my transfer to Caesarea was approved. I accepted the matter with mixed feeling, even though I've been vigorously fighting for the change. I know the difficulties in advance—a small group, completely unsuitable. But I may find my place among them. Anyway, I feel it's my duty to do something worthwhile for the advancement of the place. I still don't have a clear picture of what I'll do, but I'll do my best at whatever it turns out to be.

Caesarea
January 8, 1943

The long pauses between entries are indicative of my situation. Sometimes there's no ink in my pen; sometimes I don't have a light; sometimes it's noisy—there are others in the room besides me—and sometimes I have no reason to write. Sometimes I don't have time to write, and sometimes I don't feel like writing. Not because nothing happens—on the contrary, there has been plenty happening both inside and out. But I've simply been apathetic to everything that's been going on.

I've had a shattering week. I was suddenly struck by the idea of going to Hungary. I feel I must be there during these days in order to help organize youth emigration, and also to get my mother out. Although I'm quite aware how absurd the idea is, it still seems both feasible and necessary to me, so I'll get to work on it and carry it through. For the time being this is but a sudden enthusiasm, a hopeful plan to get Mother out and bring her here, at any cost. I spent three days in Tel-Aviv and Jerusalem trying to arrange the matter. At the moment chances are slim, but who knows . . . ?

Meanwhile I've been elected Storekeeper. All my protests were in vain. I have no interest in the job, but no choice either. It's a pity to waste more years of energy and strength on something I so dislike doing, and which will hinder my development in other directions.

I'm ashamed of myself for complaining, but can't rid myself of the belief that precious years are being wasted, years that should be devoted to study and self-improvement. I'm confident that if I could study one thing thoroughly I would be of much greater value to the settlement, and also far more contented. Instead, I'm assigned to duties which I carry out with hardly any effort, and to which I can contribute little. Nor do they, in turn, satisfy me, or afford me anything whatever. How long can this go on?

'That's a lie!' cries another voice, 'I'm studying, learning about life.'

That's not true either. I live in a world of my own making, without any contact with the outside world. I live here like a drop of oil on water, sometimes afloat, sometimes submerged, but always remaining apart, never mixing with another drop.

I visited Miryam a few days ago. We were so happy to see each other. She is really my friend.

But I can think of nothing now but my mother and brother. I am sometimes overwhelmed by dreadful fears. Will we ever meet again? And one question keeps torturing and tormenting me: Was what I did intolerable? Was it unmitigated selfishness?

Sdot-Yam
February 13, 1943

I hear singing from the dining hall, a party for members of the Youth Movement. I have no desire to join them. I've nothing to do there. I don't know what to do when I'm with people.

Nonsense! The same gripe again. I don't know what's wrong with me. Loneliness is difficult, but so is contact with people. I don't like my work, and I'm annoyed that it takes up all my time. It's not worth writing about. If I could only organize my thoughts. But I've stopped thinking.

I often recall Scarlet in *Gone with the Wind*. At difficult moments she would stall until 'some other time'. I'm that way. I'll consider what life is about, the value of society, the purpose of

man, the future—at some other time. At present—much work and
little satisfaction. The place is beautiful, magnetic. I feel as bound
to it as is possible in the short time I've been here. But I wonder—
is that enough? I'm fearful of the moment my reserve will run
out—my reserve of initiative, strength, and the will to give
without receiving anything in return.

Caesarea
February 22, 1943

How strangely things work out. On January 8 I wrote a few words
about the sudden idea that struck me. A few days ago a man from
Kibbutz Ma'agan, a member of the Palmach, visited the kibbutz
and we chatted awhile. In the course of the conversation he told
me that a Palmach unit was being organized to do—exactly what
I felt then I wanted to do. I was truly astounded. The *identical*
idea!

My answer, of course, was that I'm absolutely ready. It's still
only in the planning stage, but he promised to bring the matter
up before the enlistment committee since he considers me admir-
ably suited for the mission.

I see the hand of destiny in this just as I did at the time of
my Aliyah. I wasn't master of my fate then either. I was enthralled
by one idea, and it gave me no rest. I knew I would emigrate,
despite the many obstacles in my path. Now I again sense the
excitement of something important and vital ahead, and the
feeling of inevitability connected with a decisive and urgent step.
The entire plan may miscarry, and I may receive a brief notifi-
cation informing me the matter will be postponed, or that I don't
qualify. But I think I have the capabilities necessary for just this
assignment, and I'll fight for it with all my might.

I can't sleep at night because of the scenes I envisage: how
I'll conduct myself in this or that situation . . . how I'll notify
Mother of my arrival . . . how I'll organize the Jewish Youth.
Everything is still indefinite. We'll see what the future brings . . .

May 5, 1943

Such a long silence. I wonder why. Hasn't anything happened?
Or if it has, doesn't it matter to me? And if it does matter, doesn't

it demand expression? I have *fifteen* minutes before work. So
I'll write a few words.

My job remains the same. I don't like it, even though I
appreciate its importance. After work—a bit of reading, a great
void. I miss some good company, or, specifically, a companion. I
know—just one bold step and I would find a companion. But
not *the* companion. Or perhaps yes. The whole thing is so strange.
The boys . . . they're all right, yet the same inner voice says, 'Not
this one'. But does the one I'm looking for really exist? Or is he
someone my heart and imagination have invented? Meanwhile I'll
soon be twenty-two, and who would believe I've never kissed a
boy? It's silly, especially the way it bothers me. I joke with all
of them, but I think I'm cold, heartless. Joking, joking—but
something must be missing within me, or perhaps it's buried very
deep.

May 27, 1943

My entire being is preoccupied with one thing: departure. It's
imminent, real. It's possible they'll call me any day now. I
imagine various situations, and sometimes think about leaving
the Land . . . leaving freedom . . . I would like to inhale enough
fresh air so as to be able to breathe it even in the Diaspora's
stifling atmosphere, and to spread it all around me for those who
do not know what real freedom is.

But these are all positive thoughts about the matter, not doubts.
There is absolutely no question but that I must go. The hardships
and hazards entailed are quite clear to me. I feel I'll be able
to fulfil the assignment. I see everything that has happened to
me so far as preparation and training for the mission ahead.

May 29, 1943

I'm waiting to be called. I can't think of anything else. I don't
think there is any outer, noticeable change in me. I do my daily
work as usual, but sometimes feel as if I'm seeing things from
a distance. I look at everything from one point of view only: is
it, or is it not necessary for my mission? I don't want to meet
people. It'll be easier to leave if I don't. No. That's a lie. Now,
more than ever, I'd like someone who is close to me.

There are some things one can't express. One tends to confuse them and believe that as long as one doesn't find expression for them they don't exist. I pray for only one thing: that the period of waiting will not be too long, and that I can see action soon. As for the rest—I'm afraid of nothing. I'm totally self-confident, ready for anything.

June 12, 1943

The settlement decided to allow me to enlist. I'll soon be leaving for instruction.

Aged twenty-one   *August 24, 1943*

I'm constantly on the road, or at courses. I'm leaving now for a Working Youth seminar. Sometimes I have doubts: will I fulfil my mission? I try to have faith.

I think I'm in love, but there are many difficulties.

September 19, 1943

I arrived in the Land four years ago. Immigrant House, Haifa. Everything was new, everything beautiful, everything a world of the future. Only one figure takes me back to the past: my mother at the railway station. Four years. I never would have believed the distance between us could ever be so great, so deep. Had I known. . . . Or perhaps I knew but didn't dare admit it.

There's no sense to all this accounting. I'm now in Bet Ruthenberg, a splendid mansion, spending a month at a Working Youth Seminar. Before that, I was at another course. After this—I don't really know. Am I satisfied? It's hard to say. I spent two years in Nahalal, after that almost two years at Sdot-Yam and Caesarea. Many struggles, and considerable satisfaction, but always loneliness. No friends, no girl friends, but for Miryam.

And now I stand before a new assignment again, one that demands great preparation for a difficult and responsible mission. Again a sense of transition coupled with strong emotions, aspirations, tensions. And the everlasting aloneness. Now it's clearer to me than ever that this has nothing to do with outside factors. There's a certain peculiarity within me, and a lack of sociability

which keeps me away from people. This is especially difficult
where it concerns men.

At times I think I love, or could love, someone. But . . . There
are many objective 'buts' in the way, and I lack the courage to
overcome them. Meanwhile there are a few men who love me,
and I'm thinking of Moshe in particular . . . about whom I can
say only good things. And yet, I can't love him. All right, at
least my heart is far from breaking. But even so, there is something which terrifies me: I am twenty-two years old, and I don't
know how to be happy.

I wear a placid mask, and at times I say to myself, What is
this? Is this how my life is going to unfold? It's no longer an
external matter, but something within me. I have no complaints
about life, really. I'm satisfied. I can't imagine a state in which
I would be more content. On the contrary. And the assignment
which lies ahead draws me on. But I forget how to laugh—to really
laugh, heartily, as I once could with George while wrestling on
the couch until we rolled off onto the floor—laughing about
nothing but the joy of living, of being young and alive. Are
hardship and loneliness to blame for the lack of that particular
kind of joy? Or do I bear this sorrow from the time when—at
the age of seven or eight—I stood beside my father's grave and
began to write poems about the hardships in life? I feel I'm
just chattering. However, this is necessary too. Amid essays,
speeches, and silences, it's good to converse sometimes, even if
only with oneself.

I had a chance to talk with 'him' yesterday . . . but I left
anyway. I wanted so much to talk to him. I waited all week for
the opportunity. We chatted a few moments, and it was up to
me to continue. I really had no reason to leave. Yet I did. I
could not do otherwise. It's impossible to explain . . . but nevertheless, I understand. What a pity.

I long for satisfying work. In the last four years I've done all
kinds of work, not always out of conviction, always explaining to
myself that it was all necessary, and never gaining any real satisfaction from it. I really wanted to be a teacher. If I had to decide
today whether to emigrate to Palestine I'd do exactly as I did.
But I wouldn't go to Nahalal. Probably directly to a kibbutz.
Would I enlist? Of course. Thus, I would do nearly everything
over again.

In my life's chain of events nothing was accidental. Everything happened according to an inner need. I would have been miserable following a road other than the one I chose. No, perhaps this is an exaggeration. But had I chosen differently, I would not have been in harmony with myself.

Zionism and Socialism were instinctive with me, even before I was aware of them. The foundation was a part of my very being, and my consciousness merely reinforced my instinctive beliefs even before I knew their designations, or had the means of expressing them. Today, as I read more and more in these areas, their inner sense and logic become increasingly clear to me.

October 2, 1943

It's been about a month since I finished the seminar, and I'm home now, in Caesarea. I've worked in the kitchen, the garden, the laundry, scrubbing floors, and now I'm on guard duty. It makes little difference to me what work I'm doing. I'm happy to be home, to see people.

I bathe in the sea, swim out far, climb up on a rock and enjoy sea, air, sand, new and ancient Caesarea. Afterwards I dive back into the sea and feel fine, just fine!

No news from Mother, but new immigrants say the situation in Hungary is still satisfactory. I've stopped writing entirely. That's one of the things which depresses me.

January 11, 1944

This week I leave for Egypt. I'm a soldier. Concerning the circumstances of my enlistment, and my feelings in connection with it, and with all that led up to it, I don't want to write.

I want to believe that what I've done, and will do, are right. Time will tell the rest.

Hannah Senesh wrote the following letter in Haifa on December 25, 1943, asking that if she failed to return from her mission it be given to her brother George upon his arrival in Palestine. Her brother, however, arrived the day before she left for Cairo, and thus she let him read the letter quickly, then asked

*for its return so as to hide from him the danger inherent in her
mission. At that first, quick reading, and probably because of
the excitement of his arrival and their reunion, George did not
realize the letter's full importance—a letter of parting and apology
from one who was leaving, perhaps never to return.*

*The letter is included with her Diary rather than her Letters,
since it is the only intimation she gives of the nature of her
mission, and would seem to belong here.*

Haifa
Darling George!   *December 25, 1943*
Sometimes one writes letters one does not intend sending.
Letters one must write without asking oneself, 'I wonder whether
this will ever reach its destination'.

Day after tomorrow I am starting something new. Perhaps
it's madness. Perhaps it's fantastic. Perhaps it is dangerous.
Perhaps one in a hundred—or one in a thousand—pays with his
life. Perhaps with less than his life, perhaps with more. Don't
ask questions. You'll eventually know what it's about.

George, I must explain something to you. I must exonerate
myself. I must prepare myself for that moment when you arrive
inside the frontiers of the Land, waiting for that moment when,
after six years, we will meet again, and you will ask, 'Where is
she?' and they'll abruptly answer, 'She's not here'.

I wonder, will you understand? I wonder, will you believe
that it is more than a childish wish for adventure, more than
youthful romanticism that attracted me? I wonder, will you feel
that I could not do otherwise, that this was something I had
to do?

There are events without which one's life becomes unimportant, a worthless toy; and there are times when one is com-
manded to do something, even at the price of one's life.

I'm afraid, George, that feelings turn into empty phrases even
though they are so impassioned before they turn into words. I
don't know whether you'll sense the doubts, the conflicts, and
after every struggle the renewed decision.

It is difficult because I am alone. If I had someone with whom
I could talk freely, uninhibitedly—if only the entire burden were

not mine, if only I could talk to you. If there is anyone who would understand me, I think you would be that one. But who knows . . . six years is a long time.

But enough about myself. Perhaps I have already said too much. I would like to tell you a few things about the new life, the new home, as I see them. I don't want to influence you. You'll see for yourself what the country is. But I want to tell you how I see it.

First of all—I love it. I love its hundred faces, its hundred climates, its many-faceted life. I love the old and the new in it; I love it because it is ours. No, not ours, but because we can make ourselves believe it is ours.

And I respect it. Not everything. I respect the people who believe in something, respect their idealistic struggle with the daily realities. I respect those who don't live just for the moment, or for money. And I think there are more such people here than anywhere else on earth. And finally, I think that this is the only solution for us, and for this reason I don't doubt its future, though I think it will be very difficult and combative.

As far as the kibbutz is concerned, I don't think it is perfect, and it will probably pass through many phases. But in today's circumstances it best suits our aims, and is the closest to our concept of a way of life—about this I have absolutely no doubt.

We have need of one thing: people who are brave and without prejudices, who are not robots, who want to think for themselves and not accept outmoded ideas. It is easy to place laws in the hands of man, to tell him to live by them. It is more difficult to follow those laws. But most difficult of all is to impose laws upon oneself, while being constantly self-analytical and self-vigilant. I think this is the highest form of law enforcement, and at the same time the only just form. And this form of law can only build a new, contented life.

I often ask myself what the fate of the kibbutz will be when the magic and novelty of construction and creation wear off, when the struggle for existence assumes reality and—according to plan—becomes an organized, abundant communal life. What will the incentive of the people be, what will fill their lives? I don't know the answer. But that day is so far in the future that it is best to think of existing matters.

Don't think I see everything through rose-coloured glasses.

My faith is a subjective matter, and not the result of outer conditions. I see the difficulties clearly, both inside and out. But I see the good side, and above all, as I said before, I think this is the only way.

I did not write about something that constantly preoccupies my thoughts: Mother. I can't.

Enough of this letter. I hope you will never receive it. But if you do, only after we have met.

And if it should be otherwise, George dear, I embrace you with everlasting love.

Your sister.

P.S. I wrote the letter at the beginning of the parachute training course.

THE LETTERS

Dearest Mother and Evi! *   *October 12, 1939*

I am so glad I can begin my letter this way, that Evi is already in the city. At least I know you won't be so alone, Mother dear. I received your joint letter today, the one in which Aunt Eliz wrote a few dear lines too. I was so happy to get it.

I'll write a detailed letter now, and hope that despite the existing circumstances you'll receive it in good time. I know, Mother, that all the smallest details interest you, so today's letter will deal with all such small things in order to give you an idea of my life here.

Let's start with the daily routine: the bell rings at 5.30 a.m., my two room-mates begin to stir and I get up as well. We have a wash basin in our room, so I can brush my teeth comfortably, get washed, dress in slacks, boots, blouse, a headscarf—oh, wait, the scarf comes later since at six there is only class and for that we don't need a scarf. I pull my bedding off the bed—the mattresses are very good, and I sleep wonderfully well, using a sheet and a blanket. That is, at night only a sheet, and if towards morning I feel chilly I pull up the blanket. I haven't bought a mosquito net yet, and for the moment don't miss it since we haven't any flies in our room. But if you can, please send one as I may need it later.

At six the bell rings again: we have to go to class. So far we've had classes in four subjects: chemistry, botany, general agriculture and fruit gardening. Chemistry and agriculture are taught by a woman, the other two subjects by a man. How well each teaches I've not yet been able to judge, but I think our classes will be interesting. What I'm now learning in chemistry I already know. It's new to me only insofar as the language is concerned. I'll probably learn a lot of new things in the other subjects. We're about to have our first class in dairy farming, and nutrition (I think this is the best way to translate it) is also

* Her cousin.

included in the curriculum. Of course there's also Hebrew class—and that's all so far. As you can see, it's diversified.

The classrooms are attractive, light, and there are about three or four of them in all. But this is really enough because there are, all told, only four classes, divided into two each terms: 'A' and 'B'—according to knowledge of the language. I believe I have already written that I am in 1A, that is, in the advanced classes. One doesn't stand up when the teacher enters the room, nor to speak and answer questions.

I've already been to the blackboard once—in chemistry—and once I answered a question in botany from my desk. Though the questions and answers weren't very complicated in either case, from the point of view of language I was pleased I did well. The relationship with the teachers is quite different here. One simply calls them by their first name, and the language lends itself best to 'tutoring', thus the atmosphere is much more informal. The first class ends at seven, and we go to breakfast. The meals are all first-rate, plentiful, and varied. We economize on one thing only: sugar. For breakfast we have tea, tomatoes, butter, cheese, bread, one lump of sugar for our tea.

This week it's my turn to clean our room, so straight after breakfast I begin. First I sweep (everyone makes his own bed after breakfast), then dust, pick things up, and finally wash down the floor (it's stone). I finish all this by about eight. Then comes the red scarf, or a big hat, black sunglasses, and generally I cream my face. Then out to the fruit orchard. The work there varies. In the beginning I picked olives for several days, which is easy but monotonous work. The only thing that makes it a bit interesting is that one climbs the trees. Recently I've worked very little among the olives; instead I've been fertilizing the vineyards. Don't worry, this work is not at all unpleasant. On the contrary. And it isn't even hard to do. I don't say that after I've worked for two hours and done a row and a half my arms don't feel tired. They do. But I haven't had any real muscle pains as yet. In the morning I sort olives for a while, which is easy, and I enjoy doing it. One sits comfortably in the shade, and thus one rests as one works.

We work outside until noon—that is, a few minutes before noon—then go inside. But from 11.30 on we ask at least twenty times what the time is, and at noon, hastily washed, combed, and with a hearty appetite—and as far as I'm concerned in the best possible humour (one can't generalize about this) we sit down to eat.

There are ten of us at a table, each table covered with white linoleum. We have linen cloths only on Saturday. What we have for our noon meal is difficult to say; all I know about the food is that I eat it and like it. Exactly what it is, its ingredients, I really don't know. But, for example, yesterday's dinner consisted of boiled eggs in tomato sauce (cold), then some sort of warm vegetable-like thing with dumplings, a type of salad, and grapefruit. Today, some sort of mixed tomato-egg thing, but entirely different from yesterday's. Then minced meat, a wonderful green salad, a sort of cabbage-noodle—but much better than the Hungarian variety (or perhaps it just seemed so because I was hungry), and a wonderful cold fruit juice for dessert. This is particularly important since we don't have water on the table, and everyone is rather thirsty.

After dinner one can drink water, but although they say the water is good here, they still advise that in the beginning, until one gets used to it, it's best not to drink too much, and to be careful. We finish dinner at 12.30 and at 1.30 our afternoon work begins. Thus we have an hour's rest. Yesterday I used the time to wash my hair, today I rested a while, studied, read your letters—the post arrives just at that time. Then at 1.30 back to work in the orchard.

Today I worked all day in the vineyard hoeing around the roots, and we tied the branches. Believe me, it's a wonderful feeling to look at a completed row of vines, and the work isn't even hard.

It's not too hot now. I came at a very good time as it's beautiful, pleasant weather. I can't even believe you've already got the heating on while we're still wearing summer clothes, walking about in brilliant sunshine. Only the evenings are slightly cool—as if to remind us that winter is approaching.

We now have lemons, figs, nuts, and a tremendous number of other fruit trees, but the season is virtually over. The real fruit season will come later. Here we eat grapefruit the way we eat oranges at home. We don't make a big fuss about sugar—we simply eat the grapefruit in its natural state, and it's enormously refreshing. I don't even find it bitter any more.

At 3 we rush in for tea, because if we're not in by the time the bell rings it's more than certain we won't find a scrap of jam left as the others will have eaten it all. And this is bad because all we get otherwise is tea with bread—the poorest meal of the day. At 3.30 classes begin, and until then we shower, change our clothes, clean up in general. For the moment I'm in great shape with my cupboard—I don't know where to knock on wood! I have it all to myself, which is just great since I have all kinds of room. Here's hoping I don't have to share it with someone. From 4.30 to 6.30 we're free, two hours which we spend in various ways.

Today, for instance, I did some ironing, studied, and am now writing to you. Yesterday, Susan's brother was here. He lives in a nearby village, and works in this area building a road. Believe me, he's one of the lucky ones. A great many would be happy if they could do this, but there is a shortage of work. Of course he doesn't have a profession or a trade, and doesn't know the language. That's the way almost all of them come, and once here they can't find work. Otherwise he's a nice, pleasant lad, and we've spent a lot of time talking together. If there is any sewing to be done, or more delicate washing, I do that during this period as well. So you see, those two hours are needed.

At 6.30 we have our last class. On the whole, I understand the lessons quite well. I take notes, particularly of new words, and thus things progress. At 7.30, supper, which is also good and varied. Afterwards news on the radio, which I don't often listen to because as yet I don't understand it very well. Only what they say about France and Hungary really interests me, and the local news, of course. Heaven knows Europe is very far from here.

We listen to music, talk, study, and go to bed about 9.30. A second later we're asleep.

The reproductions have come in handy. We've made exhibits of them in the radio room. Every week we have a different painter or a different period on display, with a short description. I don't have much time to read. That is, I don't want to read in a language other than Hebrew, and that's still a bit difficult.

I see, Evi, you're completely occupied too, and what you're doing sounds extremely interesting. Letters I send Mother are meant for you as well, of course. Don't expect separate letters, and write when you have time. It would be nice to be able to talk a bit. I really would have a lot to talk to you about now. Even a four-page letter isn't long enough. This is relativity: for us four pages aren't enough, for the censor they are too many. But I do hope you'll receive this soon. I'm sending it by ordinary mail, since airmail is too expensive.

A million kisses for you all (I'm including George since you told me you forward my letters to him). Send a good many of the kisses to Dombovár too.

Nahalal

Dearest George!   *October, 1939*

I know Mother sends you my letters, but even so I'll write directly as well since there is so much to write about.

First of all, I beg of you, even though you write to Mother playfully and jokingly, and embellish your letters, write to me about your life and situation sincerely, honestly, and let me know exactly how things are with you. From your letters I judge that you feel very much alone, Old Man, and that at the moment your life there can't be too amusing. Of course this is easily understandable in the present warlike atmosphere, but just because of that write the truth about everything. After all, you know how much it all interests me, and perhaps it's good for you, too, to be able to tell someone, frankly, what you're doing, what you're thinking, what you're feeling.

I see that you, too, are very concerned about Mother being so alone. You can imagine what an awful feeling it is for me. But despite this, George, I must tell you Mother will be delighted if you stay where you are and continue your studies.

There is just one thing I want to ask of you, and I know, George, I can ask it in Mother's name as well. As I believe we discussed at home—don't volunteer for the army. Please. Mother, and I must confess I, too, would not have a single moment's rest if you volunteered, and Mother would never forgive herself for not insisting that you return home. I certainly understand the big difference between being under Hitler in Hungary and fighting against him in France. Even so, George, as long as there is any way of avoiding this step, do so, for Mother's sake, and for mine and for your own.

A few words about myself: I'm extremely busy. Even now I have time to write to you only because we happened to have a free hour from class. But this is beside the point. The important thing is that I am very satisfied and haven't regretted for one moment that I left home and came here. When one leaves work with a rake or spade over one's shoulder and looks at the Emek, the country's most fertile, beautiful area—thirty years ago all of it a horrible swamp—and knows it is Jewish land, it's a wonderful, wonderful feeling.

But I want to be honest. This work doesn't have just a romantic side. When I hoe, or clean something, or wash dishes, or scatter the manure, I must confess the thought strikes me at times that I could be doing something better. But wait . . . I didn't express myself properly. What I actually mean is that now I see, truly, that this kind of work is not as simple as I thought. One needs a knowledge of the craft, and above all, it is important work. But understand me well, George: what I'm thinking is that perhaps I could do some other type of work better. But to be quite honest I rarely think this way, for I am well aware that these automatic tasks are only for now, at the very beginning, and that later on the work will be more interesting.

The following letter was written to the 'Wizo' Youth Group of Budapest.

Nahalal
October 26, 1939

I've been planning to write you for a long time since I know you're awaiting news from me, and also that news about Palestine interests you.

People, the way of life, regions, destinies . . . there are probably few places in the world where things—all things—are as changeable. The people . . . this is where it is least possible to generalize. I must be enormously fortunate because so far, I must say, I have met all very nice, kind people.

As I reflect upon my experiences this past month, I have great difficulty choosing what, exactly, I ought to write about. It would have been wonderful if all of you could have disembarked with me in the magnificent harbour of Haifa, and marvelled, as I did, at the way it is situated, both the modern part of the city and the old. You would have been delighted, as I was, with the Hebrew signs on the stores and buses. You would have boarded, as I did, an Egged Company bus, and been driven across the Emek though primitive, makeshift settlements of Arab wooden houses, flocks of straggling sheep, and modern Jewish settlements, past huge cacti and beautiful fruit orchards. And finally you would have arrived here in Nahalal.

Now I ought to lead you by way of my letter, through the school. Of course this will be very difficult to do quickly as there are three school buildings with rooms for the students, dining rooms, classrooms, libraries and reading rooms, and countless other communal rooms. So even if you were here it would take quite a bit of time to show you everything, were we to include all the farmlands and orchards, the garden, nursery, forestry school, dairy, beehives, poultry farm, creamery, the fields and buildings that belong to the main house, such as the laundry and the wonderful kitchen. So you see, I really can't adequately describe all of this by letter.

I would like to write a few things now about the indoor life. We have a tremendous amount to do: six hours of practical and three hours of theoretical work, and preparation for classes. So not much free time remains. But whatever hours do remain after work are always pleasant. (Don't misunderstand. This does not mean that the time spent working and studying isn't pleasant as well.)

The nicest time is Friday evening. Before supper there is an *Oneg Shabbat* with singing and music, followed by a delicious supper. That night the gate is open until eleven, and one spends the evening any way one likes—generally very pleasantly. The Hora, and other dances, plus songs, are part of the Saturday programme, though at present the atmosphere is not very gay since there are a great many Polish and German girls here who have had no word from their relatives and family; it's understandable that the general mood is somewhat depressed.

One day films were shown here, and recently we went to a beautiful performance given by *Habima*, the National Theatre. There are also lectures given in the moshav, so you see there are ample opportunities to pursue a cultural life.

Sport is represented by a ping-pong table, and we generally play on Saturday. But then we have plenty of 'physical activity' if our work can be classified as such. We prefer using our Saturday holiday for reading, resting and taking walks.

Perhaps you expected big words about the adventure of Aliyah, and instead I've given you particulars about the life, just as they happened to come to mind. But these are exactly the circumstances under which we live here. The Hebrew language, newspapers, the radio, our work, our Saturdays—these are the things that lead us towards the goals we have all set ourselves. That's why I think all this will interest you.

With warmest greetings of *Shalom* to you all.

Nahalal

Dear George,   *November 7, 1939*

I think of you so much; you must feel so alone. You know, even when I was home I know how very difficult your life must have been—alone in a strange land. But now I understand your situation even better, though I believe it is considerably easier for me. After all, I'm not in a strange land, and I'm not even alone. But even so it's sometimes difficult, and at such times I always think of you, George, and that you never wrote about your loneliness, never complained. It can't have been an easy year for you, and you can't be having easy months now. Not even your friends are there, and due to the war perhaps life has become more difficult from other aspects as well. I have now learned from experience how happy I am when news comes from home, or when I get a letter from you. That's why from this point of view I am not going to be sparing. On the contrary. Particularly as at present I'm financially quite well off. I have nearly five pounds, and besides, I get pocket money from the school. Actually money is not at all important to me from a personal point of view, but very important in order to get you and Mother here soon as possible.

You see, George, I have switched from the most sentimental to the most prosaic material matters. But perhaps it's useless to write about sentimental things. It would be wonderful to sit down for a bit—or for a very long while—and talk. Among the many things we would talk about and discuss would be the things it is so difficult to write about—not only because there are no words for such things, but because one is so stupidly shy that one is ashamed to write about one's feelings, even to those who are closest and dearest. For instance, I am ashamed to write to you that here, beside the typewriter, I've been crying. Though I could not tell you why, because I like being here and am fine, and not disappointed in anything. But I think you'll understand how it is just the same, and that what I really miss is you and Mother. George, I almost said I miss you even more than Mother because I saw Mother two months ago and it's been so long since I spent any time with you, for those days in Lyon, although they were beautiful, were too short to really overcome this enormous distance.

Don't be angry, George, that I'm so selfish, and that I make it easier for myself through you, and thus make your heart even heavier. And I beg of you, don't think I am always in this mood. I'm just taking advantage of you, writing to you now that I feel this way.

Concerning your Aliyah: I think it can be considered only after you've completed your studies. At that time, however, if your views have not changed—and I heartily hope they won't— you *must* come. Perhaps life is easier somewhere else, perhaps one must struggle more here to make a living, but whatever one finally does attain here one can freely enjoy. I think with a profession, a knowledge of Hebrew, and with a bit of improvement in conditions, it won't be so difficult, and I know that for you, too, other things besides the materialistic factors are exceedingly important.

The following letter was sent to the Maccabee Society of Budapest.

Nahalal
December 18, 1939

Don't imagine that just because I don't write I don't think of you often. On Tuesday evenings I always think you must all be talking about us, and by 'us' I mean those living in Eretz Israel, and it's a wonderful feeling to be able to include myself among them.

I must honestly confess that since being here I am considerably less preoccupied with the history and ideologies of Zionism than I was at home. But on the other hand I speak a good deal more Hebrew and I am much closer to the pioneer way of thinking and living. But then of course this is only natural. At home we prepare for the 'Aliyah', and construct a foundation upon which we can build when we get here. I feel I brought with me a pretty strong foundation, strong enough to build a good and contented life upon; a foundation that enables me to participate in the communal work.

Perhaps after the tone of our discussions at home you'll feel my letter is not enthusiastic enough. Perhaps you'll think I am disappointed, or that my idealism has cooled. I am not disappointed in anything, and I have not lost my faith in Eretz Israel. But I now realize that one must not always talk about a dream State when one mentions Palestine, since there are those who imagine the Land to be constantly under brilliantly blue skies, whereas there are days, such as today, for instance, when it's pouring with rain, the wind is blowing, and it's quite cold. On such a day they would feel deeply disappointed in Eretz Israel.

Yes, there is bad weather here too, and there are many economic difficulties and mistakes. But we are at home, free; we have goals; we have a future.

Nahalal
Dearest Mother, *December, 1939*

Perhaps so far you've judged my letters to be superficial, Mother dear. After all, I'm almost always writing about what I do, how I live, where I've been. But I am sure you're waiting for an answer to an unasked question. After all, you made a sacrifice when you let me leave home, and I made a sacrifice when I parted from you. And now I'm sure you would like to know whether it was all worth it. Perhaps I don't have the right to answer this question yet. It really takes a good deal more time to make a decision, but I'll attempt to answer sincerely according to how I feel at this moment.

My answer, dearest Mother, is unequivocally, Yes. I won't deny that there are times when I would give a great deal to see you all for a bit, or at least to have the knowledge that you're all somewhat closer. But at such times I think that a year or two away from you, spent in fulfilling the very reasons for which I came, is not too long a period, and try to imagine how wonderful it will be when we can all be together again.

It was worth coming for the sensation of feeling that I am the equal of all men in my own country (at the moment this last is merely a feeling, not a fact), for that peaceful feeling with which one can walk down the street without wondering whether the person coming in the opposite direction is a Jew or not, and for the knowledge that the smallest matters are not decided by the criterion of whether one is a Jew or not.

However, this factor—that there is no anti-Semitism—may not even be enough of an answer. The most positive answer is that a healthy, new Jewish life is developing here, which one can best express by stating that in the Diaspora Jews were sad if they had no particular reason to be good humoured, and here, on the other hand, people are good humoured if they have no particular reason to be sad—as people are in most lands.

Nahalal

Dearest Mother,   *January 10, 1940*

My work is smashing! When dressed in trousers, boots, or rubber apron, I wash down the cows (I'm not a bit afraid of them. In this I'm not your daughter!). I think of my old class-mates at home and how they would turn up their noses at such work, which to me now seems absolutely natural. If at times a cow, regardless of all the nudging and pushing, refuses to stand up or lift a leg, or is reluctant to fulfil any other of my wishes, I take advantage of the opportunity to speak Hungarian, a language not often understood in this area, and wish the cow that which in Hebrew I don't know anyway because as yet I haven't learned to swear in the language! But fortunately the cows don't under-stand either, and thus the relationship between us is most peaceful.

Today I really made a mess of things with the calves. When I went to clean out their stalls I had to take them into another barn. This work, I later learned, is always done by two people so the little calves won't stampede or run amok. But I, unaware, opened the gate and began driving them ahead. In one second the five little calves ran to five different corners of the barn. You've never seen such mad running about. It took my room-mate (who is now working there) and me at least ten minutes to round them up and get them into their proper stalls, both of us running around like mad. We really worked up a sweat, but it was actually great fun.

I am enclosing a flower with this letter, sending it not only because it's already spring here, but also to take the place of that flower I would ordinarily take to Daddy's grave at this time of year if I were there. On the 18th* I'll be thinking of you, dearest Mother, even more than usual, if that's possible.

Nahalal
Dear Mother,   *January 20, 1940*
This afternoon is free thanks to a sad event. The wife of one of our instructors (old Nahalal settlers highly regarded and respected by everyone, and from all accounts a most outstanding woman) died yesterday. The funeral was today, which the entire village, and the greater part of the school, attended. It was an entirely different kind of funeral from the ones we know. People came in work clothes, the men, for the most, bare-headed, and the entire procession marched through the village and along the main road to the rather distant cemetery. In the Hebrew funeral service, that boundary between a prayer and an oration which was once customary in the Jewish ritual, became somehow indistinct. Otherwise I think a rabbi officiated, though I am not sure since I could not see him distinctly in the great mob. Standing there among the graves I thought that a year ago, on almost precisely the same date, I had stood beside Daddy's grave, and perhaps at just that moment you were at the cemetery again, Mother dear, and it was so sad to think neither George nor I could be with you at such a time.

Nahalal
Dearest Mother,   *February 28, 1940*
Distant . . . far away . . . One can no longer use old words. They have acquired new meanings with the new times. Today, when worlds separate next door neighbours and the world's oceans are spanned by the love of united peoples—today one must be careful of the word 'distant'.

Perhaps the distance is great in miles, and borders have become

* Her father's birthday.

insurmountable obstacles, but if I look at myself in the mirror
and see my tangled hair I can actually feel your disapproving
gaze upon me. If I meet someone for the first time the thought
flashes through my mind, What would Mother think of him? If
I do something I know is right, I know you, too, would approve,
and I feel that our thoughts are meeting somewhere, perhaps
midway, above the sea. I feel how strong and resilient is this
unseen thread that binds us, and I feel how unnecessary it is for
me to write about all this, for you actually know about everything
anyway.

So is it possible to say we're 'far' from each other?

What am I sending you for Purim?* Just these lines. And the
fervent request to heaven: Let the time come as quickly as
possible when we will again be together and letters and words will
be unnecessary.

Nahalal
Mother Dear,   *March 31, 1940*
In a letter he wrote some time ago Mike asked a question which
I don't want to leave unanswered. But I don't want to write a
separate letter so, dearest Mother, it must be included in this
one. Mike was shocked by the lack of religion among the youth
here, and asked why fathers don't take their sons to religious
services. The question is extremely complicated. First of all, I
must report that there is a religious element here. But let us
speak of the irreligious. Under no circumstances can the fathers
take their children to services as this is the very generation whose
only religion and only God is work, and this is its strength as
well.

Perhaps this generation was also influenced by the agnostic
or atheist movement of Europe, and instinctively cast off everything that reminded it of the Diaspora and of the outer manifestations of religion. Besides, according to the national structure
the observation of religious laws is more difficult here than it was
in the Diaspora where, if necessary, there was someone to take
over duties and to do the work when there were Jewish holidays
to be observed.

* *Purim*—a festival commemorating Queen Esther's successful intervention
on behalf of the Jews in ancient Persia.

Thus the fathers are the ones most to be blamed for the lack of religious training. But now I must say that they, themselves, feel this drawback, and even the youth seems to be a little in search of religion. Thus there is hope that between the two extremes the pendulum will find a healthy medium at which to stop. As far as I'm concerned, this should not be left to chance. There should, instead, be a complete revision of the religious laws. But to achieve this someone should be appointed who has great religious authority, who could find the middle road between orthodoxy and complete atheism, and whose decision would be acceptable. As far as I can judge, the present form of religion is not observed on all points, which makes life here much more difficult.

An example: I heard about one of the Mizrachi* kibbutzim where over a long period they dumped hundreds of gallons of milk on Saturdays because the cows had to be milked, of course, but according to the religious laws the milk could not be used. They no longer do this, yet no one from that kibbutz will travel on a Saturday, though they have no other holiday, which means being totally tied to the spot. Even if they did spend a Friday evening and Saturday in Tel-Aviv they couldn't go anywhere if they wanted to because theatres, cinemas, museums, etc., are all closed, and buses don't run on the Sabbath either. Thus they would merely waste an entire free day, which they certainly would not be pleased to do, no matter how great their religious belief.

Nahalal
Dearest Mother,   *April 5, 1940*
We have just completed a magnificent excursion and I want to write you about it immediately so that I don't forget a single thing.

Last week I was restless and so decided to go to Haifa to visit Ilonka and the family on Saturday. Miryam could not come with me that morning, so I went up to the road alone, where a lot of my classmates had already met and joined forces. We waited a while but nothing came. That is, nothing in the direction of Haifa.

* The orthodox segment.

Suddenly a beautiful car approached, going in the opposite direction. On the spur of the moment I decided to wave it down, and the car stopped. It was on its way to Tiberias, so three of us got in. We had barely recovered from our joy and wonder when we were already speeding towards Tiberias. I could write pages and pages about that drive, or I wish a fine impressionist painter would immortalize the constantly changing vistas that emerge around each bend, each hilltop. Here and there it is only an enlarged splash of colour: wonderful green, blue, brown; in another place a tiny detail, a miniature, with little dolls' houses, fruit trees, gardens. We three happy passengers constantly exchanged glances, wondering whether or not to believe our eyes as the incredible beauty of the panorama intensified. Then suddenly Nazareth appeared. Blinding-white monasteries, churches, old stone houses, Arabs, monks, nuns—this is the superficial picture one gets of Nazareth, and beyond this we saw nothing since the car did not stop.

We continued the journey towards Tiberias along winding roads, up and down. That is from Nazareth to Tiberias up, and then all at once, after a sudden bend, a wonderful blue springs into view: Yam Kinneret, the Sea of Galilee. And on its shore the town, sparkling-white.

Then from the hill a sudden descent: Tiberias, which lies below sea level. Our driver (an Englishman with whom we exchanged barely a word) put us down, and we would gladly have run right into the lake, whose colour, situation, surrounding hills and vegetation reminded me of Garda. We ate in a park, even bought ice cream, oranges, and very fine white twist bread—all for about a piaster each. After stuffing ourselves we decided to see everything worth seeing. An elderly Jewish police 'type' was standing in the road. We approached him and asked what was worth seeing, and whether it would be all right to walk about the Arab section—whereupon he offered to act as our guide. Of course he was off duty, or perhaps he was not even a policeman. At any rate, that's of no consequence. The important thing is that he knew everything and everyone in town, and proved to be a wonderful guide.

First we went down to the lake by way of the Arab quarter, and that's a chapter in itself. It is composed of narrow, dirty streets lined with balconied stone houses so close together they practically meet overhead. The houses all have deep hollows and recesses where merchants have settled in—though one sees rather attractive modern shops as well. Still, it was strange to hear a popular English tune coming from a café at the end of a narrow alleyway. The same mixture is visible as far as the people are concerned: modern European dress alongside ancient Arab garb, and in most places the two completely mixed.

Our guide took us first to an Arab-Christian cloister, or, to be exact, the home of soru monks. But more interesting than the houses and furnishings were the Eastern faces we saw there. I have rarely seen as many wrinkles on a face as I did there, wreathed in white hair and long beard. All this, along with the habits, makes an exotic picture for me, though it is certainly not very unusual here.

After that we went to the Eastern Jewish quarter (don't think of this as Eastern European, but as the quarter of those who have come from East of Palestine). Outwardly it is a little more orderly than the Arab quarter, though here, too, there is plenty of scattered orange peel decorating the streets, but the streets are wider than those in the Arab quarter, and the houses roomier. Nor is the entire quarter as old as that of the Arabs. The inhabitants dress in European clothes but speak Arabic. Hebrew is used only for religous ceremonies, though naturally the children already speak Hebrew.

We also visited the synagogue. It is very interestingly furnished, square-shaped, benches placed along the walls and covered with all sorts of coloured and chequered pillows and arm-rests, in true 'oriental' comfort. In the front section there is an attractively decorated Torah shrine, in the centre the dais for the rabbi, which differs from the European only in workmanship. There is no balcony for women, since only men participate in the services. After that we went to see the Ashkenazi synagogue which, on the other hand is exactly the same as, let us say, the one in Dombovár. That is to say, nothing unusual. There was what we imagined to have once been an interesting, beautiful synagogue, but it is now only a ruin (a few years ago it was destroyed by floods, as was a large part of the lower town); only a few columns, bare walls, and the Torah shrine remain. We could imagine the whole only from the carvings on the columns, and the Torah shrine.

We didn't even begin to see everything of interest in Tiberias.

But we didn't dare go any further since we had wandered so far
from Nahalal (about an hour's ride by car) and had to think about
getting back. For a while we hung around the park in the hope
of seeing the car we had come in, as its owner said he would be
returning to Haifa and had told us to watch for him. But we
waited in vain. My two classmates were beginning to get extremely
worried, but I refused to be upset, and climbing onto a post-box
sat in the shade and sang. Perhaps this contributed to the ill-
humour of the others! However, the whole atmosphere changed
in a flash when an attractive little car appeared around the bend
with a young man at the wheel. My two classmates began waving
at the poor thing, whereupon he fearfully stopped and opened
the door. I then jumped from my hiding place and in a moment
we had installed ourselves in the three remaining seats. The
poor fellow hardly knew where to put his brand new hat, which
had been on the seat beside him. He hurriedly slammed the door,
afraid someone else would appear, but we assured him there were
only 'three little girls'.

Our driver turned out to be quite a decent chap. We even
stopped once in the Balfour Forest and had a little walk, then
sat down, and looked down into Ginegar, which is just beneath
the forest and is Jewish territory. The sheaves of wheat seemed
very far away, a large part of the grain meant for fodder already
gathered and stacked. After the romantic beauty of the Kinneret
the Emek stretched before us with its great fertile fields. Its
beauty seems forever new, forever a thing of wonder to behold.

Dearest Mother,   *May 6, 1940*
I ought to give you the smallest details about a most beautiful and
highly successful holiday but due to lack of time I can only sum
it up briefly.

Thursday afternoon I went to Haifa, visited a friend on the
Carmel, spent the night there, and in the morning at about nine
went down to the highway just under the Carmel which leads
towards Tel-Aviv. I quickly got a lift to Tel-Aviv in a nice
private car, the driver a most sympathetic gentleman who has
lived in the country for a long time and was extremely interesting
to talk to. Thus I arrived safely and continued my journey to

Jerusalem in much the same way, all the way to the home of Uncle Michael*.

Uncle Michael and his family received me most warmly, and we spent the afternoon and evening talking, with new people constantly dropping in, joining in the conversation, as the Fekete house is most hospitable.

The following morning we went with friends to see the Old City. I'll describe it for you in detail another time. In the afternoon we went to one of the city's suburbs with friends who have a car, and spent the afternoon and evening visiting. The next morning they took me through the university, and in the afternoon I went to Givat Saul to see friends who then insisted I stay for supper. After supper we went to town to dance, and that was very pleasant too. Monday morning we went to the Bezalel Museum where, apart from the usual Jewish historical items, there was a most interesting Chinese-Japanese exhibit. In the afternoon we went to Bethlehem to visit a very lovely old church.

Next morning I went to see the Tnuva Dairy Centre. It was so interesting to see everything we do in such a primitive way being done by modern, sophisticated methods. Everything is done by machines, so one rarely sees a human being around. From there I wandered along to Keren Kayemet Hayesod, the beautiful modern building of the Jewish Agency, which I investigated inside and out. Then onto the garden of the King David Hotel— and nearly turned to stone in wonder, as I have never in all my life seen such a beautiful garden. But then the entire hotel isn't bad! In the afternoon I attended the conferring of doctorates in the amphitheatre of the university, and afterwards went walking in the grounds of the Hadassah Hospital, at the same time inspecting the beautiful, modern building.

In the evening I went with Uncle Michael and his family to a lovely concert given by the Palestine Orchestra. Wednesday afternoon we visited Rockefeller Museum, and went once again to the Old City. In the afternoon there were visitors, and then a film. And Thursday morning I came home.

* Dr. Michael Fekete, professor of mathematics at the University of Jerusalem.

Dearest Mother,
Nahalal
June 29, 1940

Everything is fine with me. Sometimes I am even surprised that the day's tiny events continue to interest me. At the moment farm work chases away all one's dark thoughts. I'm working in the hay press, gathering the fodder, and so on. I'm brown as a berry, and the pitchfork feels as comfortable in my hand as the pen once did. The best parts of the work are the overture and finale: driving back and forth to the fields in the tractor. But the work itself, with its monotonous rhythm, is good and not hard. The mule-stubbornness of the horses sometimes disturbs the monotony, plus a thousand small details about which I just don't have the patience to write now. Today's happenings do not encourage one to write about the little things in life. And about the big things it's hardly necessary to write.

I ask only one thing, Mother dear: be very sceptical of the things you hear—or will hear—about Palestine. So far there is the most absolute peace here, yet one already hears entirely different news from the outside about us.

Dearest Mother,
Nahalal
August 15, 1940

Day before yesterday I started working in the bakery. It's very interesting, nice, and quite difficult work. One can learn a great deal, and it's a joy to work there. We knead by hand, bake in electric ovens, and use either 65 or 130 pounds of flour daily (the latter if we bake for two days at a time). Two girls do the work, and we're relatively independent, though of course the supervisor, Lea, is present for the most important tasks, particularly when one is rather new. But even so, we're much freer, and can make our own working arrangements.

Apart from learning Hebrew and baking, we are now engaged in preparing a performance (actually a sort of celebration for the recently graduated class) which is a lot of trouble, and as usual I'm involved in it. George is right when he says anyone who spends time doing this sort of thing is mad. It takes a lot of time, and I'm afraid produces few results.

Saturday afternoons we have basket-ball matches, in the evenings we go for walks, sometimes talk with Hungarian boys

Egy virág is van a levélben, ezt nem csak azért küldöm, hogy lásd, milyen tavasz van nálunk, hanem a helyett a virág helyett, amit apuka sirjára vinnék ki most, ha otthon lennék. 19.-én még többet fogok Rád dondolni anyukám, mint máskor, ha ugyan az lehet.

Ami Gyurka vizsgáit illeti, nem is csodálnám, ha a gyerek a mostani körülmények között nem tanult volna olyan rendesen, de remélem, hogy mégsem olyan veszélyes a helyzet, mint gondolod. Ezerszer csókolom őt is, remélem megkapta a levelemet, amit nemrég irtam.

Számtalanszor csókollak

Part of a letter Hannah Senesh wrote from the Nahalal Agricultural School, adorned with sketches and light-hearted comments about falling into a manure heap and having to be helped out (left), and about her work with the cows (right).

Hannah at work at Nahalal (left) and relaxing in the fields of her kibbutz.

Hannah and George's final meeting: he had just reached Haifa from Europe, she was on the point of departure.

Hannah Senesh lies in state in Haifa. Her body was brought to Israel in 1951, where she was buried with full military honours.

in Nahalal; but I don't spend much time with them because they always speak Hungarian. Now and then, just to please me, they try to speak Hebrew, but for many it's still too difficult. Occasionally we arrange big debates, they on the offensive, and me trying to parry the attacks. They are dissatisfied with a good many things here. They expected and imagined things would be different because they are the victims of the romantic Zionism of the Diaspora, in which much was promised to the immigrants and nothing demanded of them.

Here, on the other hand, life demands a great deal more than it gives, at least according to the vocabulary of Budapest, and he who constantly compares and weighs, who wants only to receive and not to give, finds it very difficult. These boys are now working for the peasants in the village, without pay, but with keep, until they learn farming. This is satisfactory during *hachshara* (training), and I think after six months they are already paid a wage. If they find work, that is. The important thing is for them to remain farm workers in the villages, but of course many decide to go and live in the cities.

Nahalal

Mother Dear,   *October 25, 1940*

I want to write you about my work. After all, I've barely accounted for it. At the moment six coops are entrusted me (there was a time when I took care of eleven), fifty to sixty hens in each. There are larger coops, made of concrete, but mine are very cleverly constructed wooden coops, the invention of our instructor. They are easy to take apart, to move around, to keep clean, and require barely any work.

In the morning I give the chickens fresh water—of course I first wash the pans—feed them (I think it is unnecessary to say with what and when) and leave them in peace to walk about and to scratch in the yards. I always find something to do—there is never a lack of work—until 9.30 when we prepare a mixture for them all (hens, pullets and roosters), and amidst the greatest imaginable excitement I begin distributing it. I can hardly walk among the jumping white feather balls since each would like to be the first at the feeding trough. By the time I finally distribute all the feed it seems as if their necks are nailed to the troughs. They

stand in double rows and won't move until every speck of food
is gone. Meanwhile I fill the water dishes, gather eggs, and get
extremely irritated because despite all my efforts they barely lay,
since at the moment they're moulting.

We keep an exact record of the eggs, a separate one for each
hen-house. We stop working at 11 and at 2.30 start all over again
—feeding, watering, gathering eggs. The little chicks are fed
greens, and since this is their favourite food they nearly eat me
along with it.

At 4.30 our work is done. Apart from the daily routine outlined
above, once a day we prepare the feed, sometimes carry out the
manure, take care of the gardens attached to the poultry yard,
and attend to whatever other work there is about the place. We've
already started the incubation period—for experimental purposes
rather early in the season.

To her cousin, Evi Sas

Nahalal
October 30, 1940

Recently we celebrated the first anniversary of my arrival. Based
on the foundation of affection and enthusiasm I had for the
Land even before coming, during the year I've been here, slowly,
imperceptibly, a true love has evolved, and I now feel completely at home in Eretz Israel. I have grown to love the country,
the people, the way of life, the language, and village living. I see
now that even at home I was not at all a city person, lived in
Budapest as if it were a village, and for that reason even here
I've missed nothing of city life.

I've really made great progress with the language, and have
had and have a good deal of joy from it. I am beginning to know
Hebrew poetry, and have been reading the poems of Rachel,
Tschernichowsky, Simonovits, Bialik, and Shneur. I had no idea
Hebrew literature was so rich. The most valuable, however, is the
Bible, with which I was not at all familiar until now, and must
seriously tell you it is most enjoyable reading. Perhaps it means
more in the original, and it is also important to note that here
the Bible comes to life. The Land, the people, geographical names
—all are in daily use, so one does not have the feeling that it
dates from ancient times, but that it's part of the present.

Of course all this is the shining, attractive part. That there are times when it's not all so nice and easy, you can imagine. But that is all fleeting, and the work helps one overcome the rough spots. You've probably heard from Mother how delighted I am with the work in the agricultural school. But I still maintain, or at least want to maintain, that I would like best of all to combine the work I am now doing with teaching children. My table of values is the following: I am interested in plants, but more so in animals, and most of all in people. I believe my thinking is quite realistic because apart from the various schools, there are many institutions where children are taught farming, and boys and girls study agricultural pursuits.

When I begin writing I find a great deal to write about—but enough for today!

The following letter was written to a young man in the forced labour battalion in Hungary

Nahalal

Dear Friend, *December 6, 1940*

You ask for a detailed account of my experiences. This is very difficult because one can judge things a thousand different ways, and I am wary of making superficial judgments; it is impossible to really know the Land while one is at school.

Had I come here as a tourist, attracted by the natural beauty of this Land, I could tell you about the hills of Galilee, about the Kinneret, about the fabulous, richly planted shores of the Jordan, about the sunset in the Emek, about the ocean, about the view from the amphitheatre at Jerusalem.

Had you been interested in the historical patina of the Land I could write pages about the Old City of Jerusalem, not to mention the fact that the entire land is history. Were I a student of nature, or of geography, I would certainly marvel at the fact that nature crammed so many different kinds of plants and weather into such a tiny area. Had I the eyes of an industrialist I would see how little, so far, the economic possibilities have been exploited, as well as the agricultural and industrial potential of the country—though one doesn't really need the eyes of an industrialist to judge all this.

But I cannot write about everything, and I did not come here for reasons of tourism, nor for purposes of exploration, nor for reasons of economy. So, if you would like to hear of my experiences based upon my year here, I'll try and tell you about them.

I, like every other Zionist, am searching for a home, a country, and I will try to explain what it is in Eretz Israel that offers this —or can offer it. For those Jews born who were from here (the 'Sabras'), this is not a question, just as it is not for any people living in its own land. For the Sabras this land is their natural heritage: it is their country, the language is their language. So for them there is no question of 'searching for a home', and their daily lives express this truth better than any words can.

For those who, from free choice or conviction, or by reason of necessity (one can't draw a sharp line between them), came to the Land, it is more difficult to answer the question. We have two basic characteristics: we want to get something from the Land, which is natural. But we must give too, which is our duty. If we can accept from it what it can give us, and can give it what it needs from us, then Eretz Israel can become our home.

We can receive from Eretz a framework for an independent, healthy way of life; the possibility of a calmer, better balanced view of social problems, and a better chance of solving them. We can acquire a feeling of freedom here, and we have prospects of seeing the first results of a new culture. We can also feel responsible for all that is happening here, not only to us, but through our efforts. I don't think any of this is at all new. This is exactly what we look forward to while in the Diaspora. After a year here I remain convinced that Eretz can give us all this, but only to those of us who give faith, work and love in exchange, to those of us who know this is not a dream state, but that here, too, there are six working days and one Sabbath; to those of us who can forget a good many memories, but can remember a good many vital things. Briefly, to those of us who want to feel at home here. Everyone gets as much from the Land as he gives. We could have learned in those thousand years in Exile what it means to put the weights on one side of the scale and always notice too late that the other side has not moved.

Don't think I am writing empty words. I see endless examples of people adjusting as quickly as possible to the life of the country, making its problems their own, learning the language, satisfying the requirements. All this because they have the will and the love for the Land. And sorry to say, I see exactly as many examples of 'outsiders', those who remain homeless, who merely gaze at the work in progress, strangers in language and in their thinking because they were not strong enough and young enough to be spiritually renewed.

To be absolutely objective, I must state that Eretz is a difficult country—climatically, economically, politically. One must accept and adapt oneself to the hardships one cannot change, and acknowledge all other difficulties in order to overcome them.

I don't want to stretch this letter much longer, but above all else I want to bring one thing to your attention: in my opinion your duty and most concrete assignment before your Aliyah becomes a reality is to learn Hebrew. I don't think I can emphasize this strongly enough. Knowledge of the language makes everything so very much less difficult, makes it so much easier to sink your roots into the Land, that it's worth every possible effort to learn it before coming. And you must not forget that in the very beginning one is so absorbed by new conditions that it is difficult to give enough time to learning the language after you get here.

The second assignment (at least as important as the first, or perhaps more important) is to be absolutely clear in your mind about the Movement, and about yourself; to know exactly what you want in Eretz, and to acquire a foundation upon which you can build here. I feel I lack a good deal of knowledge. A year of Zionist-Jewish training was totally inadequate. I am now trying to make it up, but not everyone has the opportunity to go to school for two years after arrival. And school, after all, is not as confining as a regular job.

One more thing of vital importance is a trade or profession. You can tell everyone who asks that with a knowledge of farming, a trade, a craft, everyone can find a place for himself here. But crash courses in general knowledge are just not enough. What the country desperately needs is people who have been thoroughly trained in the trades and professions.

Nahalal
April 29, 1941

My Darling George,
In all probability I'll soon be unable to write you, and the know-

ledge that perhaps you'll both be worried about me worries me a
great deal. I am prepared for the war to come closer, but if I had
to be born in the age of this war I'm happy to be in a country I can
call my home, and which I feel *is* my home. You know the words,
'in this wide world there is no room for you anywhere but
here. . . .'* This is a matter of fact for us and there is little
to be said about it except that here everyone knows and feels it.

Our daily life continues unchanged. It's amazing how calming
outdoor work can be. It makes one forget everything else. If I
had learned only this during the two years I've been here, that,
in itself, would have been reason enough for coming (though
perhaps it has always been a part of me). But though the time
spent here has seemed outwardly monotonous, actually it produced an active inner life due to the considerable and constantly
changing impressions, and the changes in my outlook on life. It
would be good to discuss all this, George dear.

If difficult times lie ahead and Mother reproaches herself for
letting me come, you, George, will have to explain to her that
for me this was the only solution, the only possibility, and that I
have not regretted my decision for one single moment. It hurts
that during these difficult times you are both so far from me,
and I pray you both will weather these days in good health and
sound spirits.

Don't think my mood is always this serious. Just last night we
had a gay, delightful evening, and we are generally cheerful. One
tries to forget the things that cause one to write such letters.

Darling Mother,   *December, 1943*
I want to write about something important without any preamble.
At the moment there is a real possibility for you to come and
join me. I have taken all the necessary steps, and it's likely the
journey can be arranged within weeks, perhaps even days.

I know, my darling, that this is very sudden, but you must
not hesitate. Every day is precious now and there is a growing
likelihood that the road will be momentarily closed, or that other
hardships will suddenly arise. George will be here in the nearest
possible future too. I don't know whether there is any need for
further arguments.

* Quotation from a Hungarian poem.

Mother dear, be brave and quick. Don't allow material questions to stand in your way. In today's world that must be your last concern, and you must have confidence in us that here you won't have any financial worries.

I'm sure, my darling, there is no need for further discussion. I don't want to ask you to do this for us—do it for yourself. The important thing is for you to come. Bring what you want to if you can do so without difficulty, but don't let such things stop you even for an instant. I just can't write of anything else now.

I kiss and hug you. With inexpressible love.

The following letter was written to Professor Michael Fekete.

Dearest Uncle Michael, *January 15, 1944*

I know you don't approve of what I have done, and it is very difficult for me not to be able to explain in detail the reason I did it. But I hope you will still maintain the old friendship for your 'soldier-foster-daughter'.

My plans concerning my mother have not changed. On the contrary. My new situation will create certain opportunities which I will naturally attempt to take advantage of as quickly as possible. I hope, meanwhile, that George will be here too. However, it's quite possible that I will be leaving the country. Don't think for a moment, Uncle Michael, that I am taking this question lightly. You know how I have been awaiting the arrival of George and Mother. Even so, I would like to believe I have done the wise thing. Perhaps upon another occasion I will be better able to explain the reasons.

I would like you, Uncle Michael, to be familiar with the financial situation so that should I not be here when George or Mother arrives they will be able to have access to my money without having to wait for me. The amount that has been in my name up till now, according to the enclosed receipt, is at the Keren Hakibbutz, from where it can be taken at any moment George or Mother present proper identification.

I have one more thing to tell you in case I am not in the country when my mother arrives, or am unable to get leave immediately: the Mazkirut Hakibbutz gave me their most solemn promise that when my mother arrives they will assist her in every possible way, either to get settled, or to find work, or in whatever way necessary.

And if by any chance I don't write—which I hope will not happen—only they can give exact information concerning anything to do with me.

I would like you to know there is a suitcase at K's which may be of some use to Mother, and another suitcase in the kibbutz (Caesarea) with Daddy's books and a few specific personal belongings.

Please don't be surprised by the 'testamentary' tone of this letter, but since in the foreseeable and immediate future I shall be in Egypt, I don't want George or Mother, when they arrive, to be totally without information about these matters which, when one first reaches Eretz, can be important.

Please forgive me for burdening you with so many things. I have become accustomed during my four years here to turn to you, Uncle Michael, and you have really spoiled me with your kindness and willingness to help.

Warmest regards, and deepest gratitude.

                                                        Cairo
My Darling George,   *January, 1944*
We arrived safely after an approximately ten-hour ride by car. The drive was pleasant since I came with a group of good-natured people. We sang, talked, and even slept (of course this last is not a sign of good spirits, but it made the trip pass more quickly). I drove a part of the way, though of course not all the way because there were three drivers besides myself. I had plenty of time to think, and thus naturally thought about you. Again and again I thanked Providence that we could at least meet, even though only for such a very short time.

You can imagine how interested I am in your first impressions of the Land, and of the kibbutz. You don't have to hurry too much in forming opinions; try to know the country first—which will not be an easy achievement. (I'm not thinking of knowing it geographically, but its way of life and its society.)

At the moment it is difficult for me to write because everything is considered a 'military secret' and I'm afraid the censor will delete something. In short, I am well, there are a lot of

soldiers (boys and girls) here from Eretz among whom I can find
a good many to be friendly with. During the day I'm busy, at
night we go to the cinema, or I stay home and read. Fortunately
I am not in the barracks but in the city, so I can take advantage
of my free time.

George, please write about everything. You know how much
it all interests me. Did you send Mother a telegram? I will try
to write more in the immediate future, and will send a picture
as well.

A million hugs.

Cairo

My Darling George,   *February 27, 1944*
The only fortunate thing is that there are so many soldiers here
from Ma'agan, and that one by one they take trips home so I
can send you a letter, and along with this one a little gift. I
would like to send you every nice thing I see, to make up for
the many years I could send nothing. But I don't know what you
need, and of course I am not exactly wealthy so my gifts are not
very impressive. I am also sending you my fountain pen as I
have been given a new one.

I received your first letter with the greatest possible joy. It
took about a week for it to arrive which is not terribly long. But
send one back with Yona and that way I'll get it even more
quickly.

Not long ago I talked to someone who has just returned from
Turkey and asked for news of Mother's arrival. He said everything possible has been done, but that so far there has been no
sign that Mother has even thought of Aliyah. Of course one does
not know anything to the contrary either. I hope my letter, which
Mother probably received, has convinced her of all the advantages
of coming as quickly as possible. That it's impossible at the
moment to come through Bulgaria is a great obstacle, but there
is some hope that there will be a new way soon.

As for me, there is a good chance we will soon be leaving
here, and in that case I will be writing shorter letters. But in
any event I'll make every attempt to keep you informed of my
well-being. I'm preparing several letters for Mother which you'll
have to send her later. She must not know, under any circumstances, that I've enlisted.

I hope you're guarding those addresses I gave you in connection with matters to do with you and Mother. You can use them safely at any time should you have need of them.

I hug you. With everlasting love.

Cairo
Dear George,   *February, 1944*
Today I went on an excursion again. This time to the royal graves of Luxor. They are interesting, monumental creations. But as a matter of fact I don't have the patience for such things now. As far as I can see, we're moving on next week, and I am tensely awaiting the new assignment.

Should Mother arrive during my absence you will have to explain the situation. I know, darling, this is a difficult task for you, and I don't know if Mother will understand what I've done. I can't find words to express my pain at the thought that once again I am going to cause the darling so much worry, and that we can't be together. All my hopes are that you two will soon be united.

Unending love.

The following letter was written to the secretary of the kibbutz, who arranged her mission.

Cairo
Dear Braginsky,   *March, 1944*
Before my departure, I would like to send you a few words. This is not goodbye; we already said goodbye in Eretz. But I feel the need of saying a few words to you, my close good friend.

I know that uncertain situations can arise. To be exact, difficult situations which can affect our fate. I know in that event you will ask yourself certain questions—and I want to answer them beforehand. Not on behalf of others, only on behalf of myself, even though everyone feels as I do.

I leave happily and of my own free will, with full knowledge of the difficulties ahead. I consider my mission a privilege, and at the same time a duty. Everywhere, and under all conditions, the thought that all of you are behind us will help.

I have something to ask of you which it is perhaps unnecessary to ask, but I must. We have grown used to the fact that a lot of comrades know about our affairs since we all live our successes and difficulties together. But you must be aware that in fulfilling the curiosity of those who are interested in knowing our fate we might well have to pay a very high price. You know how much all information or disclosure of fact can mean. I don't want to multiply these words.

Before my departure I must express my appreciation for your help, for all I've received from you, and for the friendliness you always extended to me.

We will talk about everything else upon my return. Until then, warmest regards from Hagar*.

Dear George, *April 2, 1944***

As I thought I would, I left my former place. I am well and like my work, which is all I can tell you now. I know this laconic communication doesn't say much, but you, darling, can write to me about everything. How are you fitting into the new life? It should be easier for you to judge things now that you have had time to become acquainted with the good and the bad. I think the people are quite decent there, which helps considerably to create a feeling of being at home.

I don't envy you the approaching summer. One doesn't exactly freeze in the Emek Hayarden. But Kinneret is close by and that's not exactly bad! Any news from Mother?

My darling, a thousand hugs.

Dear George, *May 10, 1944*

Though air-mail traffic is not too good I've received three letters from you, and I am so happy I've finally had news of you. It makes me feel well to know everything is in order, and that you're content. I, too, am well, but it hurts that we are so far from each other. I've enjoyed some fine and interesting experiences, but we'll have to wait until I can tell you all about them.

* Hagar was her code name during the mission.
** The following four letters were sent from Yugoslavia. At the time, though, her whereabouts were a military secret, and even her brother did not know where she in fact was.

Darling, I am as concerned about Mother as you, and it's terrible that I can do nothing for her. Without knowing any of the details I can envisage the horrible situation. You can imagine how much I think of both of you, and more than ever before of Mother.

Forgive this brief letter, but by now you must be used to these succinct messages. Some day I will make up for all the omissions.

Thousand kisses.

George Darling,   *May 20, 1944*
Again a short letter so you'll know everything is all right with me, and that's all. I have a suspicion all my friends and acquaintances are annoyed because I don't write. Perhaps they are even angry with me. Please try to explain the situation, and if you can't perhaps they'll forgive me later.

I don't write to Mother at all, so your letters will have to take the place of mine. In fact I even give you permission to forge my signature with the hope that you won't one day take advantage of this to 'extort large sums'.

It is unnecessary to tell you how much I would like to see you, talk to you, or at least be able to write in more detail. I hope you know all this anyway. Your letters arrive with great delay, but sooner or later they do get here and I am always so happy when I have news from you.

A thousand kisses, and warmest regards to our friends.

The following letter was written the day before she crossed the Hungarian border.

Darling George,   *June 6, 1944*
Once again I'm taking advantage of an opportunity to write, even though I have nothing to write about.

The most important thing: most heartfelt wishes for your birthday. You see, I was so hopeful that this time we could celebrate it together, but I was mistaken. However, let us hope we can next time.

I would be very pleased, George dear, if you would write a

few lines to M. at our kibbutz. It has been a long time since I wrote but think a great deal about all of them. I am well. I have reason not to write to them at this particular time.

Any news of Mother? I beg you, please write about everything. Your letters reach me sooner or later, and I am always so happy to read them.

My darling, I wish you the very best of everything. A thousand kisses.

This letter was written to her comrades in Caesarea an hour before she flew from Italy to Yugoslavia

Dearest Comrades: *March 13, 1944*
On sea, land, in the air, in war and in peace, we are all advancing towards the same goal. Each of us will stand at his post. There is no difference between my task and that of another. I will be thinking of all of you a great deal. That's what gives me strength.

Warmest comradely greetings.

This letter was written the day she parachuted into Yugoslavia and was received by her mother very much later; it was forwarded by an unknown route.

Mother Darling,   *March 13, 1944*
In a few days I'll be so close to you—and yet so far. Forgive me, and try to understand. With a million hugs.

THE MISSION

The Last Border

Reuven Dafne

I had the privilege of serving on the same mission with Hannah during World War II, spending months with her slogging through the land of the Yugoslav partisans, and remaining with her until the terrible day she crossed the Hungarian border, and fell into Nazi hands.

I first met Hannah when the emissaries chosen to be paratroopers convened to plan their mission. I was not yet a member of the group, but because I knew Yugoslavia well I was invited to talk to the members, advise them, tell them where I thought it best for them to land in order to avoid capture. I was a soldier at the time, and my duties concerned the partisan front in Yugoslavia, where I knew the lie of the land perfectly.

During my sessions with the group, a girl—the only girl in it —attracted my attention by her alert participation throughout the long discussions of the problems involved in the execution of the daring plan. At first it didn't occur to me that she was also an emissary. I thought she, too, had been called in to give information concerning one of the countries the mission was heading for. When I realized she was actually one of the group I began talking to her, and was enormously impressed by her great fervour.

Several weeks later we met again in Cairo, and Hannah implored me to join the group, strongly emphasizing that the participation of someone who was completely at home in Yugoslavia would make things much easier for the group assigned to that area. That evening I joined them on a trip to the Auxiliary Transport Service Unit. I distinctly remember how much Hannah impressed me that evening. I still didn't know her well, nor did I understand what motivated her. She was happy, cheerful, joked with all of us, including our Arab driver, yet didn't take her mind off the mission, making suggestions and planning details for action. Her changes of mood astounded me. One moment she would be rolling with laughter, the next aflame with the fervour of the mission. I felt that a kind of divine spark must be burning in the depths of her being, motivating her.

It was finally decided to send me on the mission too, and I joined the group. Hannah expressed her happiness about the decision, and I'll never forget the way she helped me overcome my enormous psychological tension before and during practice jumps. She, more than any of the others, showed a lack of fear of jumping. During those dreadful, difficult moments when my heart would pound with trepidation before a jump, I would think of Hannah, her comforting words of encouragement, and feel relaxed, reassured.

The way things turned out, we left for Yugoslavia together. One night all five members of our particular mission were flown to Bari, Italy, accompanied by Enzo (Hayim) Sereni* who was Italian-born and represented the organization behind our mission. We reached the Italian coast after a thirteen-hour flight, and spent the next day in a village near the city.

Sereni breathed more easily in his native land, felt free and stimulated. He chatted with everyone he met, played with the children, patted them, gave them sweets. From time to time he would return to report what he had seen and heard. That evening he and Hannah had a heated argument about our attitude towards the Italians. Hannah could not accept his forgiveness and tolerance after the cruel bombing by the Italians of defenceless Tel-Aviv, which was still fresh in her memory.

The next day we set out for the nearby city to make final preparations for our departure. I'll never forget the discussion on the way between Hannah and Enzo on the subject of whether or not there is a God. Enzo was an extremely astute man of great experience, a student of philosophy, and he fervently postulated God's existence. Opposing him with clear, penetrating logic was 22-year-old Hannah. Observing her forcefulness,

* A few weeks later Sereni parachuted into German-occupied Northern Italy, was captured, and murdered in Dachau on November 18, 1944, about ten days after Hannah's execution.

determination and passion, I began wondering whether I would
be able to work with her. Where, I thought, does this young
girl, still so inexperienced, get so much self-assurance? Where
does fortitude, and the courage of her convictions come from?
I was convinced it would not be easy to work with her, that she
would be difficult to sway from her stand once her mind was
made up about something. Eventually I became positive this was
so, and frequently we exchanged heated words. I told Sereni
how I felt, and he answered, 'She certainly won't be easy to
work with, but believe me—and don't ever forget—she's an
unusual girl.'

That was true. She was fearless, and none of us was as positive as she that our mission would succeed. Never once did she
consider the possibility of failure; never once did she allow us to
become dispirited or discouraged. She would explain with iron
logic how we could extricate ourselves from any predicament,
and her inner conviction would reassure us. Of course she
experienced moments of discouragement, but renewed strength
constantly welled from the depths of her being.

When, on the night of March 13, 1944, we were told to get
ready to leave, she was overjoyed. She sang the whole way
back to the village where we were quartered, and made us sing
along with her. That song, in the course of our mission, became
our group's theme song.

But I was not in the mood to sing. The hand of fate felt
heavy on my shoulder. I had been informed the day before that
my father and older brother, neither of whom I had seen in nine
years, were in a concentration camp near Trento. I had hoped to
have some time to visit them but our orders kept me from doing
so. Again it was Hannah who understood—and how well she
understood—my feelings, and tried to prop up my spirits and
comfort me.

At the airport we met the officer in charge of our operation.
Despite his British reserve he couldn't restrain his surprise at
seeing a woman among us. The British boys working in the
large parachute storeroom where we were taken to put on our
harnesses couldn't take their eyes off Hannah, nor hide their
amazement. The Scottish sergeant who helped me into my
parachute said simply, and with considerable emotion, 'I can't
believe it. I've been working here a long time, and I've fitted

hundreds of parachutists, but never a woman among them.' And he added, 'If I told it to my Jewish friends in England they wouldn't believe me.'

A group of paratroopers, evidently Americans, were equally surprised, but assumed she was a paratrooper's wife who had come to see him off. When they met us again, just before we took off, they were shocked to see her, and one of them, extremely moved, walked over to her and wordlessly shook her hand. Hannah didn't understand the handshake, but her charming and simple reaction threw the astounded American completely off balance.

In the last moment before take-off we wrote final letters to those we held dearest, and Hannah, too, wrote several letters, including the one to Caesarea.

Finally it was take-off time. We parted warmly with dear, good Enzo Sereni, embracing him (I can still hear his parting words:'Remember, only he who *wants* to die, dies!'),and climbed aboard the plane in sequence so as to facilitate jumping. Hannah and I were to jump first—I ahead of her. Y. and A., and the accompanying Britisher, were to follow on the second pass over the target.

We sat inside the crowded plane, parcels all around us, some for the partisans, some for our own needs. We felt weighed down. What with the harness on our backs, the weapons, and our heavy winter clothes, we had almost no freedom of movement at all.

The thunderous roaring of the engines killed conversation. I studied the faces of my comrades, all deep in thought, and felt our hearts must be pounding in fateful unison. My eyes rested on Hannah. Her face was aglow, and she exuded happiness and excitement. She winked at me, waved her hand encouragingly, and a delightful, impish smile enveloped her features. Below her paratrooper's helmet her face seemed smaller, her expression almost elfin, and her luminous smile reminded me of a little girl on her first merry-go-round ride. Her excitement was contagious; we were all infected by it. Gradually tension relaxed, and the air seemed lighter. Fears and black thoughts receded, finally disappeared, and we began feeling peacefully confident.

Time ticked by. Fatigue and tension had taken their toll; blessed sleep embraced us, one by one.

We awoke to find the crew tossing parcels out of the hatch, and the plane circling its target. I'll never forget the moment I made that jump, Hannah standing by, so slim, her face wreathed in a huge smile, her expression calm, happy, thumbs up—her favourite victory sign.

I jumped . . . and she was right behind me. A few moments later we were on the soil of Yugoslavia, land of the partisans.

For months we wandered across that land together, witnessing the cruel yet wonderful, ferocious partisan battle for victory and liberty. We saw incredible heroism, victory, tragic defeat. We saw destruction—entire towns and villages in total ruin, flames consuming the labour of generations. We encountered attacking as well as retreating forces, joined up with caravans of brave, simple people escaping from the relentless enemy, or returning to repossess their hills, fields, villages. Everything we saw touched us deeply: the cruelty, the terror, the humanity and tenderness. Our goal lay further on . . . our mission was to try to save at least some of our brothers.

A great number of people—partisans and civilians—were fascinated by Hannah, the young British officer smart in her army uniform, pistol strapped to her waist. She fascinated them. They had heard about her before our arrival, and she became something of a legend. When she encountered members of the high command she aroused their respect, and although the Yugoslavs had taken women into the army on an equal footing, and partisan women marched into battle alongside the men, there was a special, mysterious quality about Hannah which excited their wonder and respect.

Hannah was to continue on into Hungary, the neighbouring country, but we encountered a wall of reality at the very outset. We had to reach the Hungarian border on foot, and the partisans informed us that there was no possibility of crossing the border because the Germans had recaptured the entire region. 'You'll just have to wait', they said.

A few days later we were sitting at the partisan headquarters when the news reached us that the Germans had occupied Hungary as well. It was catastrophic news for all of us—and it was the first time I saw Hannah cry. I thought she was crying solely because of her mother, whom I knew she adored, and to whom certainly anything could happen now. But amidst her sobs she exclaimed, 'What will happen to all of them . . . to the million Jews in Hungary? They're in German hands now—and we're sitting here . . . just sitting.'

Her conscience knew no rest. It was as if the earth beneath her were on fire. She constantly sought ways to cross the border, but we were entirely dependent upon the partisans, and our objective was foreign to them. Besides, we couldn't discuss our mission, and the so-called 'real purpose' of our assignment—that is, the one they were told about—didn't help pave our way either, since they were intent upon their own purpose.

Meanwhile we roamed that beautiful land of mountains and forests beset by rebellion and battle, awed by the magnificent landscape. We lived through amazing experiences—some disillusioning and depressing, others encouraging, inspiring. Our emotional fare was certainly varied. One evening we were invited to a partisan festival. Men and women in uniform, fully armed, thronged the town, their laughter and loud voices adding to the festive bustle. As we—four members of our group—entered the hall, the crowd cheered us as representatives of the British Empire. We felt sad that we had to keep our true identities secret, that we could not share with them the full purpose of our mission.

By then we were well known among the high command, and the colonel asked Hannah to come forward and speak. This she did, with me acting as interpreter. Her every sentence was greeted by the crowd with appreciative, cheerful enthusiasm, and afterwards they formed circles and danced. The joyful gusto that filled the hall was as compulsively exciting as the beat of the music, and it was wildly exhilarating to watch the men and women dancing their folk dances, rifles strapped to their shoulders, hand grenades swinging from their belts in rhythm with the music. Hannah slipped into the main circle, quickly adapted to the beat, and worked off some of her pent-up emotions and tensions during hours of dancing.

In contrast with those few happy hours of relaxation, there were cruel, fearsome, endless days under fire, facing death.

In our wanderings we joined a partisan unit and found ourselves in a village near the border, within enemy territory. There was a surprise attack, and a hail of bullets burst upon the village. The partisans had to retreat, seeking shelter wherever possible, and the majority escaped. The villagers ran about in total confusion, sliding down the hillside or sheltering under rocks. We were completely alone, cut off, surrounded by the enemy. We slid down a rope, continued running in an open valley, entirely exposed to the firing from the encircling hills. We tried desperately to catch up with the retreating partisans. All around we heard cries of fear from clusters of bewildered civilians who stumbled along, clutching pathetic belongings, their children, driving their thinning herds of cattle. The cries of the wounded and the groans of the dying filled the stillness; people dropped like wounded birds. All about us there was horrible panic.

In the mad race to save my own life I forgot everything. Suddenly I stopped, horrified at the thought that I had been cut off from Hannah. I turned, saw her running behind me, breathing wildly, gasping for breath. Her instinct for self-preservation, goaded by the firing and sounds of battle, spurred her on. With our last ounce of strength we reached the forest and, we hoped, protection from enemy fire. We fell to the ground, exhausted but safe.

For a short while we lay silently in the bushes, clutching our rifles, looking about us, listening to the incessant tattoo of bullets, the moaning of the wounded. Suddenly a group of German soldiers came into view, and my finger tightened on the trigger. But Hannah, calm, in control of her senses, stopped me. Firmly, quietly, she said, 'Stop it! Don't shoot!' Her eyes reminded me of that which I had forgotten in all the chaos: our goal was to rescue our brothers; shooting at the enemy could only endanger our mission.

I vividly recall another memorable occasion. Four of us were lying alone, cut off in a thick forest, hidden behind tree trunks, our guns aimed. Our nerves were at breaking point, alert to the possibility of meeting enemy units hunting down partisans. There were moments when we thought we would be unable to hold out another instant, but we plodded on, praying for a miracle. At the edge of the forest the Germans, shooting wildly in all directions, were so close they could have stepped on us—but miraculously they missed us. I'll never forget Hannah's amazing composure. I would glance at her from time to time, lying there, pistol cocked, a heavenly radiance on her face. I was literally overwhelmed by wonder for this unique girl. Her remarkable strength of character, her courage, her integrity and unwavering dedication to our mission aroused my utmost admiration and respect.

One evening we found ourselves in a village under the command of a woman partisan. When she stepped into the room where we were seated I was astounded. I knew her! We had been childhood friends, had lived in the same district, had played together in the streets of the capital. The years of terror had left their mark on her face, and despite her youth her hair was streaked with grey. In the course of conversation it turned out that all of us in the room were Jews. We became very excited by this discovery, and felt united by an almost sacred bond. She revealed to us, who had been so protected in Palestine from reality, the horrible suffering of the Jews in the Diaspora, and we, whom she had thought to be British officers involved only in military affairs, told her about Eretz, and the Homeland we were building.

Hannah was deeply impressed by this encounter. A couple of days later she handed me the four-line poem, *Blessed is the Match*, which revealed the passion within her.

At long last the day Hannah had been hoping for came—the day for her to cross into Hungary. It was June 9, 1944. At the end of a four-hour trek we reached a village near the border, and found members of our unit sitting in the room of a little house with two Jews from the Hungarian underground, and an escaped French prisoner of war. We were making our final preparations, and I, to be quite truthful, felt uncomfortable. I was not satisfied with the arrangements we were making for Hannah's departure. But by then it was quite impossible to restrain her. She absolutely refused to wait another day, another hour, and all my efforts to persuade her to wait a trifle longer were in vain. She had firmly decided to cross over without further delay—if necessary even without an escort. That was that. The matter was settled.

Hannah, in high spirits, joked with everyone, teasing the

British officer in our unit. But beneath the banter there was a
sharp edge to her jesting, a steady note of earnestness.

We had an early supper, and the minute we finished Hannah
asked me to come outside with her. In the yard we discussed
necessary details of her assignment, and arranged about future
contact. We walked in the orchard near the house, and painstak-
ingly reviewed all the possible means of communication, contact,
codes, and so on. We finally agreed on a key to our secret code:
United Kibbutz Movement Sdot Yam Caesarea. She begged me
to give her a cyanide pellet, but I refused. I knew it was my duty
to increase her self-confidence, to encourage her, to remove all
doubts of her success.

She asked me not to accompany her to the border since she
did not think it wise for us to enter a danger zone together,
unless absolutely necessary. One of us, she said, ought always
to be relatively safe so our mission could continue if one or the
other were captured.

At seven o'clock the head of the partisan group assigned to
accompany Hannah and her comrades to the border came into
the room and said they would be leaving in fifteen minutes.
Hannah was extraordinarily cheerful during those last minutes,
radiant, the epitome of a free soul. She jested, recalled some
funny incidents that happened to us in Yugoslavia, and above
all, seemed remarkably calm and relaxed—yet, at the same time,
alert, self-assured. She was bubbling with joy, forthright, impish,
and amazingly carefree. She seemed to be like someone about to
embark upon an experience she had been looking forward to
for years.

She created a dream for the future, for the day we would all
return and meet in Eretz Israel. 'We'll rent a big bus,' she said,
'and drive up and down the country. First we'll visit all the
settlements that sent members on this mission. Then we'll arrange
celebrations in those settlements, and we'll tell them everything
that happened to us, and spin tall tales. In addition, we'll visit
the entire country, from Dan to Be'er Sheva. We'll spend a
month travelling.'

We left the house together, but walked in the opposite direction from the border, just in case one of the villagers was watching. We shook hands, and thanked each other for shared
experiences. She said, 'Till we meet again—soon, I hope, in

enemy territory.' I watched her march confidently towards her unknown fate, and at the bend in the road she turned and waved farewell.

I didn't know I would never see her again.

How She Fell

Yoel Palgi

Leaden clouds covered the sky as our car skidded along the rain-drenched road, slicing through the desert. Only the skill of our driver kept it from rolling into the ditch. My bones ached from sitting so long, and the desolate view tired my eyes, dulled my brain. The cold increased, penetrating my very soul. An unpleasant shudder of foreboding passed through me. I felt utterly depressed, and struggled to stave off the nagging thought that things were beginning badly. The superstitious belief that ill omens at the outset of an assignment indicate an unsatisfactory outcome—a belief acquired during dangerous engagements at the front—overwhelmed me from time to time, no matter how hard I fought it.

We sped on towards Tel-Aviv. The pouring rain cloaked everything in sadness, and as we neared the city my depression increased. Fragments of thought flashed through my mind: I'm going to paratrooper's training school . . . tomorrow or the day after I'll jump from a plane for the first time . . . the parachute won't open . . . it won't open . . . it won't open . . . I'll drop down . . . down . . . down. And this time I won't wake up, as I did from those childhood nightmares in which I jumped—always waking up in the nick of time, before my feet touched the ground, my heart pounding, but alive, alive!

I knew I could never tell anyone about my fear, and that there was no way out. I was no longer my own master. I had been entrusted with a mission. If I failed, we would all be put to shame and would all suffer. And who knew where that might lead? I feverishly repeated to myself, 'It won't open . . . it won't . . . I must jump! I'll jump and be smashed. Then they'll get someone else for the job, and it won't be my fault. . . .'

The car wove its way carefully through the city streets, its wheels splattering mud on passing pedestrians. The atmosphere was oppressively sombre. The flamboyant Hebrew city did not receive us with a smile, and I greeted her disconsolately, as a stranger, without the joy I had always felt when returning from afar.

I was allowed half-hour's respite before resuming the journey northwards to the school, and decided to visit Zvi and let him know I was back. Tired, dejected, I groped my way up the dark stairway. He wasn't there; the workroom looked forlorn. But a strange girl was sitting in the darkening room. I asked for Zvi and she said, 'He'll be right back.'

I lit a cigarette, watching her out of the corner of my eye. There was something enchanting, captivating in the way she sat, her long, pretty legs crossed, her hands resting gracefully on the little table. She was a soldier in the British Air Force, and the blue-grey of her uniform matched her blue eyes. Her light brown hair flowed in soft curls around her refined, elongated face; there was something delightfully harmonious about her. I liked her at once, without being able to determine exactly what it was about her that had charmed me, or why she was so completely pleasing to the eye.

The door opened and Zvi entered. He greeted me, surprised, and bombarded me with questions. When did I get in? How long was I staying? Where was I off to?

She looked at me curiously, suddenly stood up, her face aglow with a wonderful smile. 'Are you Yoel?' she asked.

I looked at her again, finding her even more attractive than at first glance, and was struck by the thought, 'That's her! Of course!' And with the same note of surprise in my voice said, 'And you're Hannah!'

Neither of us bothered with answers, but Zvi asked in amazement, 'What, you haven't met?'

The whole of that day's oppressiveness lifted at once. I answered with a broad smile, 'No!' and my 'no' blended with hers. Our handshake became a prolonged handclasp as our eyes met and held. This wonderful girl who had captivated my heart at first sight mystified me. A torrent of questions came to mind, and I felt sure there was much that she too wanted to say. Yet I knew then, as I was sure she knew, that our bond was not one of

love, but rather the deep covenant of those engaged in war against
a common enemy, the unvoiced pact of fellow soldiers.

'I have so much to ask you. Are you spending the night in Tel-
Aviv?' she asked.

It was only then that I remembered I had to hurry. The car
was waiting for me. I had to move on, to paratrooper's school.
'No,' I answered hesitantly. 'I have to leave at once. I'm going
to learn how to jump.'

Apparently she sensed my sudden fear, perhaps even noted a
tremor in my voice. 'I've just finished the course,' she said. 'It's
nothing. You go up in a plane, you jump, and you're right back
on the ground. I'll never forget how Nahalal looked from the air.
It was a great experience. You'll love it.'

She spoke as naturally and plainly as if she were describing
what she had had for breakfast that morning. I was ashamed,
feeling that if this girl could jump, then I could too. All the same,
I suspected she was putting on a show for my sake, and was sure
that she had also been afraid, and if she could be afraid, so
could I!

I went on my way in high spirits, wrapped myself in blankets,
feeling fine. The rain pattered on the car roof, and washed its
windows. It was good to know that she would accompany me on
the long, hard road ahead.

It was the eve of departure. We were all tense at the thought
of leaving Eretz. None dared admit to the other how difficult it
was to leave; everyone wondered whether he would ever see the
Land again. We were all parting from our dear ones, our settlements, our land. It was a silent parting, one that neither relieved
tensions nor lightened spirits. We had to avoid arousing curiosity
and questions. The mission itself was a silent one; no one must
know we were going armed with a sling to do battle with the
powerful enemy. Behind us lay days and nights of tense preparation, including endless discussions with ghetto fighters. We had
studied conditions, countries, roads, carefully preparing for all
eventualities.

Whenever we went out together, Hannah always proved a
cheerful and charming companion. At such times we would try
to divert our minds from the mission that lay ahead, but of

course it was difficult. Hannah's face would occasionally turn sad. Once she told me that her mother was still living in Budapest, alone, and that she was supposed to come to Eretz. She was frightened her mother would arrive when we were who knows where and that there would be no one to meet her. She also told me about her brother who was due to arrive any day, and probably would—straight after our departure. She said she had written him a letter in which she tried to tell him about the Land and guide his first steps. In fact, the very day the car came to take us on the first leg of our mission the news reached her that the ship *Nyasa* was due in port, with her brother on it. Hannah became extremely emotional, and I hardly recognized in her the strong self-assured young woman I had come to know so well. Tears flowed from her eyes. With difficulty I managed to obtain tickets for Haifa, and accompanied her there to see if her brother had arrived. He had, and after an enormous amount of manoeuvring we were able to spirit him out of Atlit camp immediately. The custom then was to detain immigrants for as long as two weeks.

We managed to postpone our departure for twenty-four hours to enable Hannah to spend a little time with her brother. Whoever reads her diary and senses the uniquely deep brother-sister relationship will be able to appreciate the remarkable will-power of this girl in foregoing any additional delay. Even when she requested permission for the one-day leave it was with profuse apologies, although she had not seen her brother in years, and no one could tell when—if ever—she would see him again.

The car sped southwards. Gradually the sparkling-white houses in the Jewish settlements gave way to drab Arab villages. We all felt the seriousness of the moment, but probably no one more so than Hannah, who was leaving such a complex personal issue behind. But she said nothing as we sang, joked and planned all kinds of projects for after our return. We decided that at the end of the war we would return in a big bomber, and each of us would parachute into his own settlement. There were five of us in the car, plus two British drivers, to whom we paid scant attention. We were soldiers, arrogant and ill mannered, and we failed to take the Britishers' feelings into account. But Hannah

did not, and was careful to translate all our jokes for their benefit
so they could laugh with us, understand our silly plans, feel
involved, one of us.

After we crossed the southern border she declared suddenly
that she wanted to learn to drive! We protested vigorously, saying
she would endanger our lives. But she insisted that it was as good
a time as any to learn. She slid behind the wheel, listened as one
of the drivers explained what was what, and began driving. We
were amazed at her dexterity and ability to grasp everything so
quickly. After a few hundred yards of careful, if at first unsteady
driving, she accelerated, evidently feeling entirely secure and at
ease. We begged her to drive more slowly, to let the driver take
over. But she ignored us and sped on furiously through the desert.
Whenever another car approached we all trembled, and more than
once I closed my eyes expecting the worst. But she was quite
confident and having a wonderful time with her new toy. We soon
realized she knew exactly what she was doing, that she had a
firm hand on the wheel—and we all relaxed.

She drove for hours on end, without tiring, and only handed
the wheel back to the driver when we reached the Suez Canal.

A difficult period lay ahead. Our departure was delayed from
day to day, from week to week. There were rumours that Rumania
and Hungary were on the point of surrender and it was of the
utmost importance that we reached there before this happened,
or at least immediately after, so that we could save as many of
our people as possible. But this was of no concern to the Allies.
What was a matter of conscience to us was, to them, a routine
matter. We knew our lives and the lives of our people hung in
the balance, and that the British were certainly attempting to
protect us as individuals. But in so doing they were preventing
us from helping our people, and naturally there were endless
arguments, even serious clashes between our British sponsors
and ourselves.

Hannah was the chief rebel. And she was not always right. On
the contrary. More often than not, she was wrong. At the time
I could not even distinguish between her tense impatience and
dedication to our mission—which to her was the only thing that
mattered. She was totally unconcerned about her own safety.

Sometimes I wondered how I would ever be able to work with her once we were in enemy territory. She didn't appear to be sufficiently cooperative, she seemed concerned only with her own goals; she was totally lacking in caution, and refused to accept discipline. She insisted that we divide up the fields of activity in advance, so we would not have to waste time on such matters once we were dropped. She wanted to be sure she got her share of the action, that she would not be left out. Apart from Hannah, we were all products of youth movements, and accustomed to certain methods and routines of working. Being unfamiliar with these, Hannah was afraid she would be brushed aside.

As things turned out, she was fated to precede me. Our parting was rather emotional and eased the tension that had gradually been built up between us. 'See you in Budapest', I said when we parted, and to the surprise of those of my comrades who knew how strained our relationship had become, remarked later, 'She's really a good kid . . . I'll miss her.'

Several months later Hannah and I met again somewhere in the forests of Yugoslavia. We had changed, and so had our plans. Hungary had meanwhile been occupied by the Germans, and we knew only too well that sentence had been passed on nearly a million Jews—the last great Jewish community in Europe. We knew Jews beyond the border were waiting for deliverance, and that it was up to us to help them. But there was little we could do. We had been through a great deal since parting, and had discovered a strength in ourselves we had never dreamt of. We had become accustomed to marching for forty-eight consecutive hours, without rest, without food, in rain, through swamps, under enemy fire; we had witnessed acts of personal and national heroism we were never to forget. In the partisans' eyes we represented a great Empire, and we learned to protect its honour.

Hannah was unmistakably our leader. She was the only woman who had ever parachuted into Yugoslavia from a friendly country, and she knew how to talk to a general as well as to a private. Her reputation preceded her, and everyone was familiar with her progressive views. She did more for British propaganda in Yugoslavia than all of Churchill's announcements, and even more than the inferior weapons the Allies sent to aid the partisans. Thanks to Hannah we learned to control our desire for revenge when confronting the enemy. It certainly was not easy for us to refrain from using our arms, to control ourselves to the point of not shooting when we came face to face with the Nazis. But she always said, 'That's not what we came for. We must save ourselves for our mission, not place our lives in jeopardy.' And we always bowed to her wisdom.

When I finally arrived in Yugoslavia I did not find the old Hannah, the Hannah I had come to know so well. Her eyes no longer sparkled. She was cold, sharp, her reasoning now razor-edged; she no longer trusted strangers. She was the first to suspect the partisans of unwillingness to help and of misleading us. We argued with her about this, but she was adamant, and finally succeeded in making us suspicious as well. Only weeks later it became clear how right she had been, and that we were, in truth, being completely misled by the partisans. They regarded us as allies, but they didn't trust anyone—including their allies. And if Hannah was difficult to get along with before, she was ten times more so now. At first she had only sensed the forces that lay dormant within her; but now she was fully conscious of them and had unlimited faith in herself.

Just what brought about this change in Hannah is difficult to say—perhaps the German occupation of Hungary, or being so often under enemy fire, but whatever the reason her missionary feeling intensified. She was impatient, unwilling to listen to suggestions that she should delay crossing the border—no matter how sound and reasonable the advice. She had her own theory: 'We are the only ones who can possibly help, we don't have the right to think of our own safety; we don't have the right to hesitate. Even if the chances of our success are minuscule, we must go. If we don't go for fear of our lives, a million Jews will surely be massacred. If we succeed, our work can open great and important avenues of activity. Thanks to our efforts, multitudes will be saved.'

I felt that she was wrong, and that if we crossed into enemy territory and failed, we would end the entire action—as had happened in other lands. But it was impossible to oppose her. She turned against anyone who disagreed with her point of view. I told her I thought she was wrong, but that I was not going to fight over it, even though her decision made my departure mandatory.

We waited for the planes that were supposed to bring us the

supplies we needed to replace those we had lost during our many
wanderings and encounters with the enemy. We went to the field
where the containers were to be dropped, and as we marched I
looked at this amazing girl who could be so feminine, but who
was now marching with us in her grey uniform, an automatic
strapped to her waist, always at the ready. We marched out of
step, battling mud, discussing this and that. She told us about
the secrets of the poultry trade, and we debated political issues
in Eretz. From time to time we would pass a partisan sentry, and
she would respond to his salute with a curt yet charming motion,
always turning her head to look straight into his eyes.

Everything was ready for the plane's arrival. It was a cold,
clear night, and the partisans had made a bonfire and were sitting
round it. They began singing, and the wild song penetrated the
silence, the voices bewailing the anguish of an oppressed people.
That night we liked the partisans very much. They were simple
people, most of them illiterate, but they had learned the truest,
most profound lesson a nation can learn: the need to live as
free men, and to be willing to sacrifice their lives for liberty.

A pretty blonde girl of about seventeen sat facing us, her
features were refined, her bearing elegant. We knew her well. She
was an upper-class city girl to whom we had often spoken—her
English was fluent. She suddenly fell asleep, her head resting on
the shoulder of a partisan. He, a simple man of the forest, did not
move for hours so as not to waken her.

We sat with them, warmed ourselves at their fire, tried to
sing along with them. Suddenly Hannah got up and asked
me to walk with her. As we walked side by side in the still,
dark night she poured out her heart, saying many of the things
she had said before, only that night she spoke differently. It was
not the cold, logical woman talking, the stubborn young officer
who was unwilling to accept another point of view, but a sensitive
young woman, perceptive and tender. She said she was overwhelmed by inner turmoil and struggle, that although she was
aware she was not always sensible, ours was not a sensible, reasonable time, that she felt incapable of waiting on the sidelines
while thousands were being slaughtered. 'It's better to die and free
our conscience,' she said, 'than to return with the knowledge we
didn't even try. Each of us is free to act as he thinks best, and I
quite understand the way the rest of you feel about discipline.

But for me this is not a question that can be decided by authority.'

I took her hand and said, 'Let's go!' She was right, even though her opinion ran counter to logic. She was happy I understood her, and began describing to me the things she had imagined, the things she hoped would happen. She drew imaginary portraits of Jewish partisans sitting around campfires, singing songs of Eretz, the forests of Europe echoing the sad songs of Jewish freedom fighters.

I set out the next morning. We decided to go separately so as to open up different routes of escape and rescue. I sensed the fatefulness of the parting—but we had made up our minds, come what may, whether or not the road seemed right. We sensed, though we could not be certain, that beyond the border the fate of the Jews was probably sealed. That was May 13, 1944, the very day—as I learned later—that the expulsion of the Jews from most of Hungary's cities had begun. But of course we were unaware of the situation, and agreed to meet after the Sabbath service at the Great Synagogue in Budapest. And if Jewish services were no longer being held there, we would meet on the same day, at the same time, at the Cathedral.

That morning we parted as dear, close friends, a closeness produced by kinship in mission, in interests and hopes shared.

I waited in vain for her at the Synagogue, I looked for her at the Cathedral. And when I was thrown into jail, battered and broken in body and spirit, I kept thinking, it's a good thing she doesn't have to suffer all this. Who knows whether she could have stood it . . . it's a good thing she isn't here. She probably turned back for some reason . . . crossed later . . . when she comes she'll succeed where I failed . . . and the world won't be able to say there is no way of helping, no way of saving Jews. She'll succeed, she *must* succeed. . . .

One of the guards looked into my cell and saw me lying there blood-soaked, in tears. He took pity on me and came in to console me. He told me it would soon be over, that they wouldn't torture me indefinitely, that in a few days I would be transferred to another prison, that no one would bother me anymore.

'No', I replied, 'They'll just hang me!'

'What are you talking about?' he said. 'We don't hang people so easily, so don't worry. There was a girl here from Palestine, a few days ago, and she was only sentenced to five years.'

The guard had meant to console me, but I was shocked. I guessed that the five-year sentence was something he had just invented, but not the girl from Palestine; I knew it must be Hannah.

So all was lost. Hannah and I were both under arrest. Who knew when Peretz's* turn would come? Even if he managed to avoid them, he would still be forced to flee. He would be unable to do anything because the police would be on to him.

I felt completely helpless. The moment I was arrested I knew my life wasn't worth a jot. But we were responsible for far more than our own lives. The rescue project depended, to a large degree, upon us, upon our failure or success. And we had failed. I, the careful one, the one who had wanted to preserve my life, not only because I had no wish to die, but also because it was no longer mine alone but dedicated to a cause—and Hannah, who had been so ready, so willing to sacrifice herself, who had looked forward consciously to that moment when she would proudly face the enemy, the murderers—she, too, had been captured.

I was in my cell in the Gestapo prison. Suddenly I heard a loud voice calling 'Hannah Senesh!' then Hannah's voice immediately replying 'Yes.'

She was in the same prison! I frantically pounded on my cell door with my fist, kicked at it, stormed and raged. The door opened and the warder asked gruffly what I wanted. I pushed him aside and rushed into the corridor. No one was there. Had Hannah been there a moment before or was I dreaming? The question troubled me all that afternoon and night.

The next day I was again taken for questioning, and in the van that took us to headquarters met other prisoners. I asked if they knew anything of Hannah, or had heard of her. 'What a question!' one of them said. 'She was with us yesterday. They took her up for questioning. A remarkable girl. She is always talking about the Jewish problem, and tells everyone about Eretz

---

* Peretz Goldstein of Kibbutz Ma'agan. He volunteered for the mission to Hungary and was one of the thirty-two parachutists. He was caught by the Gestapo, and sent to Oranienburg, in Germany, where he died.

Israel. She really gave us hope'. The prisoners told me she was in
solitary confinement three floors above my cell. I tried in vain
to attract her attention all the next day. The following morning,
sitting in the sunlight, it occurred to me that I might be able to
flash signals with my mirror onto the ceiling of her cell. That
afternoon, when the sun was on her side, she flashed an answering
signal. Thus we established contact.

In the course of the next six weeks we held many short 'conversations' in this way, and so each of us always knew what was
happening to the other. However, this means of communication
was much too difficult to use for 'friendly chats', and we were
never taken in the van together. But I discovered from other
prisoners that she was in good spirits, that she accepted her fate
valiantly, and was utilizing every minute to encourage others.

She found an ingenious way of communicating with prisoners
whose cell windows faced hers by cutting out large letters and
placing them, one after the other, in her window to form words.
In this way she introduced herself to the prisoners, learned their
troubles, gave them information about happenings outside the
prison walls, and also told them about Palestine and kibbutz life.
Her window became an information and education centre, and
from morning till evening prisoners looked towards it for news.
Opposite her were some members of the Zionist Movement who
had been arrested for underground activities and were awaiting
sentence. She encouraged them, gave them new heart.

Her behaviour before members of the Gestapo and SS was
quite remarkable. She always stood up to them, warning them
plainly of the bitter fate they would suffer after their defeat.
Curiously, these wild animals, in whom every spark of humanity
had been extinguished, felt awed in the presence of this refined,
fearless young girl. They knew she was Jewish, but they knew
also that she was a British paratrooper who had come to fight
them. Having been taught for years that Jews never fight back,
that they will accept the vilest treatment, they were taken aback
by her courage. The warden of the prison, a notorious sadist who
was credited with the death of many he had tortured with his own
hands, considered it a privilege to visit her cell daily to argue
with her fearless criticism of German rule, and her prophecies of
an allied victory.

Those were days of change in internal Hungarian politics. The government the Germans had set up after occupying the country was thrown out of office, and replaced by a new government charged with preparing Hungary for surrender. The Nazis tried to continue the deportation of the remaining Jews, but the new Hungarian government prevented this—not because they had any love or pity for the Jews, but because they hoped to use those remaining as evidence of their good intentions. In vain the Gestapo attempted to transport some of the prisoners to Auschwitz—as was customary after questioning was completed—but Hungarian soldiers and police surrounded the prisons and prevented the extradition of the inmates.

The time had come for decisive action. With the agreement of the political prisoners with whom I shared a cell, I sent a secret letter to the Hungarian Regent, Admiral Horthy, describing our situation. I stressed that if anything happened to us, even at the hands of the Germans, he would be held responsible. The reply was not long in coming, though in an unexpected manner: on September 11 a warder ordered me to pack my belongings. He informed me I was being handed over to the Hungarians. My heart pounded. Evidently liberation was near. I knew what it meant: Hungary would surrender to the Allies, and we would be taken to a safe place out of reach of the Germans.

I was standing to attention in the corridor, my face to the wall (the customary procedure in Nazi prisons),when, out of the corner of my eye, I suddenly saw Hannah coming down the stairs. I turned my head. She looked so young and lovely, though very pale, smiled brightly, and nodded in greeting. She skipped lightly down the steps, wearing a raincoat and carrying a black case—as if she had just returned from a journey and was stepping from the train—then paused beside me, as I reached out my hand. She just managed to grasp it when the Gestapo officer roared at us, drew his pistol, and cocked it to prove it really was loaded.

We were herded into a closed van generally used for transporting dangerous criminals. It was divided into compartments, and I was put into one directly next to Hannah's. We communicated by tapping quietly on the partition. I was happy we were together, that she was alive and evidently in good health, and I was confident we would soon be freed. It was good also to see Peretz's face peering from a compartment opposite and signalling, 'Where to now?'

We were led, two by two, through the latticed entrance of the Hungarian army prison. This was the building in which I had been tortured so much during my previous interrogations. But this time, though still a prisoner, I felt superior, as if I were entering as a guest of honour, positive I would soon be able to avenge myself upon my torturers. All the prison officers stood on the stairway, shook hands with us, and received us as friends. Everyone wanted to show his goodwill, hopeful it would stand him in good stead after the surrender.*

We took advantage of the relaxed conditions, saying we wanted very much to talk since we had not met in a very long while. Our request was granted. Hannah and I sat down in the corridor and held a lengthy conversation, a continuation of the one we had had in the middle of that field in Yugoslavia near the campfire. It was to be our last.

We told each other what had happened since that night. Happiness and deep sorrow were mingled in our talk. We were all too aware of the mistakes we had made; we had learned from experience. She told me the shocking story of her capture, and only then did I come to know why she had been unable to keep our rendezvous at either the Synagogue or the Cathedral.

After we had parted, the little Palestinian group with Hannah became aware that the partisans had no intention of helping them cross into Hungary. We knew that all the border runners were in everyone's employ, including the Germans', and could no longer be trusted. Then, one day, Hannah came across a group of refugees who had escaped from Hungary. Among them were three young men who were willing to join the rescue mission—a non-Jewish Frenchman and two Jews who had been planning to reach Palestine. All three agreed to go back into Hungary with Hannah.

The four set out, and although the area was unknown to them they nevertheless decided to cross into thickly patrolled enemy

---

* Hungary did not surrender to the Allies, and there was again a Fascist take-over. The Nazis returned to power—including Adolf Eichmann, who had fled. On October 17, 1944, directly after the new (Szálasy) government took power, Eichmann resumed the deportation and on the 20th the 'Big march' began, when the first of 50,000 Jews were herded, on foot, from Budapest, allegedly to work in Germany, but actually to their death. Thousands died from hunger and exhaustion during the march, or were shot to death for 'not marching fast enough'.

territory, a map and a compass as their only guide. I still don't understand how, in the circumstances, they managed to reach their goal—a Hungarian village—without encountering German patrols. But somehow they did. It was decided that Hannah and the Frenchman would hide among some bushes on the outskirts, while the other two went into the village to contact friends who were to provide them with permits to travel to the capital. However, on the way the two men were stopped by Hungarian police. What took place in the mind of one of the boys we'll never know. What we do know is that instead of trying to bluff his way through, or even to use his guns against the few policemen, he shot himself instead. Farmers then came forward and told the police that the men had been accompanied by another two partisans whom they had seen hiding in the bushes. Hannah and her companion suddenly found themselves surrounded by soldiers, with no chance of escaping. That was how she was caught, only a little while after she finally reached Hungary.

She suffered dreadful tortures, and she didn't want to talk about them. The tooth missing from her mouth testified to this. I heard from others how they had tied her; how they had whipped her palms and the soles of her feet; bound her and forced her to sit motionless for hours on end; beaten her all over the body until she was black and blue. They asked her one thing, only one thing: what is your radio code? Yes, the code was important to them, for they had found the transmitter she hid just before she was caught—and now they wanted to use it to send out false information, to mislead bomber squadrons so that they could be greeted by fighters and anti-aircraft guns. Hannah was perfectly aware of the value of her code, and she didn't reveal it. When she was being transferred by train to Budapest she tried to kill herself by jumping from the window, because she didn't know how long she could hold out. But she was caught in the act and beaten even more. 'You don't have the right to destroy yourself', her guard told her. 'You are state property; we'll do away with you when we no longer need you, not before.'

But her most awful test was yet to come. They brought her to the jail—to Budapest. But it was not the meeting with her home-town that Hannah had dreamed of. Upon arrival they threw her into a room and there, to her horror, she found her beloved mother. She hugged her and could find only the words: 'Forgive me, Mother, I had to do what I did.'

The Germans knew their business. They threatened that if she did not reveal her secret, they would torture her mother before her eyes and kill her. Still Hannah would not yield. Only someone who knows how deeply she loved her mother can fathom what went on in her heart. I was completely shattered on hearing her story and stared at her in astonishment. How could she have remained so resolute and calm? Where did this girl, who loved her mother so much, find the courage to sacrifice her, too, if necessary, rather than reveal the secret that was not hers, that affected the lives of so many? As it was, Hannah's fortitude saved her mother. Had she broken down and surrendered her secret, they would doubtless have executed her immediately and sent her mother off to the gas chambers of Auschwitz.

But the Germans didn't give up. They kept Hannah and her mother in the same prison, believing that prison, hunger and the fear of death would humble her. Friends in the prison—there were some prisoners who had known the family before the war, or had heard of them—did what they could to make things easier for them, and even managed to have mother and daughter transferred from their separate, distant cells to nearer ones, thus making it possible for them to meet. Once or twice a week prisoners were allowed to stroll in pairs in the tiny prison yard, the eyes of the SS guards fixed firmly upon them. Every snatch of conversation was firmly punished.

During the afternoon, I would often hear the footsteps of the women prisoners and climb up to my window to observe Hannah secretly. I saw her walking with another woman, their fingers intertwined. I assumed that was her mother. Interminable hours of waiting, long days and nights, preceded their meetings. When they did meet, Mrs. Senesh could not contain one, burning question, which she asked again and again: 'Why?' And her daughter would squeeze her fingers and say, 'Eventually I'll explain it, and you'll understand.' She sensed that her mother feared she was a spy, and tried to reassure her. 'You'll be proud when you know what I've done.'

To mark her parents' 25th wedding anniversary, Hannah sent her mother some gifts—a beautiful vase she had fashioned from an empty can and silver foil, some colourful paper flowers, a poem. She improvised dolls and other toys from paper and rags, and those prisoners 'in the know' provided her with the raw material. Whenever possible she would pass a note to her mother. But these, together with the poem, were destroyed by her mother for fear of searches and recrimination.

All this I learned as I sat with Hannah in the corridor of the Hungarian military prison. The next day we were taken to different prisons which were to be our permanent places of detention. Hannah was dropped off first, at Conti Street. She stood at the gate, looking so young, so brave. As the van moved off, she put down her bag and gave us an encouraging thumbs up sign, her lovely face wreathed in a smile.

It was the last time I saw her.

I don't know what happened to her between September 11, the day we parted, and October 28, the day of her trial. I later placed inquiries in the newspapers, hoping to find people who had been in prison with her during that period—but in vain. Only one man responded: he had been a court house official and had seen her just once; but she made such a deep impression on him that he himself wanted to discover whether anything was known of her last days. I found out only that after Mrs. Senesh was released, she had gone to see Hannah who had requested one thing—a Hebrew Bible. Her mother searched all over Budapest for one, without success.

On October 28, 1944, Hannah was brought before a military 'court' in Budapest. We know very little about her trial. There are people who were present at the time, but they were taken from the room at the most dramatic points, leaving her to face her judges alone. We know that she admitted her 'crime'. But she explained boldly what had brought her to Hungary, analyzing in a penetrating way the political-moral decline of Hungary during the preceding years. And she stressed—in the very midst of Fascist rule—the great crime in which the Hungarians had participated, concluding that those responsible would pay for their actions, as would those who could have prevented them. She admitted that she had come to save Jews, not to save Hungarians from suicide. But in so far as it would have been compatible with her task, she would also have saved Hungarians—and to a degree, the Hungarian nation—from the heavy blame now on their heads.

There is no doubt that in closed session Hannah insulted the judges even more brazenly. They were taken aback, both by her character and her convincing words, aware that there was justice in the world, that someone would avenge the dead. They grew confused. The era was a bloody one. Our cases had come up for trial on orders from higher up; so they couldn't impose a light sentence. Yet a death sentence might mean that one day they would face judges whose judicial powers and views of justice were quite different from their own. There was consternation in the court, and an unprecedented action was taken; the court announced, after extensive consultation, that sentence would not be passed for eight days—until November 4. By then, the judges calculated, the verdict would be made for them. American bombers had been pounding the city, and Russian cannon could be heard booming on the outskirts.

In the corridor outside stood a black-clothed mother awaiting news of her daughter's sentence. Those were times when Jews were not allowed on the street; but she, the mother, had come.

While the court was in consultation the defendants had been taken out into the corridor. The Hungarian sergeant assigned to Hannah turned a blind eye as mother and daughter embraced and had what was to be their last conversation. Hannah had noted the consternation she had caused her judges, and was confident of victory. 'Why worry about a sentence when we'll all soon be free', she encouraged her mother.

The news spread like wildfire. Before the defendants had reached the prison corridor we all knew of the strange decision and had understood its significance. They did not dare to execute her, and they did not have the courage to pronounce any other sentence. They were afraid. Not a bad sign! We all felt much more optimistic.

The days that followed were difficult. We heard continually about the progress of the Red Army, and of its powerful attacks, but no one knew exactly what the situation was. Confusion reigned. To our amazement, the judges who had tried Hannah fled the country. There was no one left to try Peretz and me. Prison boilers became pyres for court records that had been kept since the beginning of the war. Artillery thunder increased hourly until our window panes rattled. We heard that they were preparing to move all prisoners westwards. Then came the news that Conti Street Prison had been evacuated and that Hannah was among the last prisoners transferred to Margit Boulevard Prison, where I was. We had two fervent wishes: that they would not move us before the Russians arrived, and that they would bring us food. We suffered desperately from hunger. Because of the frequent bombardments we were sometimes given soup only once a day, and in the penetrating cold of late autumn we trembled with hunger and increasing weakness. It sometimes seemed that even if we were lucky enough not to be moved, we would starve to death before the Red Army broke through.

November 7 was a dark, cloudy day. We sat around quietly, leaning against the wall, huddled together in an effort to conserve the little body heat we had. Suddenly we heard shots. We looked at each other, frightened and bewildered. What had happened? Had someone been executed? Impossible! This was not their method. Last respects were always paid. There was always the marching of the firing squad, the reading of the sentence, prayer and a bugle call accompanying the dark moment of execution in the grey courtyard beneath our cell window. Someone climbed up to the high window, and looking down informed us that he could see a table with a crucifix on it, but no sign of an execution. At the same moment we heard voices in the courtyard—an order to rearrange the straw. Apparently a guard had fired a bullet by accident and the reverberation had amplified the sound.

That afternoon one of our cellmates went to the doctor. Every day one of us would go for treatment or a pill because the clinic served as a centre of information and communication. The return of that 'patient' was the most important event of our day. That afternoon we waited even more eagerly than usual for our cellmate's return. He was back within half an hour, pale and shaken, as if he really were ill. He leaned against the wall for support, removed his hat, and announced in a faint voice, 'They've executed Hannah. That was the firing we heard'.

We were stunned. Hannah? Executed? No! Impossible! Why Hannah? Why not us? 'It's a mistake . . . a mistake. . . .'

After the first wave of shock I became sure it was an error, that my cellmate had misunderstood, and I mumbled over and over again, 'It's a mistake . . . a mistake . . . a mistake . . .' until the Frenchman, imprisoned with me at the time, gripped my hand and whispered, 'Calm down, control yourself.'

We pounded on the door until the guard came and asked what we wanted.

'We want to know who was just executed'.

'What do you care? Shut up,'he roared.

We pleaded with him and for the first time since we had come under his protection he heard from us the official formula prisoners were ordered to use when addressing a guard: 'We respectfully request . . .' The guard sensed that something had undermined our self-confidence, that we were frightened, and he consoled us; 'Don't worry. She wasn't one of yours. Just some young girl . . . a partisan, they say . . . a British parachutist. But that's surely a lie. Whoever heard of a young girl being a British officer?'

So it was Hannah after all. Wonderful, sparkling Hannah, who had encouraged us with her upraised thumb when we had last parted. She was the first to go. She, who had been so sure we would return to tell our comrades of our exploits, to spin tall tales. I felt I had to speak. But the words, strangled in my throat, left me stuttering. I saw them all staring at me, and I managed to utter, 'She was the most wonderful person I ever knew'. And they repeated after me, as in prayer, 'She was the most . . .'

We rose and stood in silence for a long while, honouring her memory the only way we could. Then we just sat down, speechless, stunned. Tears would not come. I couldn't find anything to say. All I could hear were my cellmate's words over and over again, 'They executed Hannah . . . they executed Hannah . . .'

I spent seventeen more days in that cell. It slowly emptied until there were just two of us left, the Frenchman and myself. When you are in prison for a long period, the quiet becomes unbearable. You feel as if you are trapped in a cemetery, you sometimes have the need to make a noise, to talk, to sing, to disrupt the silence. Yet during those seventeen days not a sound was heard in our cell. One by one we parted from comrades, and although we knew our parting might be final, we still shook hands in silence. I parted from Peretz—never to see him again. No one dared disturb the silence of that cell. It was as if the silence were her monument, a constant reminder of the frightening fact: Hannah is gone.

About two months earlier, at the clinic, I had fallen into conversation with a young man who was accused of betraying his country. He had tried to convince his friends that it was their duty to rebel against the German invaders. During our conversation he mentioned that he lived not far from the prison we had previously been in, at 30 Bimbo Street. Amazed, I recalled Hannah's words at the entrance to the prison, as we parted; 'If we get out, look for me at my mother's house, 28 Bimbo Street'. I asked him if he knew his neighbour, Mrs. Senesh. Of course, he had done for many years. 'And her children?' He knew them, too, and told me enthusiastically about both of them, about the son who was in France, and about the daughter who had gone to Palestine. He told all this at length, for they had been childhood friends, and he was shocked when I told him he was mistaken, that Hannah was not in Palestine—that she had returned on a mission and was now in prison.

That young man served as a prison orderly (most of the menial tasks were done by prisoners), and in fact he was the last person to see Hannah alive. He was on cleaning duty immediately outside her cell—Cell 13, the Condemned Cell, where she had been taken on November 7—when the prosecuting officer, Captain Simon, entered. He testified to Hannah's stand in her last moments.

Simon began tonelessly:

'Hannah Senesh, you have been sentenced to death. Do you wish to ask for clemency?'

'Sentenced to death? No, I wish to appeal. Bring in my lawyer'.

'You cannot appeal. You may ask for clemency'.

'I was tried before a lower tribunal. I know I have the right to appeal'.

'There are no appeals. I repeat: Do you or do you not wish to ask for clemency?'

'Clemency—from you? Do you think I'm going to plead with hangmen and murderers? I shall *never* ask you for mercy'.

'In that case, prepare to die! You may write farewell letters.

But hurry. We shall carry out the sentence in one hour from now'.

Motionless, Hannah sat alone in her cell, her eyes fixed to a point on the wall. What she saw there, what she was staring at, we shall never know. Perhaps her mother's face. Perhaps the scenes of her childhood—the sea, the sand, the places and the people so dear to her.

She asked for paper and pen and wrote letters—to her mother and to us. No one besides Simon ever saw the contents of those letters for they never reached their destination. In the letter to her mother I imagine she explained why she had chosen the path she had. She wanted her pardon, and knew she would obtain it only if her mother understood that her conscience and way of life had compelled her to take the steps she had . . . that ideals and a sense of moral obligation had prompted her actions.

The letter she wrote to Peretz and to me—a letter that was probably intended for all of us, for the entire pioneer movement—also failed to reach its destination, and disappeared with all the files on Hannah's case. But after her death Captain Simon told the Seneshs' solicitor: 'Hannah Senesh remained rebellious till her last day. About to die, she revealed that evil purposes had directed her steps. She wrote to her comrades: "Continue on the way, don't be deterred. Continue the struggle till the end, until the day of liberty comes, the day of victory for our people."'

The hour allotted her passed. At 10 a.m., the same officer stepped into her cell a second time, and silently signalled her to follow him. Two soldiers escorted her into the courtyard. Next to the grey brick wall, near the little prison church, stood a wooden sandbox. They drove a post into the sand, tied her hands behind her back, and strapped her to it. Hannah observed all the gloomy preparations with wonder. She looked straight into the eyes of the officer, who stepped towards her with a blindfold. She shook her head defiantly and lifted her blue eyes to the cloudy, foreboding sky as the three rifles spat.

Half an hour later, a car arrived and took away her body.

Hannah was buried in Budapest's Jewish cemetery, in the Martyrs' Section, among the many anonymous victims of the Germans. We don't know who brought her body there. The Jewish Burial Society was functioning no longer; Jews were not allowed to leave their houses. Perhaps an admirer did her this final kindness.

I've tried to trace her family and her home. The mystery of her personality, the riddle of her life, have baffled me increasingly. The more I discover about her background, about the scenes of her youth, the less I understand her. I saw how she had lived—the villa in a wealthy neighbourhood, the huge country house where she spent half her childhood: her family respected in Jewish and non-Jewish circles alike. I don't know what compelled her to go to Palestine. Whether it was the anti-Semitism she encountered at school, the discussions she had with a girl from Palestine, whether it was some other unknown factor. Only when she reached Palestine is the picture complete and clear and it is there that her character was finally shaped. For this reason, Hannah's death symbolizes a great deal for those of us who continue to live there, but not only for us. She was the product of an assimilated Jewry that had long turned its back on Judaism. This Jewry, to whose aid she came, began to find a new path for itself, apparently, with Hannah's death. Her death alone was not responsible for this: 800,000 Jewish corpses paved the road for the survivors. They said in Budapest that Hannah was Hungarian Jewry's swan song. But that is not how we see it. She represented a new era, the return of a Jewish community to its people, to its land. Thus, her image and her actions lit the way for the Hungarian Jewry for whose rescue she came and for whom she sacrificed her life.

1945

Meeting in Budapest

Catherine Senesh

From the autumn of 1939 to the spring of 1941 there was a
steady flow of cheerful, reassuring letters from Hannah in which
she described, in minute detail, her work and life in Palestine.
These letters helped, in some measure, to fill the great void left
by her absence.

Our correspondence continued uninterruptedly while Hungary
remained neutral. But after November 1940, when Hungary
joined with Germany, I received letters from Hannah with
decreasing frequency; those I did get were brief, and heavily
censored. Then, after the summer of 1941, letters ceased entirely,
and were replaced by occasional 25-word Red Cross communications. But I was not at all worried. On the contrary. My gratitude that Hannah was in the safest possible place, and happy,
grew apace with the increasingly rapid gathering of ominous clouds
over Hungarian Jewry. By then my fears and anxieties were entirely centred on George who, in the winter of 1942, disappeared
from France, without a trace, and my letters to him were returned
unopened. Then, at the end of January 1944, a telegram from
Hannah informed me he had arrived in Palestine. I was happy and
grateful that my children were safe and together at last, and
excitedly prepared to join them.

I had received word from Hannah in December 1943, through
secret channels, advising me that I should prepare to leave at a
moment's notice. I had also been contacted by the president of the
Zionist Organization, who intimated the same thing. But the time
limit for Hungarian Aliyah was fast running out, and the anxiously
awaited Immigration Certificate failed to arrive. Then March 19,
1944, greeted us, the day of the German occupation of Hungary.

All the humiliating, discriminatory, annihilating laws it had taken
the Nazis years to institute in other countries were put into effect
and enforced in Hungary with fantastic speed.

The compulsory wearing of the Yellow Star struck us with
paralyzing force, and there were those who would not under any
circumstance be seen wearing it in the street. Arrests, house-
arrests, evictions, deportations, suicides marked each day of
German domination. Visiting my relatives in the provinces was
no longer possible, and by May I heard they were all in the ghetto.
Then rumours spread that Jews in the ghetto were being
transported by freight car to unknown destinations. And a
few days later Jews in Budapest were ordered to move into
Yellow Star-designated houses. I, too, packed a few essentials,
ready for any eventuality, but was uncertain what to do, how
to proceed.

Old friends—a husband and wife—tried to convince me not
to move into one of these houses but to obtain false documents
stating I was Aryan. They wanted me to escape with them to
Rumania, assuming that it would be easy to make our way from
there to Palestine. I thought the plan unfeasible, even absurd, yet
out of desperation agreed and obtained the forged papers. But I
had not as yet reached a definite decision.

For the past several years I had been renting part of my home
to Margit Dayka, a well-known, popular actress who, in those
tragic days, demonstrated infinite sympathy for those of us who
were being hunted, and was unfailingly helpful and kind. On the
night of June 15, Margit remained home with me. Perhaps she
was aware of how completely dispirited I had become since the
disappearance of my relatives, or perhaps she didn't want to leave
me alone, knowing that only a few days previously the Gestapo
had come to requisition a part of the house in which I lived, and
had only been prevented from doing so by her heated intervention. She made me promise that I would not, under any circumstances, allow anyone to enter the house during her absence. The
following day we agreed that she should go to the Housing
Authority and demand that the part of the house in which I lived
be placed in her name too. 'And of course I'll take care of your
things, Kate,' she said, 'so you'll find everything intact and in
perfect order when you return.' She was touchingly gentle and
understanding.

I slept little that night. Not only was I exceedingly troubled,
but I was on air-raid duty as well. Next morning, June 17, I got
up at about eight and began dressing. The bell rang. I hurried to
the window and saw a stranger who, on catching sight of me, said,
'I'm looking for Mrs. Béla Szegö.'

'She doesn't live at this address,' I answered.

'Of course she does,' he insisted, taking a slip of paper from
his pocket. Then, 'Oh, wait a minute. Not Szegö . . . Senesh.
Mrs. Senesh is the name of the woman I'm looking for. I'm a
State Police Detective. Please open the door.'

I showed him into the entrance hall.

'You're being summoned to the head office of Military Headquarters as a witness,' he said. 'Please come along.'

'Witness for whom? In what matter?'

'I don't know,' he said, shrugging.

It was beyond my comprehension. Certainly I knew no one in
the Armed Forces, and Jews had long since been drafted into
the Compulsory Labour Forces. The thought flashed through my
mind that the summons might have something to do with George,
who was of military age. However, he had left the country six
years previously with permission from the proper authorities. I
wondered whether his escape with false documents from France
to Palestine, by way of Spain, had something to do with the
summons.

I asked the detective to wait while I finished dressing, and
rushed to wake up Margit. Hearing what had happened, she
threw on a dressing gown, rushed downstairs, and asked the
detective to be seated in the drawing room. She tried to find
out why I was being taken for questioning but could obtain no
information either. Before leaving he assured us both I would be
back home very soon. Even so, I had the presence of mind to give
the forged papers I had acquired for the planned escape with my
friends to Margit.

The detective took me by tram to the Military Headquarters
in Horthy Miklos Boulevard, which was half an hour's ride from
my house.

What did I feel? Perhaps curiosity as much as fear since I could
not imagine why they wanted me. But in those days arrest without
reason was a daily occurrence, and there were few among us who
were not afraid of being picked up and taken to the police or

military headquarters for questioning. We began to accept the disappearance of relatives, friends, acquaintances; our ranks were thinning daily. What could happen? The only thing of great importance was the safety of both my children—and that was assured. Whatever happened to me did not matter.

Those were the thoughts that raced through my mind as I chatted with the detective about Margit. He was interested in her career, in the plays and films she had starred in, and in the theatre in general. He was really quite courteous, even considerate, and immediately agreed when I asked permission to telephone Margit. It seemed even more important now to have the house put in her name, and I wanted to remind her about it.

I stopped at a tobacco shop to make the call, but when I began dialing the proprietor shouted, 'What's the matter with you! Don't you know anyone wearing a Yellow Star is forbidden to use a public phone?'

I really hadn't known, but neither had the detective; he said I could use the phone in his office.

When we arrived at the Military Headquarters Building we walked up to a second-floor office where two policemen were having their mid-morning snack of smoked bacon and green peppers. The detective went to announce my arrival and when he returned asked the police to leave. He also allowed me to phone Margit, and after I talked to her, asked whether I had any children. When I replied in the affirmative he asked where they were. There happened to be a large map on the wall and I smilingly pointed to Palestine.

A very tall civilian of military bearing entered the room. His name, I soon learned, was Rozsa. He indicated a chair and settled himself behind a typewriter. The interrogation began. After taking down the usual data concerning family and background, he first questioned me about George, as the eldest, but quickly turned his attention to Hannah. Much to my surprise, he questioned me endlessly about her, stopped the pretence of typing, and asked what specific reasons she had had for leaving home. 'I can understand a boy leaving home: to see the world, to complete his studies, to prepare for his career. But a girl . . . why should a young girl want to leave her home, her mother, her friends?'

'For the very reasons you mentioned,' I replied. 'Jewish youth has no future in Hungary, no opportunity of making a living. And much as it hurt me to part with her, particularly after having had to part with my son, I'm happy she's not here now to see and experience the terrible suffering of the Jews.'

A scornful smile spread over his unpleasant face, and the interrogation continued. The majority of questions revolved around what Hannah had been doing during the past few years, where she was at present, what she was doing now, and above all, how, from where, and how often I received news from her. The thought struck me that perhaps one of her letters had been intercepted and contained something that displeased the censor.

But there was no time for conjecture as the interrogation intensified and its tempo increased, the snapped questions becoming more incisive. What had Hannah done before leaving Budapest? Who were her friends? Her teachers? What had she been interested in? With what had she primarily concerned herself? What profession had she thought of following? What were her ambitions?

To all questions I simply answered that she had always hoped to be a teacher, and had studied with that end in mind.

There was further questioning in the same vein, which I finally put an end to by saying, 'Perhaps you'll construe this merely as a mother's normal pride in her child, but I can tell you my daughter is an unusually gifted girl and in every respect a very remarkable young woman. You need not take my word. You can question her teachers who will, I am sure, verify my statements.'

He was finally satisfied with the interrogation and instructed the detective to type a summary of what I had said. He then warned me I would have to swear under oath that my testimony was the truth, and sign it.

I summarized my statement, and the detective typed it on a long sheet headed 'Hannah Senesh'. We had barely finished when Rozsa returned, carefully read it over, made me swear to its veracity, and sign it. 'Now then,' he said, 'where do you *really* think your daughter is now—this minute?'

I repeated that to the best of my knowledge she was on an agricultural settlement in the vicinity of Haifa.

'Well, if you really don't know, I'll tell you. She's here, in the adjoining room. I'll bring her right in so you can talk to her and persuade her to tell us everything she knows. Because if she doesn't—this will be your last meeting.'

I felt as if the floor were giving way under me and clutched the edge of the table frantically with both hands. My eyes closed, and in a matter of seconds I felt everything—hope, faith, trust, the very meaning of life, everything I had ever believed in—collapse like a child's house of cards. I was completely shattered, physically and spiritually.

The door opened. I turned, my back to the table, my body rigid.

Four men led her in. Had I not known she was coming, perhaps in that first moment I would not have recognized the Hannah of five years ago. Her once soft, wavy hair hung in a filthy tangle, her ravaged face reflected untold suffering, her large, expressive eyes were blackened, and there were ugly welts on her cheeks and neck. That was my first glimpse of her.

She tore herself away from the men, and rushing to me threw her arms around my neck sobbing, 'Mother, forgive me!'

I felt the pounding of her heart and her scalding tears. At the same time I noted the expectant, avid expressions on the faces of the staring men as they watched us—as if they had been watching a scene in a play. Again the floor seemed to sway, and it took all my strength to maintain my self-control and remain silent.

Rozsa said, 'Speak to her! Use your maternal influence and convince her she had better tell us everything, otherwise you'll never see each other again.'

I had not the faintest idea what was happening. Not even in my wildest imaginings would it have occurred to me that Hannah, the fervent pacifist, was a volunteer in the British Army. Nor did I know a woman could become a member of the British Armed Forces. What puzzled me was how she had suddenly been catapulted from the far distance into the hell that was then Hungary. Certainly no one told me anything, or explained anything, and I could not possibly have guessed the truth. But of one thing I was absolutely certain: if there was something Hannah did not want to reveal, she had good reason, and under no circumstances would I influence her otherwise.

'Well,' Rozsa snarled, 'why don't you talk?'

My voice sounded strange when I answered, 'There is no need to repeat yourself. We both heard you.'

'All right, but talk to her. We'll leave you alone for a while.'

They led us to facing chairs and then left the room, only the detective remaining.

We couldn't find words. Then suddenly it occurred to me that Hannah, upon hearing about the horrible things happening to the Jews in Hungary, might have volunteered for a daring, even reckless mission, in an effort to rescue me. I was only too familiar with her extraordinary courage, will-power and perseverance when faced with seemingly insurmountable obstacles. And regardless of the considerable distance that had separated us, I was always aware of her love and constant concern.

'Hannah, tell me, am I the cause of what's happening here? Did anxiety about me bring you back?'

She quickly reassured me. 'No, Mother! No! You're not to blame for anything. Not anything at all.'

'But how did you get here? I received a telegram not long ago to say that George had arrived in Palestine. Isn't he there now either?'

'But of course he is, darling. I sent the telegram myself. You needn't worry about George, believe me. He's fine.'

I noticed one of her upper teeth was missing, obviously a result of the same beating that had produced the welts and bruises on her face and neck. The presence of the detective inhibited our conversation, but despite him I said, 'Of course your tooth was knocked out here.'

'No, not here,' she answered.

Seeing her in such battered condition was heartbreaking. I stroked her hands, the nails broken, the skin like sandpaper. The purple-black bruises on her face were like knife wounds in my own flesh, and I leaned over to kiss her. The instant I embraced her the door burst open and Rozsa rushed in with his four henchmen. He had evidently been spying on us. He pushed us apart and said, 'Whispering is not allowed here! Anyway, that's enough for today.'

They took Hannah away, and Rozsa turned back to me. 'I could detain you as well, but I'm taking your age into consideration. Go on home! If we have further need of you we'll telephone. Of course everything depends upon her. If she refuses to confess at subsequent interrogations we'll probably have no further use for you. But I warn you, you're not to tell anyone anything that has happened here today. Not a word! Not even that you've set foot inside this building. Understand?'

'Yes, I understand. But someone already knows that I'm here.'

'Who?' he asked in astonishment.

'Margit Dayka, the actress.'

'How is that possible?'

'Mrs. Senesh is her housekeeper,' the detective interrupted. 'She was there when I picked up the witness.'

'Will she ask questions when you return?' Rozsa demanded.

'Undoubtedly. After all, she isn't accustomed to seeing me hauled off by a detective.'

'If she asks you anything just tell her you've been forbidden to say one single word. Remember that! Not a word. You can leave now.'

He left the office and the detective, seeing I was barely able to move, said, 'Rest a moment. We don't have to leave immediately.'

His kindness gave me courage to ask what was going on. But he protested he didn't know, and at that moment several policemen came in saying the room was needed. The detective accompanied me down the stairs and attempted to comfort me. 'Don't take the threats too seriously. Things don't happen quite that fast around here. Everything will be straightened out—you'll see.'

In any event, it was reassuring to know there was someone left who behaved like a human being.

I stumbled home. It must have been about one in the afternoon. A small group of neighbours and acquaintances were waiting in front of the villa together with Margit. They ran towards me, clamouring to know what had happened.

'It was all a misunderstanding,' I told them.

But immediately Margit and I were alone in the house I said, 'It wasn't a misunderstanding. A horrible thing has happened, but I'm not at liberty to tell you about it. Perhaps I won't be able to keep it to myself, but at the moment I can't possibly tell you.'

The bell rang. Margit ran to open the door. I heard voices. I went to my room but Margit followed. The producer of her recent film had come to take her to the studio to see the rushes. 'But I don't want to leave you alone now,' she said. She told my sister later that I had changed so incredibly in the short time I had been away that she had difficulty believing I was the same woman who had left with the detective that morning. Of course

I didn't know my appearance had been so affected, and when she insisted on staying home with me it required superhuman effort to control myself: all I wanted was to be left alone. I begged her to leave and promised if anything happened I would somehow get word to her. She returned the forged documents I had entrusted to her that morning, and finally left.

But I wasn't alone for long. There was a knock on the door, and the caretaker led in the husband of the couple who wanted me to escape with them to Palestine. He had come to see how I was getting on with my preparations, since the attempt had to be made in the next day or so. In answer to his repeated questions I told him firmly that after giving the matter most careful consideration I had decided not to leave Budapest. He attempted to persuade me, to convince me that so far as he could see it was the only step for me to take. Once again he detailed the bright prospects of life in Palestine. 'We have neither friends nor relatives there,' he said, 'but even so, we feel it is the only place for us to go. You, on the other hand, have two children there. If there is anyone to whom it's worth the risk and the gamble, you're certainly the one. And don't forget the efforts Hannah has made to obtain an immigration certificate for you.'

While he talked I considered the advisability of telling him what had happened. I felt as if Providence had sent him. I so desperately needed someone to confide in, to consult. And if he and his wife ever reached Palestine they could at least tell George what had happened. I knew him to be a serious, level-headed man who could be trusted absolutely with my secret, and finally decided to tell him everything. He listened with rigid attention, and then spoke. 'I hardly know what to say. This is really a catastrophe, and of course I understand now why you don't want to leave. It's difficult to find an explanation for what has happened. I promised not to betray your confidence so of course I won't tell a soul, but I don't agree with your decision to maintain complete silence. On the contrary; I think you ought to confide in those who might possibly be able to help you. First of all, I think you ought to tell Margit, who probably has connections in military circles.'

I accompanied him to the door, and we were standing in the entrance hall, saying our goodbyes, when the bell rang. I looked out of the window and saw a closed car surrounded by SS men.

One of them rasped, 'We are looking for Mrs. Senesh. Please let us in.'

'I'll get the key right away,' I stalled.

I ran into the living room, quickly gathered up the forged documents, which were still lying on the table, and hid them in Margit's cupboard. Then I ran to unlock the front door. My friend wanted to leave but one of the Gestapo men, whose name, I later learned, was Seifert, scrutinized him, and barring his passage asked, 'And who are you?'

'Mrs. Senesh is a close friend of my wife. I came to enquire how she was, and I was just leaving.'

Seifert debated whether to let him go. We waited tensely, knowing that those who happened to be in the company of someone being arrested were often taken to prison as well. Finally Seifert let him go, and then entered with the four others, saying, 'Come along immediately for interrogation.'

I was alone in the house. The caretaker, who lived in a flat at the side, had gone shopping. I desperately wanted her to witness my departure. Then if I failed to return, she would tell Margit, who would, in turn, notify my sister. 'I can't possibly leave now,' I said with assumed naïvety, 'since I'm entirely responsible for the house and personal belongings of Margit Dayka, the actress, and she's not at home.'

'But you'll be brought back straight after the interrogation,' Seifert promised. 'Just get ready to go.'

I went to my room slowly, Seifert on my heels. I tried to decide whether to tell him I knew why I was being taken for questioning, or whether to feign ignorance. Remembering Rozsa's threatening tone I decided to say nothing. Seifert began inspecting the house, strolling from room to room, shouting out questions about the furniture, the contents of drawers and cupboards, finally demanding to know which of the rooms were mine.

I replied that all the rooms but one were occupied by the actress. He then asked about the front door, and all the other doors in the house. Of course I was aware there would be a thorough search of the premises as soon as I left. Suddenly Seifert held a photograph directly in front of me and asked, 'Do you recognize this girl?'

It was a picture of Hannah looking the way she had that morning.

'Who is it?' I asked.

'Have you a daughter, Hannah Senesh?'

'Of course,' I answered, 'but if this is supposed to be a picture of her, she's unrecognizable. Where did you get it?'

Instead of answering, he urged me to hurry, ordered me to lock all the doors, and asked who had keys to the house.

'Only the actress and I. There is a separate entrance to the caretaker's quarters.'

'When will the actress come home?'

'Probably by evening.'

Fortunately the caretaker returned, and I was able to exchange a few words with her. I gave her Margit's number, and asked her to telephone immediately after I left. She, on the other hand, knowing I had not yet eaten anything that day, rushed to the kitchen, prepared a few sandwiches, and slipped them into my large handbag. We left the house, and I locked the front door. Whereupon Seifert asked, 'Why are you taking the key along?'

'Didn't you say I would be back before evening?'

'Of course, of course,' he answered hastily, aware he had betrayed himself, 'take the key.'

We climbed into the police van, and in a few minutes arrived at the prison. Only after we had got out did I realize how close it was to my house. The car had stopped at the freight entrance of the Budapest County Department of Justice Building, which led directly to the German Police Prison. Seifert got out with me but spent some time taking leave of the others, exchanging jokes, discussing Saturday night plans, and wishing them a happy weekend. Then he conducted me to an upstairs office. All this took place at about five o'clock on a Saturday afternoon.

Seifert asked for and examined my identity papers in the presence of a gaunt, fearsome-looking young SS man with a Death's Head badge on his cap*, a young German soldier, and a middle-aged, corpulent civilian. He put my documents in a dossier marked 'Very Urgent', asked for my house keys, and left.

The young Death's Head man, whose face resembled his badge, took over. He asked for all my personal belongings, examined my handbag, turned it inside out. He confiscated my money, fountain

* Death's Head units (*Totenkopf SS*) carried out the acts of atrocity in concentration camps.

pen, watch, and wedding ring. He asked whether I had any more money. I wore a little bag around my neck in which I carried the maximum amount of money Jews were allowed. After an instant's hesitation, I handed it to him. The reward for the momentary delay was a powerful slap across my face. I spun completely round on my own axis, but strangely enough didn't feel the blow at all. After that morning's encounter with Hannah I felt nothing: as if a stranger had taken my place, or a mechanized puppet. But the young soldier was embarrassed, and the corpulent civilian repeatedly blinked and motioned me to disregard the abuse. (I learned later that the civilian was a Jewish prisoner, formerly the general manager of an important firm, who had been drafted for office work in the prison.)

A meticulous record was made of the things and amount taken from me, the small change returned, and I was told by Death's Head that when I was released (if ever) everything, without exception, would be returned to me. He then gave the soldier the number of the cell to which I was assigned: 528. As we were climbing the stairs the soldier asked if I had anything else concealed on my person because, he warned, I would be searched, and he wanted to spare me a repetition of what had happened downstairs. I assured him I had nothing more but the clothes on my back and my handbag with its innocent contents.

After being carefully searched by two Swabian women guards, I was conducted by one of them to a wide corridor on the fifth floor. The lock of a heavy steel door creaked open, and I stepped into a surprisingly spacious, bright room. With its six white iron beds it looked (apart from the bars on the window) more like a hospital ward than the prison cell I had imagined. A number of inquisitive-looking women turned expectantly towards me, but I soon learned they always did this—and so would I—upon the arrival of a new 'roomer'.

One of them jumped up and ran towards me, and I recognized her as Baroness Böske Hatvany, divorced wife of Baron Lajos Hatvany. Some of the women were seated on two of the beds, playing bridge, though, like any kind of activity, it was strictly forbidden. Baroness Hatvany had cleverly drawn numbers and figures on bits of paper, and made playing cards. The women killed time this way, since from five in the morning until bedtime they were officially supposed to sit on the benches placed around the table in the centre of the room, doing absolutely nothing. From time to time the matrons observed us through the peep-hole in the door to see whether we were breaking rules. Despite this, we took turns to lie on the beds, but even in our dreams we heard footsteps, and automatically jumped up and ran to the table.

When I entered the cell the women surrounded me, and questioned me about events on the outside. Böske made the introductions: Mrs. Eugene Vida, wife of the only Jewish member of Parliament, whose ex-butler had denounced her for making an allegedly anti-Nazi remark. Countess Zichy, of Jewish origin, who was arrested while attempting to hide valuable paintings; the widow of Lehel Héderváry, accused of collaborat-ing with the Allies; the sister of Jacques Mannheim, the Parisian banker. These are some of the names I still remember. They all wondered how I came to be among them. After all, I was not a membe: of the moneyed aristocracy, nor politically involved. It was also generally known that since my husband's untimely death I had led a most retiring life. Of course I didn't dare reveal the reason for my imprisonment.

It was getting dark, and I had eaten nothing since the night before. I was famished. I found the sandwiches, and bit into one of them. Twelve pairs of eyes fastened upon me. Hungry as I was, the mouthful caught in my throat. I handed the small packet of food to Böske, who carefully divided it. She seemed to be the 'officer in charge'.

Later that evening a heated argument developed concerning next day's cleaning of the room and adjoining toilet. It was the turn of Countess Zichy, but she violently protested, stating that she would not, under any circumstances, clean the toilet—not only because she had never performed such a task, but also because she had not the faintest idea how to go about it. Someone offered to do the work for her, but Böske insisted that no one could be exempted from the work detail for any reason but ill-ness. She then explained the use of the brush, disinfectant and scrubbing powder.

Everyone joined in the debate, pro and con, and had the situation been less tragic it would have been extremely funny. Due to my state of mind, I was not yet able to make contact with prison life; my thoughts were certainly elsewhere. I crouched in a corner, and remained silent.

After a completely sleepless night I was routed out of bed at
five. Sunday was a day of rest even for the Gestapo interrogators,
but as my dossier was marked 'urgent', the consensus of opinion
was that I would be taken to Schwab Hill for questioning early
the next morning.

Worry and uncertainty weighed so heavily upon me that I
could no longer stifle my secret, and told Böske everything that
had happened. She listened in shocked silence and promised to
tell no one. Whether she did or not, I don't know. But that
Sunday evening Clara Zichy apologized to me for making such a
fuss the previous evening, and all the others seemed particularly
kind.

I observed them through a haze of preoccupation, my thoughts
wholly centred upon Hannah, wondering whether she was still
alive. Certainly she would never divulge what they wanted to
know, and they would show no mercy. What use was there in my
going up for interrogation the following morning? I shuddered
at the thought of being questioned, and decided it was senseless
to endure further torment. Even if Hannah were alive, I could
be of no help to her whatever while imprisoned.

Small shelves, which prisoners used to keep toilet articles on,
had been fixed on facing walls of the cell. There were not enough
of these for everyone in the overcrowded cell, so those who had
been imprisoned the longest had prior claims on them. One of
the few things one could do to pass the time was arrange and
rearrange the little odds and ends sent in the fortnightly parcels
prisoners were allowed. Clara Zichy said that among the things
she had received, the most useful was a razor blade, which served
as a knife, pencil sharpener and scissors. I glanced at it out of
the corner of my eye as it lay temptingly in view on the left side
of her shelf. That night, while everyone was absorbed in the
complicated business of placing mattresses on the floor (it was
roomier and more comfortable sleeping that way than sleeping
two in one bed), I managed to take the razor blade without anyone noticing. Since I lay directly next to the open window I was
able to hide the blade on the outside ledge.

The light switch was in the corridor; because the guards never
bothered to turn it on, we all went to bed immediately it grew
dark. That night, when everyone seemed to be asleep, I tried to
put an end to further misery and suffering. Locating the main

artery in my wrist I slashed it and felt the blood flow—but it did not gush forth as I had expected. My neighbour sat up, and for a while I feigned sleep. Then, after a considerable interval, I tried once more. But again there was only a trickle of blood. Before I could bring myself to make yet another attempt, the prisoners began stirring.

Böske, an alert woman, looked towards me inquiringly, and noticed something wrong. Fearfully she rushed over and grabbed my wrist. While tightly binding it with two small handkerchiefs, she berated me, saying that what I had foolishly attempted to do could have got them all into serious trouble. She advised that when I was taken for questioning I should wear my long-sleeved raincoat in order to hide the bandage.

At seven o'clock a soldier appeared and read my name from a list. A cellmate immediately gave me my day's ration of bread; they all knew from experience that during the morning-to-night interrogation on the Hill I would be given nothing to eat. However, hungry as I was later that day, the bread was so mouldy I could not eat it.

Prisoners rounded up for questioning were made to assemble in the second-floor corridor, ordered to face the wall, and the slightest movement, gesture, or even flutter of a hand in attempted salutation was forbidden. About forty of us were crammed into a huge police van and transported to the Gestapo headquarters. The van was windowless, but there were a few narrow air vents near the top. When we were under way I noticed that postcards (previously written and addressed) were collected and slipped through the vents in the hope they would be picked up by people humane enough to forward them.

There was a separate, crowded waiting room for women where I sat all day awaiting my turn. During the morning a woman deliberately squeezed in beside me and began asking questions, whereupon a prisoner across the aisle gestured and placed a finger across her lips. Later she explained that my inquisitive neighbour was an informer.

I was not questioned that day. The same evening I was handed a postcard and told this would be my one and only opportunity to notify someone of my whereabouts, and to ask for food parcels, clothing and toilet articles. Packages were accepted every other Wednesday morning, from 10.00–12.00, and delivered to the prisoners immediately. It was already Monday evening and I wondered if the card would be delivered in time. Nor did I know to whom I should send it. I was afraid of sending it to my closest relatives, and did not want to involve Margit by writing her a card from a Gestapo prison. After considerable speculation I addressed it to the hairdresser in my neighbourhood, and asked her to please give it to the lady who lives in my house.

On parcel-day there was tremendous excitement in the prison. Although consignments could not be distributed until after 10.00, the tension of waiting and expectation began early in the morning—not only due to hunger, but because the awaited package was the only means of communication with the outside, the only link between the prisoner and his family or friends. Every parcel was carefully examined and thoroughly pilfered. Paper and string were confiscated, and what finally remained was distributed. There were those who received two or three parcels, and those who received none, and were consequently panic-stricken.

By noon that first Wednesday I gave up hope of receiving anything, concluding that the card had arrived too late, or had not been delivered. But at the last moment a parcel arrived, apparently delivered by taxi. There was a jar of soup in it, still steaming, and everything else was fresh and wonderfully appetizing, particularly after the incredible prison fare. I was surprised, however, that most of the clothing Margit had sent consisted of worn things I no longer used, and had put aside to be given away. I learned later that the room I had indicated to Seifert as mine, and which did, in fact, contain most of my clothes, had been thoroughly searched and subsequently sealed by the Gestapo. Thus Margit was compelled to send whatever she could find in the mending room, plus some of her own things.

Every day, after the midday meal, we were allowed a ten-minute walk in the prison yard, along with prisoners from cells on either side of ours. This exercise period was the highlight of our day. Though conversation was forbidden, we managed to exchange bits of news which, amazingly enough, filtered into the closely guarded cells. One soon came across forgotten acquaintances, and from day to day, as new prisoners arrived, friends and relatives one hoped had managed to escape joined the ranks. Gradually the number of inmates grew, and before long there were about twenty in our cell, which was not intended for more than six. But prisoners also left. On the morning of June 23, Böske Hatvany and Mrs. Vida were taken away. Where, no one knew. It was rumoured that there were twice-weekly deportations, as well as twice-weekly selections for shipment to the Kistarcsa internment camp in the suburbs. To be ready for any eventuality, we all packed little bundles each morning since one had to leave instantly if one's name was called.

The morning Böske was called I was summoned again for interrogation. When I followed the soldier down the stairs to the second-floor corridor to join the assembled group, a young prisoner who was scrubbing the floor whispered, 'Auntie Kate, Hannah is here too. I talked to her last night.' I could barely control myself. I glanced at Böske and longed to run over and tell her, but she, as everyone, was facing the wall, and I was only too well aware that talking was strictly forbidden.

That day I was interrogated by Seifert, who was in charge of my case. He questioned me for hours on end, lingering interminably over the slightest detail. Though the interrogation was infinitely more thorough and painstaking than that conducted by Rozsa, Seifert's manners and method were more polished and courteous. Because of this I had the temerity to ask, 'Won't you please tell me what has happened? What the charge is against my daughter?'

He weighed my questions silently, and finally, instead of answering directly, said, 'According to my interpretation of Hungarian law, your daughter's life is in no danger. German laws are more stringent.'

I breathed more easily.

That very evening Hilda, a Hungarian prisoner of German origin, and the prototype of German beauty, unlocked the door of the cell, and in a sharp, strident voice called my name. Because of her beauty and fluency in German she was exempted from physical labour and assigned primarily to office work and errands of considerable responsibility. Now and then, when the matrons were at meals or busy elsewhere, she was even entrusted with keys to the cells.

When I stepped into the corridor and the door of the cell was closed behind me, she whispered that I was to stand by the window of the cell and look across. Looking out of the window was generally forbidden, but then so many things we ventured to do were forbidden that I did as she bid. At the window directly across the yard, and exactly opposite mine, I saw Hannah. She smiled and waved.

Early next morning I stationed myself in the window again, and after a brief wait she appeared and wrote huge letters in the air, carefully outlining each with her index finger. I answered the same way. Knowing we might be watched we were exceedingly careful and 'talked' only of inconsequentials. At least in the beginning.

It seemed strange that Hannah's window was so different from the others. It was immediately beneath the ceilings, horizontal, and considerably smaller than ours. I was told that all prisoners in solitary confinement had such windows to prevent them from looking out. How she managed to look out of hers we couldn't fathom.

My cell mates stood beside me and watched our 'correspondence' with great interest. Hannah noted the Yellow Star on our clothes and asked what it signified. I explained and enquired whether she was excused from wearing the discriminatory emblem. She answered that she was no longer a Hungarian citizen, thus not bound by such 'laws'. One of my companions wrote in the air, 'You're lucky not to be branded.' Whereupon Hannah drew an enormous Star of David on the dust-coated window, and there it remained until weeks later when the window was washed. As soon as she had drawn the Star she disappeared from the window, and although I watched for her all day she did not appear again. The next evening the beautiful Hilda again called me sharply: in the corridor she whispered that I could talk to Hannah for a few moments in the bathroom nearby.

At last I could hold her close, kiss her. Hannah hastily explained that she was a Radio Officer in the British Army, and had volunteered for a mission which 'unfortunately I could not complete.' She continued, 'I'm reconciled to my fate. But the thought that I've needlessly involved you in all this is unbearable.' I convinced her that I was perfectly all right, and the one consolation in the entire tragedy was that I could be close to her, could see her now and again, even talk to her. Had I been allowed to remain free I would probably not have been able to obtain visiting privileges, and there could even have been the horrible possibility of deportation and separation for ever.

She smiled sadly, and looked almost like her old self. The visible marks of the beatings had healed. Her hair was clean and well combed, her expression calm. But the gap in her mouth disturbed me. In answer to my question she said she had taken a course in parachute jumping while still in Palestine, and had lost the tooth completing a jump. Obviously she did not want me to know the truth, and sensing my doubt she smiled and said, 'Dearest Mother, if all I lose during this venture is a single tooth, we can both be really grateful.'

I asked if she had been repeatedly tortured, and how severely, beyond the obvious. 'Believe me,' she answered, 'compared to the mental and emotional anguish, the physical suffering is negligible.' She related that at the time of their arrest, before she and her companions were charged with anything, the sudden suicide of one of the boys in the group triggered the subsequent catastrophe that caused them all to be suspect. Consequently they were all searched, and in the pocket of one of the boys the radio earphones were found.

At this point Hilda knocked and we said goodbye.

During the following days I hardly saw her; in fact there were days she did not appear in the window at all. I learned she was taken to the Hill daily for interrogation and did not return until nightfall. She became acquainted with several of my cellmates, either in the police van or else in the waiting room. From them I discovered she had parachuted into Yugoslavia and had lived for months with the partisans there.

Occasionally she appeared at the window for a few moments early in the morning. She cut out huge paper letters and held them up to form words, but often she would duck down suddenly in the middle of a word or sentence. I learned she could reach her window only by putting the table on her bed, and on top of the table a chair. Since the chair was used as a washstand, and she had only a short time early in the morning to use it, she would quickly jump from her perch when she heard the guard returning for it.

On the rare days when there were no interrogations, I could stand at my window and watch her walking in the yard after lunch. Or, to put it more accurately, I could watch one corner of the yard, for as the line turned I could catch a momentary glimpse of her in that corner. The prisoners walked in pairs but she brought up the rear alone. As a prisoner in solitary she was forbidden to have direct contact with anyone, nor was she given the remotest possibility of talking. She knew I was watching her, and each time she reached the corner she would look up. They were particularly careful not to let us meet, but on one occasion our groups chanced to be in the yard at the same time. By then the majority of the inmates knew us or had heard about us. Consequently everyone who was aware of our relationship watched excitedly to see if we could manage a meeting, an exchange of words. It seemed hopeless. I was at the head of my double column, she alone at the tail-end of hers. The matron stood in the centre of the vast yard, watchful; the armed military guards were stationed at various points.

Hannah continually stepped out of line, evidently troubled by her shoelace. Meanwhile the line kept going ahead, and she kept taking a step backwards each time she stooped, until we were side by side. My partner stepped back, and Hannah slipped into her place. It was done so smoothly, so effortlessly, one would have thought it had been carefully rehearsed. We chatted softly, but I kept my eyes on the matron. Whenever her gaze caught mine I became silent, whereupon Hannah said, 'Listen, Mother, we're in the greatest possible danger here anyway, so we might as well talk freely. We've nothing to lose.'

She told me that a day or two after our first meeting Rozsa had wanted to interrogate me again, and had telephoned my home while Hannah was in his office. Margit had answered, and obviously told him I had disappeared. When, upon further questioning, she could not give him the information he wanted, he became furious, slammed down the telephone, and raged, 'That damned Jew hireling! She's probably got her hidden!'

July 17, Hannah's birthday, was drawing near. I wondered what little gift I could send her. I had already shared my last parcel with her, but had providentially put aside a jar of marmalade. When my cellmates saw me preparing the carefully guarded bottle, they contributed gifts from their own precious stores: a handkerchief, a sliver of soap, a sponge—in prison each a cherished, rare possession. One of the matrons agreed to deliver the gifts.

That afternoon she summoned me to the peep-hole and dropped in a piece of paper upon which Hannah had written a few lines to thank us for our thoughtfulness and generosity. She said the marmalade particularly pleased her, not only because it was so good, but because it reminded her of Palestine. She continued that she had summed up and weighed the events of her life, and upon looking back over her twenty-three years decided they had been very colourful and eventful, her childhood happy and beautiful. Her accounting with life at such a tender age was like a dagger in my heart.

During the exercise period in the yard I began noticing children at Hannah's left and right, grabbing her arms, clinging to her. Two, in particular, struck me: a Polish boy and girl. One was eight, the other six, and they had been wandering for years with their mother, from camp to camp, prison to prison. They immediately sensed a friend in Hannah and would not leave her side. Sometimes they even played tag, and the guards would 'benevolently' look the other way. To please these children Hannah began making dolls, concocting them ingeniously from bits and pieces of string, paper, rags, crayons.

Eventually I heard, via the grapevine, that she had been placed in the communal cell where the children were, though I never did learn why. At once she began teaching them to read and write, played with them, told them stories. She thought of things to occupy the adults too, and entertained them with anecdotes and songs about Palestine. She was soon back in solitary confinement, but the manufacturing of dolls continued, and our 'window correspondence' flourished once again.

Of the three matrons, each of whom worked eight-hour shifts, the most dreaded and implacable was Marietta. She was so unrelentingly cruel to the prisoners that many sacrificed the longed-for daily ten-minute walk if she was on yard duty. She used to stand in the centre of the yard, bullwhip in hand like an animal trainer in the circus, directing the prisoners, 'Faster, slower, still faster, on the run!' Often she made them run in circles. On one of the rare occasions Hannah and I met in the yard Marietta was the matron on duty, and Hannah related an incident she had had with the woman. One morning she was so completely absorbed in our 'window correspondence', that she failed to hear approaching footsteps. Suddenly the door burst open and Marietta, who had already seen her in the act of 'writing' through the peep-hole, stormed in, completely beside herself. She began shouting at the top of her strong voice, demanding an explanation from Hannah who, she said, knew only too well that signalling, or communicating in any fashion through the window, was strictly forbidden. She demanded the name of the person, or persons, with whom Hannah was attempting to make contact, and Hannah shouting from her perch in equally energetic tones, answered that she was trying to 'talk' to her mother, whom she had not seen in five years.

Marietta left without another word, and from then on, whenever she came on duty, she would immediately take a chair into Hannah's cell. This same Marietta, learning that the female British officer did not receive any parcels, assembled a package with an exceptionally fine assortment of delicacies pilfered from prisoners' parcels, and sent it to her. The materials Hannah needed to make her dolls were supplied by the generally feared matrons.

One day I received some paper dolls: a boy and girl walking hand in hand. I was enchanted. My cellmates were equally delighted, the monotony of prison life being such that everything and anything outside the deadly routine aroused comment and admiration. I sent Hannah a note thanking her for the dolls and added, 'Though I have always dreamed of the day you would present me with grandchildren, for the time being these substitutes will do.'

Gradually more and more of her dolls turned up, and the more she made the more ingenious, varied and colourful they became. She sent them not only to the prisoners, but also to the matrons, who cherished them equally. She made Biedermeier dolls, Rococo dolls, ballet dancer dolls, Carmens, Madame Butterfly dolls, Toscas, and so on. But most popular were her Palestine dolls, likenesses of the boy and girl kibbutzniks, shouldering picks and shovels. She told me once, 'I'm glad my time here isn't entirely wasted. I've converted a good many people to Zionism.' At the same time she said she could not understand that no sign or word had reached her from the outside. She was sure 'they' were unaware she was in prison.

The next parcel-day I slipped a note into the empty suitcase in which Margit had packed clean clothes and toilet articles, and which she would pick up the next day. I thanked her for her efforts on my behalf, and asked her to send two parcels henceforth since I shared everything with Hannah, and one was not quite enough for both of us. The suitcase passed inspection, and reached Margit. She immediately sent the note to my sister, who generally contributed to the parcels, and helped assemble them. My sister, secure in the belief that Hannah was in Palestine, was shattered to think I had lost my reason and imagined my daughter was in the same prison as I. Not for an instant did it occur to her there could possibly be any truth in my note—until the following day when, quite by chance, she heard the same thing from an entirely different source. For this was already the first week in August, and—with the occasional release of prisoners— bits of news had begun to filter out of the prison.

The next time we met in the yard I questioned Hannah about the mission for which she had volunteered.

'I can't tell you because it's a military secret,' she said. 'But the war will soon be over and then you'll know everything. However, even if I could, I wouldn't tell you, since it's difficult enough to maintain silence during interrogations anyway, and the less you know the better off you are. In fact it's best if you know absolutely nothing.'

'Even if you don't tell me,' I replied, 'I'm sure your enthusiasm for the British didn't prompt you to volunteer in the army. There must be some sort of Jewish affair behind all this.'

Pressing my hand she said, 'If that's the way you feel . . . you're on the right track.'

'The only question is whether it's worth risking your life for your boundless fanaticism.'

She answered softly but categorically: 'Look, Mother, it's worth it to me.' She added, 'But you can rest assured, I've done absolutely nothing that can in any way be injurious to the interests of Hungary. On the contrary. And remember, what's considered a crime today will probably be considered a virtue in the near future, justified by coming events.'

At another meeting she told me that during her first interrogation she actually fell into a trap. When they were unable to force an explanation from her concerning the earphones, they said, 'It doesn't matter, we know enough already. One of the boys has confessed everything and he'll be executed tomorrow.' She took the bait. 'He had absolutely nothing to do with the matter. The radio is mine.' Subsequently they tortured her in an effort to make her divulge the code.

Once during a 'window conversation', she asked whether I would like to learn Hebrew—pointing out that I would never have a better opportunity, considering all the time on my hands. Though I was not exactly in the mood to study anything, I knew if I agreed she would be pleased. From then on excellently organized and prepared lessons arrived daily.

As a widow I had long since stopped observing my wedding anniversary. But during the first week of that sad August in prison, Hannah remembered my silver anniversary in a most touching manner. She covered an empty talcum powder tin with silver foil, attached white buds made of paper onto twenty-five blades of straw pulled from her mattress, and fitted these into the holes in the top of the can, which then looked like a delightful little bouquet of white roses. She glued a lace doily, also made of tissue paper, to the bottom of the can. Accompanying the 'flowers' was an exquisite little paper doll bride with a long veil, carrying a minute bouquet of tissue paper roses. (For some reason one of the few things one could purchase in prison was tissue paper.) The gift was surpassed by a delightful accompanying poem which, unfortunately, I destroyed, along with all communication from Hannah, since there was the constant danger of being searched, and thus of implicating her in further difficulties.

Meanwhile, Hannah's manifold accomplishments reached their zenith. Her window signals were no longer directed only to me. They served as a daily news report and were watched for avidly by every prisoner whose window faced the yard. I was distressed by her courage and recklessness, afraid that her already precarious situation would be aggravated if her foolhardy actions came to the attention of the Commandant. But my warnings had no effect upon her.

One morning she placed her middle and index fingers horizontally on her lip, then drew her hand, palm down, across her throat as if cutting it. She repeated this pantomime several times. Everyone understood she was referring to Hitler. That afternoon, during exercise time, word was passed that there had been an attempt on Hitler's life.

How did she get her information? Those known as 'free prisoners'—Hungarian political prisoners allowed special privileges —sent her newspapers, books, scraps of news. But she also heard a great deal on her almost daily trips to the Hill in the police van, and in the Hill waiting room. Many of my cellmates had occasion to talk to her under these circumstances, and they were greatly impressed by the special treatment extended her by the Germans. She was served a good lunch—which, they told me, she invariably shared—and often she was given newspapers. The guards, mainly Serbs from southern Hungary, were not too strict with her. She gained their sympathy by talking to them in their own language, which she had picked up during her stay with the partisans.

One evening, four new prisoners were brought to our overcrowded cell. Two of them were hardly more than children, who had attempted to escape and been caught at the frontier. They had already been taken to Schwab Hill for questioning, and were eager to share their experiences with us. One of them asked, 'Do any of you know a charming and knowledgeable young woman prisoner who greets new prisoners and gives them advice, encourages them, tells them how to answer questions, and seems to have a great deal of information about everything?' One of my cellmates laughed. 'That's Hannah . . . Kate's daughter. She's not afraid of anything or anyone, and knows everything.'

One of the young girls related that she had spent a couple of hours with Hannah at Gestapo Main Headquarters, where she had been taken that day by an SS guard. Hannah asked him in German, 'If it depended upon you, what sort of punishment would you give me?' And he had answered, 'If it was up to me I wouldn't punish you at all because I've never known a woman as brave as you.'

When I repeated some of these things I had heard to Hannah she laughed. 'Yes, it's true. The Germans haven't tortured me the way the Hungarians have, or used any truly drastic measures. They're trying to achieve their ends by *psychological* means.'

Seifert was her interrogator as well as mine. She told me she had kept her knowledge of German from him, and always asked for an interpreter. She insisted upon this, since it gave her time to formulate her answers. She told me that on several occasions, after long interrogations, the Nazis had offered her cigarettes or coffee, and asked her to tell them about Palestine. Lately, after protracted interrogations, they would say, 'Enough for today. Now tell us about Palestine.'

By mid-August the atmosphere seemed more relaxed, discipline less severe. Hannah was not summoned as frequently for inter-rogation, and suddenly the questions were stopped entirely. The stepped-up bombings and victories of the Allies, the rapid advance of the Russians, increased our confidence that the end of the war was near. Everyone was hopeful of being transferred to Kistarcsa, the Hungarian internment camp where, it was said, discipline was less rigid, and the treatment, in general, incomparably better. Rumour spread that prisoners under Hungarian jurisdiction were not being deported, whereas German deportations continued without pause.

By the end of August conditions improved considerably. The cell was no longer crowded; now and then I even had a bed entirely to myself. One exceptionally quiet and beautiful night I found it impossible to sleep, and had the distinct feeling Hannah was not sleeping either. I crept to the window, fearful I would wake someone in the still night. The moon was shining so brightly it was almost like daylight, and I clearly saw Hannah silhouetted against the half-opened window wearing her light blue dressing gown, her hair softly framing her lovely face. She was entirely lost in thought, and the moon appeared to form a soft halo around her head. It seemed to me her soul was mirrored in her face at that instant. Overwhelmed by infinite sadness, I returned to my bed, fell upon it, and buried my head in my arms to stifle my sobs. I was crying for my child, for her youth, for her cruel predicament and probably hopeless fate.

Throughout the period of her interrogations they promised that once the questioning was over we would be permitted to meet. But when the time came the promise was, of course, for-gotten. She repeatedly asked the prison Commandant, with whom she often carried on heated political discussions, to move her, but he said he had not been authorized to do so, and could not on his own initiative. When Hannah insisted with increasing vehemence, he capitulated. 'All right, I'll take the chance. But it will be just between us.'

At the beginning of September, Hannah was placed in a cell next to mine, but we were not allowed to share a cell. We were, however, able to take our daily walk in the same group, sometimes even to walk together, and thus managed, at times, brief, whispered conversations.

The water tap for the floor was directly opposite my cell door and three times a day a prisoner from each cell was designated to carry in the water allotment. Naturally everyone competed for this assignment since it was one of the few opportunities to leave the hated confinement of the cell. The door of my cell opened directly onto the tap. Knowing this, Hannah's cellmates self-sacrificingly delegated her as sole water-carrier. In this way I was able to look at her frequently and she would signal to me. There were even times when a matron would call me into the corridor under some pretext when Hannah was at the tap, thus giving me an opportunity to embrace her, to hold her in my arms.

A mood of optimism reigned. Food, always a favourite topic in prison, now became the primary topic. Recipes for the most gourmet dishes were discussed and exchanged. One of the prisoners, wife of a bank president, invited us all to a sumptuous supper in the near future, positive we would soon be freed. I recall a Polish prisoner (originally from Cracow) who had been roaming from country to country for years, puncturing our lovely day-dreams by saying, 'What folly! Most of us will probably end up in Auschwitz.'

Auschwitz? What was that? It was the first time I had ever heard about the Nazi extermination camps. But soon afterwards a young Polish girl came to our cell and confirmed what the woman had said, adding that Auschwitz was not the only extermination centre, but the largest of many. Nevertheless, we felt a definite change for the better, an improvement in conditions all along the line. The behaviour of the matrons became more humane, and a few prisoners were even liberated, one of my cellmates among them. Of course the ransoms demanded—and paid—for freedom were vast. We also heard that the Hungarian government would no longer tolerate citizens being transported beyond the country's border, and that our prison was surrounded by police to protect us from deportations. Then, during the night of September 10–11, all the lights were suddenly turned on, and moaning, weeping and screams slashed the stillness of the early morning. We listened in terror, and learned that most of the Polish prisoners were being rounded up for deportation. I had heard of the 'night round-ups', but had never before witnessed one. Our door was opened by a soldier who read off the name of the unfortunate woman from Cracow. He left the door open and we could see the group of victims in the corridor, wailing and sobbing.

At that very moment there was a violent bombing raid, and the lights went out as suddenly as they had been turned on. As we crouched in fear we were at least hopeful the attack would disrupt the evil project of the Nazis. It did not. It merely delayed it a half-hour.

I was told Hannah fell on the bed and sobbed when they took several of her cellmates. Those who remained were surprised, considering her usual moral strength and courage. But she pulled herself together, and was again the one to instill hope in the others.

The following morning, September 11, a young prisoner working in the corridor called me to the door and told me Hannah had just been taken away, adding, 'But don't worry about her. Wherever they've taken her, it can't be much worse than this.'

Small consolation. That afternoon in the yard her cellmates confirmed the sickening news. I was destroyed, entirely without hope, my world at an end. They attempted to comfort me with stories of her bravery and goodness. They told me that before knowing her they had been despondent, and had tried to kill the unending hours one way or another. She had brought spirit and hope to them, planned activities, taught them songs, games, dances, told them endless stories about Palestine, gave them Hebrew lessons. And proselytizing as always, she converted many to Zionism by tirelessly detailing the life on the settlements, the history of the Land, its promise for the future.

Rumours multiplied. Word spread that we were to be transferred to a better place. On September 12 they actually did take several from our cell, and two days after Hannah left my name was read from a list, along with those of many of the other prisoners in my cell. That left only three behind. A tremendous crowd was already assembled in the corridor. The roll was called, and then personal belongings that had been taken from us were returned—excepting money and valuables. I saw the civilian who had been in the office when I had arrived, and managed to ask in a whisper where they had taken Hannah. He said he had no idea, but imagined it would be a better place.

We were transported in huge vans to the internment camp of Kistarcsa, on the outskirts of the city. There, an enormous crowd awaited us, and we gazed at one another, our eyes seeking familiar faces—sisters, brothers, children, friends. Some families were reunited, erstwhile prisonmates recognized each other, old friends embraced. But there were many bitter disappointments.

After the rigid discipline of the Gestapo prison, the Hungarian camp was like a summer resort, the atmosphere relatively relaxed. We were allowed to walk about the huge fenced-in grounds without restraint, to write as many letters as we liked, when we liked, to receive unlimited packages, and in exceptional cases we were even allowed to receive visitors. I was tormented by worry about Hannah, and wrote to Margit, asking her to visit me. In a day or so I was called to the office and found Margit there, accompanied by her friend, Hilda Gobby, also a well-known actress. A prison official was with them. I happily threw my arms around her, but she failed to respond, and standing stiff as a ramrod, her voice frigid, said, 'Madame, I urgently need your signature on this contract for the flat. I've even brought a deposit along so we can settle the matter at once.'

Of course I understood immediately that she had used the contract as a pretext to gain admission. We could barely contain our laughter. However, at that time the political climate was such that the official supposedly watching us turned the other way, busied himself with paper work, and gave us an opportunity to talk freely and at length. I begged Margit to make every attempt to trace Hannah's whereabouts.

Going down the stairs Margit was surrounded by a crowd. There were many in the camp from the world of the theatre, and news of her visit had spread like wildfire. They asked for news of friends, relatives they thought she might know, and begged her to take messages. The general mood was, on the whole, remarkably good. Internees were filled with confidence, and there was even a special dinner served on Rosh Hashana, brought to the camp by the various Jewish organizations.

I was in constant touch with my sister, and in one of her letters she wrote that various countries, among them Switzerland, were issuing safe conduct papers to Jews. She said she was making every possible effort to obtain one for me, which would mean my release. But still no news of Hannah.

Towards the end of September—on Yom Kippur, to be exact —everyone was suddenly released. Thanks to an order from the Minister of the Interior, the Kistarcsa internment camp was to be closed. It was late afternoon before the roll call was exhausted and the last prisoner released. I made my way to my sister's, who then lived in one of the Yellow Star-designated houses in Alkotmány Street. She could hardly believe her eyes when she saw me, and I, for my part, was shocked by my sister's appearance. Worry and constant running from place to place in futile attempts to find Hannah and to effect my release had changed her into a prematurely aged, care-worn matron.

The important news was that Hannah had sent word. The previous day a young Hungarian lawyer named Nánay had called on her at Conti Street Prison, offering to defend her if her case came to trial. Hannah asked him to contact her family through Margit, whose address was the only one she knew, and discuss her case with them. She said it was up to them to decide about her defence.

The next day my brother-in-law (also a lawyer) and I called on Dr. Nánay. The young lawyer informed us that there were others involved with Hannah, also parachutists. They had empowered him to act on their behalf, he said, and he was preparing their defence. He produced an authorization signed by them. However, I wanted to consult our friend and family counsellor, Dr. Palágyi, before making a decision, and above all, to talk to Hannah and ask her what she wanted me to do. I explained this to Dr. Nánay, and he promised he would procure a visitor's pass for me within the next day or so—but only if I agreed to discard the Yellow Star sewn on my coat.

Then I went to visit my home, and Margit gave me an envelope which, she said, had been brought to her dressing room in the theatre the previous evening by two young men. There was a considerable sum of money in it, and Margit said the men had asked her to see that Hannah lacked for nothing in prison. The money was sent by someone named Geri, and they asked that regards from him be given to Hannah. Of course at the time I had no idea who the mysterious Geri was, but later discovered he was Reuven Dafne, her parachutist comrade who had been with her in Yugoslavia among the partisans.

A day or so later, Dr. Nánay came and took me to Conti Street Prison where I was to be allowed ten minutes with Hannah. He left me there, and I waited in a tiny room until she appeared, flanked by two guards. She looked remarkably well. Naturally, our conversation was circumscribed, but at least we could embrace, and she opened the package I brought. The war was already in its fifth year, and there were serious food shortages; but when friends and relatives heard I was going to visit Hannah, they had hurriedly brought whatever they could, including items of clothing and other odds and ends they thought might please her. I had unearthed a sewing set she had received as a child, and included it in the parcel. As an experienced ex-prisoner I knew the importance of such a thing. Everything delighted her, but this, above all. It brought tears to her eyes, and she asked, 'Does this thing still exist? Was there ever such a time . . . a time of childhood and carefree happiness?'

I asked what she needed or wanted. She quickly replied, 'Books . . . good books . . . as many as you can send. Reading is allowed here. But I warn you, you won't get them back because they're confiscated for the prison library. But more than anything else, I'd like a Bible. A Hebrew Bible.'

Hearing this, one of the guards said, 'How is it that Hannah is Jewish and you, her mother, Gentile?'

'Not at all,' I said. 'I'm Jewish, too.'

'Then where is your Yellow Star?'

I knew a recent government regulation granted exemption from the wearing of the Yellow Star to Jews responsible for cultural achievements, or those who merited special consideration for enhancing Hungary's prestige. In view of my late husband's achievements I had been recommended for such exemption. The application had received the enthusiastic endorsement of various theatres, as well as of the *Pesti Hirlap*, the newspaper with which my husband had been associated. So I replied, 'I am exempt from wearing the Yellow Star in view of the literary activities of my late husband.'

The guards believed me, and Hannah smiled proudly. One of the guards said, 'But of course! I remember Mr. Senesh. In fact I knew him well. I was a waiter in the café where he often used to go.'

I gave Hannah the greetings from Geri. Her eyes sparkled, and she beamed. Then I asked again what she would like or needed other than the books. It was the beginning of October, and the weather was turning cold.

'If possible, I'd like some warmer clothes. It's cold in the cell.' Otherwise, she said, she was well. She was not in solitary confinement. On the contrary, everyone in her cell was young, spirited, and optimistic. (Actually, during all the months she was imprisoned, I never heard her complain about anything.)

Finally, she told me the most important thing: 'I'm going to be tried soon. I need a lawyer to defend me. Decide on someone as soon as possible.'

The ten minutes were up.

Friends and relatives heard I had been released. I was inundated with advice on how to rescue Hannah. The majority insisted I must contact the Zionist Organization and ask for legal assistance.

After calling on Dr. Nánay I went to the head office of the Zionist Organization at Glass House, in Vadász Street, and was directed to a young man who assured me everything possible was being done to obtain the release of the imprisoned parachutists. When I gave him details of the case, he insisted he was completely informed about everything. But in the course of our relatively brief conversation it transpired that he didn't even know Hannah had already been in the Conti Street Prison for nearly three weeks. He thought she was in the Margit Boulevard Prison, along with her comrades. He promised again to do everything in his power for all of them.

I asked Dr. Palágyi, who had never heard of Dr. Nánay, to examine the list of defence lawyers available with utmost care, and to choose the one he thought the very best. (Jewish lawyers, of course, were not permitted to practice.) Dr. Palágyi's first choice handled only civil cases, and thus declined. Finally he

chose Dr. Szelecsényi who, he said, had recently won a string of
most complicated cases. However, before I entrusted him with
Hannah's defence, I was advised by several friends that instead
of discussing the matter with nondescript office clerks at the
Zionist Organization, I should contact influential officials at the
very top. All my attempts to do so ended in an absolute fiasco.

It is pointless to detail the events that ensued in the following
weeks, nor can I describe the tension, disappointments and dis-
illusionment. On October 12, when I was definitely convinced it
was useless to wait for the Zionist Organization to do anything,
I called upon Dr. Szelecsényi, accompanied by Dr. Palágyi, and
entrusted him with the defence of my daughter. He promised he
would see her in prison the next day, and that he would make
every effort to obtain a pass for me to visit her.

Meanwhile, I tried in vain to find a Hebrew Bible. All book
shops dealing in Jewish or Hebrew literature had been closed
months before. I even called at the home of the former proprietor
of the largest shop of this kind in Budapest, but he had fled the
country. In the well-known shop dealing in religious books in
Deák Square, I was received with surprise: they had the Bible
in all languages, but certainly not in Hebrew. Friends who had
a Hebrew Bible were, on the other hand, reluctant to part with it
for fear they would never get it back. To my everlasting sorrow,
I was unable to fulfil Hannah's last wish.

A few years later one of her former cellmates related how
Hannah had won their hearts in the very short time they were
together. She told them she was a Zionist, and being Communists
they did not know exactly what 'Zionist' meant. Thus they were
suspicious and kept away from her at first. But they soon realized
she was helpful to all of them, and though not a Communist herself, shared with them or gave them whatever she had. She
taught the illiterates to read and write, and gave interesting
lectures on the labour movement and the Histadrut institutions
in Palestine. Soon the barrier between them was torn down, and
they all felt her warmth and kind-heartedness.

During those days I received a long, censored letter from her
detailing her activities, praising her cellmates, assuring me she
kept herself busy and that she was well. Of course, she said, all
this feverish activity served to help forget reality.

Dr. Szelecsényi could not go to the prison to see her on

October 13 because of a massive air raid. So it was Saturday, the 14th, before he was able to see her. That afternoon I went to his office, and he told me he had talked to her for a considerable time since there had been another large air raid and he had been trapped in the prison. He did not go into detail, but said only that he doubted whether one man in a thousand would have undertaken and accomplished the things Hannah had. He also said that if her case went to trial she would definitely be convicted, and he had no idea what the sentence would be: five years, two years, perhaps even seven. But he said the length of the sentence was of absolutely no importance since at the end of the war political prisoners would be released immediately. 'And I don't need to tell you how the war stands now,' he added. 'There is absolutely no possibility of a death sentence. I'm not saying this just to calm your fears, but because that is my sincere conviction.'

He promised he would notify me immediately the trial date was set so I could be present. In fact he insisted I should be in the corridor during the session, and felt sure I would be able to talk to Hannah during the recess. (Captain Simon, the Judge Advocate, had refused me a visitor's pass to see her in prison until after the trial.)

The following day, October 15, the destiny of what remained of Hungarian Jewry was sealed. Szálasi came into power, and whatever hardship or atrocities the Jews had hitherto endured were as nothing compared to the atrocities and bloodbath that ensued under the rule of the bestial Hungarian Nazis, the Arrow-Crossers. Jews were permitted to leave their houses for only two hours a day—on certain days. House superintendents who had, until then, looked the other way if Jewish tenants ventured out without the Yellow Star, now insisted the brand must always be worn—which meant we did not dare to venture out on the unspecified days. This prevented me from calling upon Szelecsényi again. My sister and her husband, both under Swedish protection, and thus exempt from wearing the Yellow Star, maintained contact with him. Through them I was told the trial had been set for October 28.

I telephoned the lawyer from the home of a Gentile family. To my desperate question as to what would happen in view of the changed political situation, he said, 'It is possible that the sentence will be ten or twenty years, maybe even life. However, this does not essentially change matters.' He again reminded me that whatever the sentence, it would be meaningless in view of the military situation, and again asked me to be present on the day of the trial since there was a possibility I would be permitted to see Hannah during the recess.

On October 28, I went to Margit Boulevard Prison and was appalled by the mob milling about. I waited in the antechamber of the courtroom bearing the sign, 'Hannah Senesh and Accomplices'. I was not allowed inside the courtroom.

At eleven o'clock, when the judges retired to deliberate, the doors were flung open and I glimpsed Hannah amidst the group streaming out. She had no idea I would be there, and rushing over, threw her arms around me. The guard separated us, and said he could permit us to talk only after sentence had been passed. I was deathly pale, but she was flushed, excited, her eyes brilliant, her smile self-confident.

They were soon recalled, but after a few tense moments, appeared again. Hannah told me the judges had not reached a decision, and judgement had been postponed for eight days, which meant until the following Saturday, November 4.

This unexpected turn of events was enormously depressing, and I asked Szelecsényi, who was standing nearby, what it signified. He said the delay had absolutely no significance, and although such a postponement was rare, it had been known to happen.

Hannah said, 'Dr. Szelecsényi's defence was brilliant, Mother. Do thank him.'

The lawyer was flattered and pleased by the compliment. (He later told my sister that he had been vehemently attacked by members of the Court for accepting the defence of a 'Jew girl'.) He rushed away to another trial after advising us to make the most of the time we had left together. I could not hide my anxiety and depression. Hannah tried to reassure me by saying that, in her case, the delay made no difference, since she would not be released from prison anyway while the war continued. 'But I'm astonished that you walk about the streets so freely under existing conditions,' she chided. 'Why don't you disappear? What about all your Gentile friends? Can't they hide you?'

When I said I wanted her case to be settled before I thought of hiding, she said, 'I'll muddle through this somehow, believe me.

But I won't have a moment's peace as long as you're so careless.'

The guard (the ex-waiter) warned us our time was up, but reminded me that now the trial was over there was nothing to prevent me from visiting my daughter in Conti Street Prison. He said I could obtain a visitor's pass without any trouble at the prison office, so I promised to visit her on Monday, October 30. We walked down the stairs together, and the guard said he would run ahead to see if the prison car had arrived—to which Hannah commented that she would much rather have gone by tram and seen the busy life in the city's streets.

I was not allowed to walk across the yard with them, so watched her walk away until she disappeared from view, lost in the mob.

On October 30 and 31 there were such intensive air raids that I was prevented from leaving the house; thus I was unable to get to the prison. On November 1, I presented myself at the office, only to be told that since it was a holiday—All Saints'—visitors were not allowed. On November 2, I tried again, but was told that since sentence had not been passed it would be necessary to obtain a pass from Captain Simon, the Judge Advocate, whose office was at the Hadik Barracks.It was impossible to go there that same day, so it was not until November 3 that I applied for a pass at the office of Captain Simon. But there I was given to understand that Captain Simon was out of town, and could not be reached until Tuesday, November 7. When I explained why I had come, and asked who was replacing Captain Simon during his absence, they told me no one was authorized to issue a visitor's pass while Captain Simon was away.

In the meantime—and before the eight days had expired—I wrote to Dr. Szelecsényi and asked why he had not notified me about the date of sentence. He answered that the date had been postponed once again because a new Judge Advocate had been appointed to handle the case. He promised he would let me know without an instant's delay when he was notified.

On November 7—the eleventh day after the trial—I called again at the office of Captain Simon in the Hadik Barracks,only to find total confusion. One crammed, moving van after the other trundled out. The doorman told me it was pointless entering the building because as far as he knew everyone had already gone. Certainly the roar of the Russian guns was increasing even as we talked; the mass flight of the Fascists to the west had begun. But despite the increased bombardment, and the porter's certainty that Captain Simon was already gone, I insisted upon going to his office on the chance that he might still be there; and after a great deal of persuasion the porter agreed to let me enter the building and try the Captain's office.

There everything had indeed been packed, but I found two female clerks in hats and coats, and a young officer. All were on the point of leaving. The officer was the one I had talked to on my last visit there, when Captain Simon was out of town. So I explained once again that I still desperately wanted the visitor's permit. The officer answered that Simon had been transferred the previous day to Margit Boulevard Military Prison, and gave me the number of the Captain's office there. Then, glancing at his watch, he added, 'You had better hurry.' I understood this last to mean the Captain would soon be leaving his office and that if I wanted to catch him I should move fast.

I reached Margit Boulevard at about 10.30. It was quiet and comparatively deserted. From the sentry at the entrance to the Captain's office, I did not pass a soul, and had the impression everyone had fled the building. After wandering up and down the corridors of the seemingly deserted building, I found the right office. It was empty, but a briefcase on one of the desks, with a pair of gloves resting on it, indicated that its owner was still in the building. I waited in the corridor. A clerk appeared, who confirmed that Captain Simon was still there.

At 11.45 he returned to his office. I followed him in, introduced myself, and asked for a visitor's pass.

'The case no longer has anything to do with me,' he answered, apparently ill at ease.

'Since when?' I asked.

'Since yesterday,' he answered.

'Then who is in charge of the case?'

'I don't know.'

'Who is authorized to grant me a visitor's permit?'

'I don't know.'

'Shall I go to the Conti Street Prison and ask the warden for one?'

'You can. Go there. Try.'

His brusque, summary answers released all my bitterness. 'Captain, at least be helpful enough to direct me to the proper authorities, and tell me what I must do in order to see my daughter. As it is, I can't understand why it's so difficult for me to obtain a pass when relatives of other prisoners have been permitted frequent visiting rights. I have been granted permission to see my daughter only once, and then only for minutes.'

'Really?' he remarked, almost in wonder. 'I didn't grant you permission to see her even once?'

'And how is it possible that there still has not been a date set for sentencing? The eight-day postponement has long since expired.' He did not answer so I continued. 'Or has sentence been passed?'

'Even if it has been, I'm not in a position to tell you what it entails.'

'What do you mean? You don't mean to tell me it would be possible to keep such information from me?' Since he did not reply I repeated, '*Has* sentence been passed?'

Captain Simon then went to his desk, sat down, pointed to the chair opposite. 'Sit down.' After another embarrassing silence he continued, 'Are you a Jew? Or was only your husband one?'

'He was, and I am. We're all Jews,' I answered.

'I don't see the Yellow Star.'

I uncovered the Star which had inadvertently been hidden by my large bag.

Finally he came to the point. 'Are you familiar with your daughter's case?'

'Yes. The lawyer has briefed me.'

Ignoring this answer, he went on and summarized the case. 'Your daughter, after renouncing her Hungarian citizenship, joined the British Armed Forces and was a Radio Officer in the Parachute Corps. Last spring she flew from Cairo, via Italy, to Yugoslavia, where she was dropped, and spent a considerable length of time with the partisans. From Yugoslavia she made her way to Hungary, supposedly for the purpose of rescuing Jews and British prisoners of war. In other words, she is guilty of major crimes against the interests of Hungary . . .'

'That isn't true,' I interjected. 'I'm positive that isn't true because once, when we met in the Gestapo prison yard, I

questioned her about her mission. She said she could not answer
my questions because she was bound by military secrecy; but she
assured me she had positively not undertaken, nor committed,
any act which could possibly be detrimental to the welfare of
Hungary. On the contrary!'

'But Hungary is under martial law, and your daughter was
found with a radio transmitter. Consequently the Military Tribunal found her guilty of treason, and demanded the supreme
penalty. And this . . . penalty . . . has already been . . . carried out.'

I looked at him, petrified. The world went black.

Suddenly I remembered Szelecsényi's letter. Perhaps this man
was merely deriving some form of brutal pleasure in torturing me.
I clung to this thought as a last straw, and finally said, 'No, no.
That's impossible. It can't be. Why, only this morning I received
a letter from the lawyer telling me sentence had not yet been
passed, and that he would let me know when the day was fixed for
sentencing. Certainly the lawyer would have been informed if
anything had happened.'

'Yes, of course,' Captain Simon said. 'He knows, but probably
wants to spare you.'

'Spare me? What sense would that make? How long do you
suppose I would be spared? No. The lawyer must have told me
the truth.'

'What's the name of the lawyer?'

'Dr. Andre Szelecsényi. But I have his letter with me.' I
fumbled for it in my handbag, then handed it to him.

He glanced at the letter, made a note of the lawyer's name and
telephone number, and said, 'All right, we'll inform him by
phone.'

I knew there was no hope left. 'And this is the way it happens?
Such things exist? They can really happen?' I stammered. 'And
I wasn't even allowed to see her, to talk to her.'

'She didn't want to see you. She wanted to spare you the
shock.' (Later he told Dr. Szelecsényi just the opposite. Hannah
did indeed ask to see me. It was her last request, but they
'dissuaded' her.) After a moment's silence, he continued, 'But
you'll be given the farewell letters. She wrote several.'

After yet another terrible silence he said, 'I must pay tribute
to your daughter's exceptional courage and strength of character,
both of which she manifested until the very last moment. She was

truly proud of being a Jew,' he stated with undisguised, if puzzled, admiration.

I replied, 'I don't know the military laws and whether my daughter has transgressed them, and if she did, what that act was . . .'

'Her offence was exceedingly grave,' he interrupted.

'But that she stands innocent before man and God,' I went on, 'I don't doubt at all. Because anyone so gifted, so endowed with talent, could only have volunteered for a great and noble cause.'

'True, she was an exceptional human being. But it is just such people who volunteer for unusual assignments. Pity she chose the wrong path. Accept what has happened,' he continued. 'This war has claimed so many lives, such horrible sacrifices; consider her one of them.'

I asked for the farewell letters. He said I could pick them up any morning at Conti Street Prison.

As I staggered down the stairs, unseeing, it suddenly struck me that Simon had just come from the execution. This was later verified.

Shortly after my departure, Dr. Szelecsényi passed by Margit Boulevard Prison and saw a hearse pull out. 'What's that?' he asked the sentry. 'Have there been any recent executions?'

'Yes. They executed the British woman officer,' the sentry replied.

Dr. Szelecsényi rushed upstairs to Captain Simon and accused him of murder, stating that the 'judicial murder' had been an unlawful execution carried out without final sentence having been passed. When, after the war, Captain Simon was brought to trial, the fact of illegal execution was actually established.

A few days later, my sister and I went to Conti Street Prison and asked for the letters. They were surprised at our request, and said they must be at Margit Boulevard Prison. And they actually were, in the possession of Captain Simon. Szelecsényi, who was deeply disturbed by the series of illegal events, asked for the letters. Simon read them to him but refused to part with them. According to the lawyer, Simon took the letters, along with the documents relating to the case, when he fled the country.

At Conti Street Prison, I was given a few of Hannah's personal effects. In the pockets of the dresses I found two scraps of paper.

On one was a poem she must have written in her cell in Hadik Barracks after our last meeting, and a few undated lines of farewell:

> *Dearest Mother:*
> *I don't know what to say—only*
> *this: a million thanks, and forgive*
> *me, if you can.*
>   *You know so well why words aren't*
> *necessary. With love forever,*
>
>   *Your daughter*

SELECTED POEMS

Mother

If the world offered a reward,
A laurel for patience and love,
One person alone would be worthy:
Mother.

Let there be thanks in your hearts
And on your lips a prayer,
Whenever you hear that most beautiful word:
Mother.

Budapest 1933 (aged 12)

*translated from the Hungarian
by Peter Hay*

Now

Now—now I'd like to say something,
Something more than mere words,
More dappled than colour,
More musical than rhythm or rhyme,
Something a million people haven't already said or
heard.

Just something.
All about the land is silent, listening,
The forest gazing at me, expectant.
The sky watches me with a curious eye.
Everything is silent. And so am I.

Tatra, Biela-Voda 1938

translated from the Hungarian
by Peter Hay

Leaves

First it was green,
Then it turned yellow.
Soon its face changed to wine-red.
Tomorrow it will hide in a monk's robe,
And its next colour will spell death.

Tatra, Biela-Voda 1938

translated from the Hungarian
by Marta Cohn

Harvest

Our people are working the black soil,
Their arms reap the gold sheaves,
And now when the last ear its stalk leaves
Our faces glitter as with gilded oil.

From where comes the new light and voice,
From where the resounding song at hand?
From where the fighting spirit and new faith?
From you, fertile Emek, from you, my land.

Nahalal 1940

translated from the Hungarian
by Peter Hay

To My Mother*

From where have you learned to wipe the tears,
To quietly bear the pain,
To hide in your heart the cry, the hurt,
The suffering and the complaint?

Hear the wind!
Its open maw
Roars through hill and dale.
See the ocean . . .
The giant rocks,
In anger and wrath it flails.

Nature all arush, agush
Breaks out of each form and fence.
From where is this quiet in your hearts,
From where have you learned strength?

Nahalal 1940

*translated from the Hebrew
by Ruth Finer Mintz*

---

* This, and the following poems, were written in Hebrew.

To A Good Friend

I wounded another not knowing
Both ends of an arrow mar.
I too was hurt in the battle
And shall bear a scar.

Nahalal 1941

translated from the Hebrew
by Ziva Shapiro

For The Brothers*

Should we break,
Then take the burden
Heavy and great
Upon you.

Build upon sand
Under the blue
Sky . . . everything
Anew.

And know, costly
The road to the just
And the true.

Nahalal 1941

translated from the Hebrew
by Ruth Finer Mintz

* Written a few days prior to Russia's entry into World War II.

To Die . . .

To die . . . so young to die . . . no, no, not I.
I love the warm sunny skies,
Light, songs, shining eyes.
I want no war, no battle cry—
No, no . . . Not I.

But if it must be that I live today
With blood and death on every hand,
Praised be He for the grace, I'll say
To live, if I should die this day . . .
Upon your soil, my home, my land.

Nahalal 1941

*translated from the Hebrew
by Dorothy H. Rochmis*

To Caesarea

Hush, cease all sound.
Across the sea is the sand,
The shore known and near,
The shore golden, dear,
Home, the Homeland.

With step twisting and light
Among strangers we move,
Word and song hushed,
Towards the future-past
Caesarea . . .

But reaching the city of ruins
Soft a few words we intone.
We return. We are here.
Soft answers the silence of stone,
We awaited you two thousand years.

Sdot-Yam, Caesarea 1941

translated from the Hebrew
by Ruth Finer Mintz

Ginosar*

In the black fields on a dark night
Candles kindled, scattering light
in the furrows' festive joy.

In the dark night on white fields
Bonfires flared, flames spread . . .
Worlds were destroyed.

In the black fields,
The future's sparkling song,
The tractor sang.

In the white fields
There groaned
A dying man.

Sdot-Yam, Caesarea 1941

*translated from the Hebrew
by Ruth Finer Mintz*

* This poem was written to celebrate the winter plowing of 500 dunams
of land at Ginosar. That December in Russia the winter war was ravaging
the snowbound fields.

To Mothers In The Diaspora

A day, two days, a week, a month,
One year, ten years . . . to wait
For a line, a word, no matter how late.

Through endless plight
To gather and to store
The terror of the night.

Concealing in the dread
Vast seas of blood
A tear.

Then what word can we say?
Only a look, a word today or any day:
Mother! Mother!

Sdot-Yam 1942

*translated from the Hebrew
by I. M. Lask*

Loneliness

Could I meet one who understood all . . .
Without word, without search,
Confession or lie,
Without asking why.

I would spread before him, like a white cloth,
The heart and the soul . . .
The filth and the gold.
Perceptive, he would understand.

And after I had plundered the heart,
When all had been emptied and given away,
I would feel neither anguish nor pain,
But would know how rich I became.

Sdot-Yam, Caesarea 1942

*translated from the Hebrew
by Ruth Finer Mintz*

A Glance

How far, far have the people lagged,
Infinitely far have the seas receded.
How distant now the gay and dancing times,
How languid the once proud songs and rhymes,
How distant . . . How languid . . .

Sdot-Yam, Caesarea 1942

*translated from the Hungarian
by Peter Hay*

Walk To Caesarea

God—may there be no end
to sea, to sand,
water's splash,
lightning's flash,
the prayer of man

Caesarea 1942

*translated from the Hebrew
by Ziva Shapiro*

Seed

Seed falls, the golden grain takes root,
Not on the rock, not on the paved road.
Gather it in, black dust,
And blanket it against the heat and frost.
This speck of life enclosed within a husk.
Seed of infinity, this tiny little grain,
Pressed underneath the dust and waiting for a sign,
For mark of Spring, for ray of light, for sun,
For day.

1942

translated from the Hebrew
by I. M. Lask

At The Crossroads

A voice called. I went.
I went, for it called.
I went, lest I fall.

At the crossroads
I blocked both ears with white frost
And cried
For what I had lost.

Caesarea 1942

translated from the Hebrew
by Ziva Shapiro

We Gather Flowers

We gathered flowers in the fields and mountains,
We breathed the fresh winds of spring,
We were drenched with the warmth of the sun's rays
In our Homeland, in our beloved home.

We go out to our brothers in exile,
To the suffering of winter, to frost in the night.
Our hearts will bring tidings of springtime,
Our lips sing the song of light.

1944

translated from the Hebrew
by Dorothy Bar-Adon

Blessed Is The Match

Blessed is the match consumed
        in kindling flame.
Blessed is the flame that burns
        in the secret fastness of the heart.
Blessed is the heart with strength to stop
        its beating for honour's sake.
Blessed is the match consumed
        in kindling flame.

Sardice, Yugoslavia May 2, 1944

translated from the Hebrew
by Marie Syrkin

One—Two—Three*

One—two—three . . .
    eight feet long,
Two strides across, the rest is dark . . .
Life hangs over me like a question mark.

One—two—three . . .
    maybe another week,
Or next month may still find me here,
But death, I feel, is very near.

I could have been
    twenty-three next July;
I gambled on what mattered most,
The dice were cast. I lost.

Budapest 1944

*translated from the Hungarian
by Peter Hay*

---

* Her last poem, written in prison.

D011252323